Heroes and Scoundrels

Heroes and Scoundrels

FIVE DECADES OF FLASHPOINTS, CONFLICTS AND COMPROMISES SUPPORTING PRESS FREEDOM IN LATIN AMERICA

Edward Seaton

Seaton Publishing Company, Inc.

Photos from author's personal collection.
Maps by Seaton Publishing.

First hardback edition published September 2019

ISBN 978-1-7333329-0-3 (cloth : alk. paper)

Published by Seaton Publishing Co., Inc.

Printed in the United States of America

The paper used in this publication is recycled and contains 30 percent postconsumer waste. It is acid free and meets the minimum requirements of the American National Standard for Permanence of Paper for Printed Library Materials Z39.48-1992.

Contents

Foreword

Sometimes, just for fun, I walk into my dad's office and ask if he remembers some obscure fact—the circulation several years ago of a competitive paper in our county, for example. My dad, you see, is my boss—Edward L. Seaton, editor-in-chief of *The Manhattan (Kan.) Mercury*—and he has a very disorganized-looking office. I like to see if I can tie him in knots trying to find the right file from the piles stacked haphazardly in drawers and shelves and corners.

Somehow, he can always come up with exactly the right report, the one sitting in the middle of the three-foot-tall stack by the couch. And he's got it already paper-clipped and highlighted at all the appropriate places. I have yet to stump him.

The reason? He always does his homework. Always.

He reads every word of everything—our paper, business reports, the trade press, the news wires from Washington and Latin America, and books and stories he reviews as a member of the Pulitzer Prize board.

He's my father, so this is clearly a biased assessment. In fact, I'd warn the reader that this is more of a son's essay than it is the work of a news editor assessing the agenda of the incoming president of American Society of Newspaper Editors.

But this much is objective fact: This 55-year-old man from Manhattan, Kansas—a man who has been knighted in the Dominican Republic for his work staring down Latin American dictators over their treatment of journalists, pushed successfully for governments in the hemisphere to sign a declaration of press freedom, and spearheaded efforts to create a sort of endowment for programs to help young people in his home town—is extremely dedicated to what he does.

At Harvard he cultivated an interest in Spain, writing a senior honors thesis about the regime of Gen. Francisco Franco. Actually, Dad's interest had started young, when his father took the family to Spain for a vacation because it was cheap.

Dad and Mom spent a year on the Fulbright fellowship in Quito, Ecuador, where Dad's Spanish got a lot better. They fell in love with the country, its people and its culture. In fact, they fell in love with Latin America.

After a year at journalism school at the University of Missouri and a stint at *The Courier-Journal* in Louisville, Ky., as a general assignment reporter, Dad came back to Manhattan to join the family business. It was 1969. Dad was all of 26, and he was running the *Mercury* as editor-in-chief. He helped expand the family business, buying other papers, as well as radio stations. He now helps oversee the nine other Seaton-owned dailies and broadcast stations, all of them relatively small operations in the Midwest and High Plains.

He grew increasingly involved in the community, serving as everything from the chairman of the local and state chambers of commerce to the head of a local charity to help flood victims (in 1993) and underprivileged youth. For the latter effort, he was named Manhattan's citizen of the year in 1994.

But it's for his work on national and international causes that he's best known. In 1972, Dad got started in the Inter American Press Association, largely an organization of Latin American publishers dedicated to defending press freedoms.

And as he tends to do, he got involved and worked at it. He read the background. He volunteered to do things. And he went on IAPA missions to stand up for newspapers that were fighting dictators' censorship—or the imprisonment of their reporters. He helped win the release of Jacobo Timerman by meeting with the military dictators in a celebrated case in Argentina in 1977. He shuttled back and forth from Kansas to Nicaragua in the 1980s, when *La Prensa* in Managua was fighting with the Sandinistas.

Even in more placid countries, he kept his nose to the grindstone. I can remember vacation trips for our family at sunny beach resorts in Central America, where my brother and I would body surf and play tennis. Dad never got a whiff of a tan—he was churning away inside the hotel conference room.

"I knew he was always a leader who could be counted on to serve on any effort we needed," said William Williamson, the IAPA's former executive director. "I thought he was a great example: Here was a person from the Midwest with no financial ties to Latin America, but who was concerned about principles."

His life took a couple of crucial turns:

- In Spain studying for his thesis, he met another American woman there for the summer. They were told they could speak no English for the summer—and Dad's Spanish wasn't all that great—so she thought he was a little slow. He persisted. That woman is Karen Seaton, my mother. (Thank God for persistence.)

- Secondly, near the time of his graduation in 1965, Dad was interviewed for the Rhodes Scholarship. For some reason, he didn't prepare well, and he lost out. I think that still bugs him a little. Anyway, on his next opportunity—for the Fulbright Scholarship—he wouldn't let the same thing happen. He got the scholarship. I think that lesson has stuck with him—he certainly has told it to me more than once.

Dad said when he was sworn in as IAPA president in 1989, "If Colombians or Panamanians or Nicaraguans or Salvadorans are willing to go to jail or die for the principles of democracy, the rule of law and press freedom, the least we other journalists can do is support them."

He has also worked on related domestic issues. Dad helped lead a push for an amendment in 1987 to this country's McCarthy-era law that forbade people from entering the U.S. because of their political beliefs. That law had kept out people like novelist Gabriel García Márquez, ex–Canadian Prime Minister Pierre Trudeau and poet Pablo Neruda.

He has remained active in those efforts. He and James McClatchy of Mc-Clatchy Newspapers in 1994 spearheaded efforts to persuade governments to sign a declaration of free speech and free press principles. The Declaration of Chapultepec, as the document became known, was signed by President Clinton and the heads of state of many other countries in the hemisphere.

He was knighted in the Dominican Republic for his work of that sort. He also won the 1993 Maria Moors Cabot Prize from Columbia University, which honors journalists "for a body of work that contributes to the improvement of inter-American understanding."

When he got home from the trip to the Dominican Republic to receive his knighthood, incidentally, Mom promptly informed him that he could still take out the garbage. He does. He also shovels the sidewalk.

Ned Seaton
(Excerpted from
The American Editor
March 1998)

Heroes and Scoundrels

Introduction

A man sets out to draw the world. As the years go by, he peoples a space with images of provinces, kingdoms, mountains, bays, ships, islands, fishes, rooms, instruments, stars, horses, and individuals. A short time before he dies, he discovers that the patient labyrinth of lines traces the lineaments of his own face.

—Argentine storyteller Jorge Luis Borges

This collection of narratives is less a memoir than an assemblage of unforgettable memories. It focuses on remarkable men and women I have known, mostly heroic, who have risked their businesses and sometimes their lives to tell the truth about government and society. It recounts events I have witnessed or participated in and the history I have lived defending freedom of expression. My participation underscores my aspirations for press freedom and democracy in our hemisphere and my fight against authoritarianism.

I worry some about writing so much about my own life, but I recall the baseball great Dizzy Dean is said to have remarked, "If you done it, it ain't braggin'." I hope you take these recollections in that spirit.

For nearly five decades I have been privileged to play a part in press-freedom battles in virtually every country of Latin America and the Caribbean. When I began, darkness had already fallen over Cuba and Brazil. By the end of my first decade more than 80 percent of the region was without a free press. This was after an encouraging interlude in the mid-1950s and continuing into the democratic openings and flourishing press freedoms of the early 1960s. But by the mid-1970s fourteen of the 20 Latin American countries were under military-authoritarian rule and three others existed with the military effectively in control as the power behind the throne.

I like to characterize my years of voluntary service in this cause, especially once I became deeply involved in 1972, as years of increasing progress toward a flowering of freedom in the Western Hemisphere. But the truth is there have been defeats and ambiguous outcomes as well as victories. Recently have come the popularly elected autocrats—sometimes called "democratators." In Venezuela, Ecuador, Nicaragua and Bolivia they have used manipulation and subversion to hide behind a democratic façade in order to remain part of the international community.

It is no mystery why autocrats and illiberal democratic incumbents want to control the media. Two distinguished New York University professors studied 150 countries during two decades and learned that allowing press freedom and ensuring civil liberties reduce the chances of their survival another year in power by 20 percent.

One thing I have come to believe firmly is that press freedom requires a series of a never-ending battles. This book is the story of a number of those flashpoints, conflicts and battles and especially of the stalwarts I've known who have fought them.

Looking back on the decades, I have also seen the truth of my brilliant college professor Louis Hartz in his book *The Founding of New Societies*, which was published when I was a junior at Harvard and which played a central role in what has become my keen interest in Latin America.

Hartz is best known for an earlier book, *The Liberal Tradition in America*, in which he contends the United States was built by mostly like-minded immigrants fleeing Old World feudal restraints, royal absolutism and clerical oppression. The vast majority of those who built this country, he says, shared a Lockean liberal philosophy of individual rights, freedom, and limited representative government. To use his phrase, the United States was "born free."

In the later book he looks at other New World societies, including Latin America, where he maintains the colonial societies were established by advocates of the very systems and philosophies the U.S. pioneers fled. The conquistadors brought with them, Hartz believes, a desire to recreate the Spain and Portugal they had left. They stood firmly by feudal society, political authoritarianism and religious orthodoxy. Only later, long after these views became the root of Latin American thinking, did the modern political philosophies of the Enlightenment arrive to compete with and be grafted onto this core.

What has become glaringly apparent to me is that most Latin Americans, especially politicians and the active public, look at press freedom differently from those of us whose societies emerged from the liberal traditions. I believe Hartz's theories help one think about these differences — and clarify them.

Had it not been for Louis Hartz, I would not only think differently about Latin America, I would not have lived my life as I have. My senior year in college I had hoped to be a Rhodes Scholar and was nominated by Harvard for the Rhodes interview. I was not successful, but the experience made me realize there is homework to be done if one is to succeed in such competitions.

I then applied for a Fulbright Scholarship to Latin America. I learned that Professor Hartz would be serving on the interview committee. I already knew a great deal about his work on North America because I had taken two of his classes, but I was not at the time aware of his recently published new book. In my preparations, I learned of *The Founding of New Societies* and made a point of reading it. I won a Fulbright to Ecuador, and I have never doubted that having read Hartz's book gave me an essential leg up in the Fulbright interview. The payoff was the year-long honeymoon my wife Karen and I enjoyed in Ecuador and life-long fascination with the region.

Over this long experience, I have learned that the Old World philosophy brought by the conquistadors constantly influences the struggle for liberal ideals in Latin America. The United States and its colonial British antecedents, South American liberator Simón Bolívar observed, had been "cradled in liberty, reared on freedom and maintained on liberty alone." Latin Americans had no such history, he said, and would need to find their own way.

In the 20th century, the great Mexican writer and philosopher Octavio Paz elaborated. Writing about how medieval and scholastic philosophy and institutions have lived on to our time, the Nobel laureate concludes in *Democracy and Dictatorship in Latin America*:

"Our intellectuals have embraced liberalism, positivism, and Marxism-Leninism. Yet in almost every case, regardless of philosophical outlook, the psychological and moral attitudes of the former champions of Neo-Scholasticism are only too obvious, out of sight but still alive. The paradox of modernity: today's ideas, yesterday's attitudes."

While the United States has rightly been seen as a shining example of press freedom, it too has had and continues to experience challenges. Only in 1964 did the U.S. Supreme Court rule in *Times v. Sullivan* that, short of actual malice narrowly defined, criticism of a public official is protected. The standard is knowing the statement was false or having reckless disregard of whether it was false or true.

Although haltingly, freedom of press and transparency of government have continued to evolve and improve in the United States. But it is an endless struggle.

In Latin America freedom of the press is more an up-hill battle. But progress is occurring. A few courts in the region have adopted the actual-malice standard on criticism of government. Countries are realizing they must be more open to thrive in the global age of information. Nearly a dozen have adopted open access laws providing more transparency of government, although the follow-through has been spotty.

In the context of historical forces, especially the Iberian traditions, the accomplishments of the courageous, modern-thinking journalistic leaders this book portrays are all the more impressive. Yes, most of them have financial stakes in their efforts, sometimes very large ones. But they took risks and fought because they believe free expression is the bulwark of democracy.

Their roles in the democratic progress since the 1970s have been crucial. In fledgling democracies, the press is central in setting the agenda, shaping public opinion and keeping government accountable. It is no mere by-product of democratization. This is especially true in countries where political parties and interest groups remain underdeveloped. In this sense, the press has been the locomotive of change. Again and again, whether in Mexico, Brazil, Chile, Panama, Peru, Nicaragua, Colombia or Argentina, the press has been anything but a free-riding caboose in this process.

A prime minister of Peru even referred to his nation's press as the country's most powerful sector, by which he apparently meant the press has filled the vacuum left by the absence of real political parties.

I have been privileged to participate in a decades-long endeavor to promote the principles of press freedom. I have been in the leadership of numerous initiatives to help the hemisphere's press, the most important of which was the development and crafting of a statement of principles that has become the Magna Carta for press freedom in Latin America: the Declaration of Chapúltepec.

Democracy and press freedom are not inevitable. The late Harvard political scientist Sam Huntington[1] held that they come in waves. They surge forward, then retreat, and not in isolation. In this sense, my experience campaigning for these ends would probably not have been as successful in another era.

The first wave, Huntington contended, began in the early years of the United States. Eventually it swept Western Europe, parts of Eastern Europe,

---

1. Professor Huntington was the Harvard Government Department's grader for my senior honor's thesis about Spain's Franco regime. He had the reputation as a tough grader but was generous that day and gave me a "Magna."

Canada, New Zealand and four Latin American countries: Chile, Argentina, Uruguay and Costa Rica.

When fascism surged in the 1920s and 1930s, a reverse wave took hold around the world. Overthrow of the Axis powers in 1945 opened a new wave including in Latin America. However, a series of military coups, responding to the Communist takeover of Cuba, reversed that wave with the exceptions of Costa Rica, Venezuela and Colombia.

A third forward surge began in 1974 in response to the overthrow of the dictatorship in Portugal, pressure from the Carter administration and the end of the Franco dictatorship in Spain. This wave endured more than three decades. For the first time in history, a majority of countries in the world were viable democracies. My heroes and I have promoted press freedom and democracy during this flowering. The worldwide wave undoubtedly helped us.

Political scientists see 2008 as another retreat. Illiberal, anti-immigrant populism emerged in Europe and the United States. Attacks have come on democratic institutions including the electoral process, independent courts, the media, civil society, universities and even the police and security agencies.

In Latin America the erosion by the "democratators" began after Hugo Chávez's election in 1998, and it spread to Nicaragua and Bolivia in 2007 and 2008. These democracies today are only shells of what they once were, but democratic institutions elsewhere in the region have subsisted.

In five decades I have had the good fortune to be acquainted with many of the major figures in print journalism in the region as well as numerous dictators, presidents and other political leaders. I have worked through the Inter American Press Association (IAPA), where my initial participation was simply a means of getting back to Latin America. My interest grew and I eventually served in many capacities, including president and long-time fund raiser, to leverage moral suasion and embarrassment to preserve the independence and viability of journalists.

IAPA is a non-profit press advocacy organization founded in 1926 and based in Miami. Membership includes more than 1,300 newspapers, magazines, broadcast stations and digital outlets throughout the Western Hemisphere. Its participants are primarily executives and owners with the mission of defending freedom of the press. It is unique in that the media themselves are the members.

Other non-profit organizations play roles on press freedom in Latin America, although they also focus worldwide. Among them are the International Press Institute (IPI), the World Press Freedom Committee (WPFC), and the Committee to Protect Journalists (CPJ). I have worked with each of them.

An earlier book by Mary Gardner, *The Inter American Press Association: Its Fight for Freedom of the Press, 1926–1960,* traces the early history on IAPA.

My book is organized by geographic region: Southern Cone (Argentina, Chile, etc.), Northern South America (Colombia, Brazil, Venezuela, etc.), Central America including Mexico, and the Caribbean. Chapters are both long and short, depending on my personal involvement. Maps accompany each regional section.

Following these chapters is an essay examining IAPA's relationship with the U.S. Central Intelligence Agency (CIA)—documenting the falsehood of the long-held and unfounded allegation of cooperation between them. Then come a chapter on the origin of the Declaration of Chapútepec, a Conclusion and an Appendix relating pre-Columbian influences on press freedom battles.

At least four themes emerge in the book:

The importance of press freedom to democracy in Latin America as well as how struggles for them differ from the United States.

The roles of courageous Latin American journalists in furthering press freedom and democracy.

The importance of the Inter American Press Association (IAPA) as well as other organizations in supporting these journalists.

My own involvement in these organizations on behalf of numerous journalists—including many close personal friends—as well as my reflections on supporting these efforts for nearly five decades.

What others and I have done has had consequences, both intended and unintended. In some cases the battle has been against historical forces.

Latin America's relationship with freedom of press has been chaotic. Challenges come from diverse sources—ideology, money, affiliations, even sex. Advocates sometimes waver. Compromise occurs. This book reveals some of the chaos and challenges.

Above all, I have had the privilege to know many heroes of press freedom. This account is primarily about these people I have known, admired and tried to help. It presents their stories one country at a time.

There have been a few scoundrels, too. They go with the territory. I think

H.L. Mencken said it best: "The trouble with fighting for human freedoms is that you have to spend so much of life defending sons-of-bitches; for oppressive laws always are aimed at them originally and oppression must be stopped at the beginning if it is to be stopped at all."

Mostly, though, I think about the heroes.

SOUTHERN CONE

BOLIVIA

PARAGUAY

CHILE

URUGUAY

ARGENTINA

1. Argentina
Heroes in a Dirty War

In 1978, at the height of Argentina's "Dirty War," a colleague and I used my room at the Plaza Hotel in Buenos Aires to interview human rights workers and the rabbi of the country's most celebrated political prisoner, newspaperman Jacobo Timerman. When my wife Karen and I returned to the room after my interview with Timerman, I found a threatening message under the door. On a hotel telex form, it invited us to our own burials that night at midnight at the cemetery. It was signed by Germán Mounters Jr., which brought to mind the Montoneros, the leftist guerrillas that had brought the country to the brink of civil war.

We didn't know whether to take the message seriously, but with so many people disappearing at the time in Argentina, we were afraid to ignore it. We hesitated to call the police, because they were behind some of the disappearances. Ultimately, we contacted the U.S. embassy, and they checked with police sources they said could be trusted. These sources came to the Plaza to investigate and concluded the threat probably was not serious.

Meanwhile, I sniffed around the hotel and found a telex pad in a nearby room that had been vacated recently. Hotel management identified the previous occupants as young Venezuelan females who had checked out. I've always assumed they had observed our suspicious activities of the previous couple of days and wrote the threat as a joke. In any case, on the advice of the embassy, we made a point of being in a very public location on Florida, one of the capital's main shopping streets, at midnight. Nothing happened.

While unnerving, the incident was not our first or most disturbing brush with the reality that then was Argentina. Two years earlier, a telephone call came to me from Miami saying there was very bad news from Argentina, but that my friend Raúl Kraiselburd wanted me to know. Given his recent tragic history, my heart dropped.

Karen and I had been close friends of Raúl and his wife Cecilia from our earliest days in the Inter American Press Association (IAPA). With our classroom Spanish, we had struggled through long and substantive conversations with them in nice restaurants. We always thought they had sort of adopted us–first because we were about the same age and younger than most IAPA active members, second because they thought they might need Americans as friends, and also perhaps so they could help us develop our Spanish.

Raúl was running the large daily in La Plata with his father, David, when we first met. Their paper, *El Dia*, had been confiscated in the 1950s by Juan Peron. In 1975 David Kraiselburd was kidnapped as a political measure by the radical-leftist Montoneros, held and ultimately killed in the tumult that then possessed Argentina. Raúl went to New York later that year to accept posthumously on behalf of his father the coveted Maria Moors Cabot award from Columbia University.

Not long afterward, Raúl and Cecilia had a son and named him David. In the Jewish tradition, they could give him that name only if his namesake grandfather were dead. The baby was born in California where Cecilia had taken refuge from the violence of the Dirty War. After a year she and the baby returned to Argentina to be with Raúl, but then came the March 1976 military coup. A month before young David turned two came the disturbing message from Miami: little David had been kidnapped.

The kidnappers demanded money, publication of certain statements in Raúl's newspaper and that Raúl and Cecilia leave the country. The money was paid, Raúl and Cecilia left Argentina, but the statements were not published. The Argentine military government at the time automatically closed down newspapers that published guerrilla statements. Young David was never heard from again.

Later they told us the baby's kidnapping may have been an inside job involving some of their domestic staff and perhaps even Cecilia's family, some of whom were leftists. Even today Raúl believes the baby was probably killed the night of the kidnapping. Suspects later captured under the leadership of the military chief of police, Col. Ramón Camps, were "killed trying to escape." Raúl and Cecilia's marriage never really recovered, although they had a second son, Ernesto, who took his first steps in our home in Kansas. Raúl married again and has two more children. Cecilia went to law school, remarried and is a practicing attorney in Buenos Aires.

Raul continued his activities with the IAPA and eventually became president. While at times he has been controversial, he has always stood for the principles of democracy and free press. He was chairman of IAPA's key committee, the freedom of press committee, for five years, and in the past two decades has taken on the role of a kind of high priest on press freedom. He is listened to because he has seen so much and lost so much. He has been the person IAPA members from both the United States and Latin America have listened to time after time when the association has faced difficult freedom of expression issues. He is so bright and knowledgeable that he is looked to for insightful perspective on virtually every significant issue. In 2003 he, too, was awarded Columbia University's prestigious Maria Moors Cabot Prize. Bob Cox and I wrote his nomination. Bob is another prominent editor with horrific experiences in Argentina.

Raúl's political skills were honed in the early sixties when he was active in the student movement at Universidad National de La Plata, where he occupied various leadership positions. He was also a student representative in the university government.

My most memorable experiences in Argentina came in the 1978 mission at the request of Raul. As IAPA's freedom of press committee vice chairman for Argentina, he called for a mission to Buenos Aires to look into the disappearance of journalists in the midst of the Dirty War. Ignacio Lozano and I were asked to form the mission by IAPA President Argentina Hills, then publisher of *El Mundo* of San Juan, Puerto Rico. Nacho Lozano had recently returned to his newspaper, *La Opinión* of Los Angeles, Calif., after serving two years as U.S. ambassador to El Salvador. He knew first-hand the ways of repressive governments.

Our mission helped bring world attention to the Timerman case and played a major role, Raul Kraiselburd would later tell an interviewer, in Timerman's eventual release from custody. When we arrived in Buenos Aires, Timerman had been held in jail and under house arrest for more than a year without visits from press organizations or others except his family and rabbi. We were the first to get permission to visit him, and we were nearly in shock that we did. He was not freed for another year.

Timerman eventually became a *cause célèbre* throughout the world, especially in the United States and Israel. At the time of our visit in the fall of 1978, he was a 55-year-old newspaper owner and editor who had been dragged from his home in the middle of the night 16 months earlier, tortured, denied his property, tried and acquitted by a military court. He was then ordered freed by the country's Supreme Court, and yet remained a prisoner. In many respects he was one of the lucky ones. At the time, 22 journalists were known to have been killed, 39 had disappeared and were presumed dead, and another 40 including Timerman were known to be held by authorities.

Timerman's case was already well known in Argentina. A professional Argentine journalist for 30 years, resident of the country for 50 of his 55 years, he was acknowledged by virtually all his professional counterparts as probably the most important figure in the development of modern Argentine journalism. He was the country's best known newspaper publisher. He patterned his newspaper, *La Opinión*, after Paris' *Le Monde* and introduced interpretive journalism to the country. It was a tabloid specializing in political analysis and commentary. At its height it was one of the most important papers in Buenos Aires, with a circulation of nearly 150,000 and a state-of-the-art plant. When we visited, a colonel was running the paper and circulation had dropped to 30,000.

What made Timerman's case different from the other journalists whom the government thought to have connections to the terrorists was that he had been cleared in military court; and the Supreme Court, for the first time in its history under such circumstance, had ordered the government, under its own repressive rules, to release him. That ruling, which came two months before our August mission, stated Timerman should not have been held since the previous October.

We had a pre-arranged meeting with Interior Minister (Gen.) Albano Eduardo Harguindeguy, who by all accounts controlled the dark world of kidnapping and death. Under his watch, tens of thousands would vanish. With virtually no hope of success but as a formal gesture of support, we asked Harguindeguy to let us visit Timerman. To our astonishment, he said we could do so that very afternoon. He also revealed to us that Timerman's Argentine citizenship had been stripped, and the journalist would have to find another country willing to accept him. Although first, said the minister, Timerman would have to clear up his financial affairs in a civil court.

We were escorted through a series of guards into Timerman's 15th-floor apartment. Later I learned a cadre of 52 police were guarding him in four shifts of 13 each. Three were stationed outside the building and 10 within—in the lobby, in the 15th floor hallway and inside the apartment itself.

Timerman was alarmed to hear about his citizenship. A burly man with a round face, he now carried a gaunt appearance that conveyed a certain hopelessness. He had lost nearly 50 pounds. He was having problems with his eyes and teeth, but hadn't been permitted to see a dentist. His blonde wife Rische, so thin and nervous, could herself have been the torture victim.

Timerman, a Soviet Jew brought to South America at the age of three, described his legal state as "a kidnap victim." He told us he'd been tied to a table, covered with water and subjected to electric shock. He said the questions he was asked were those used by Nazi torturers in Germany. He said he was persecuted because he was a Jew. Thirty others detained at the same time, he pointed out, had either been convicted or freed.

He gave us a carbon copy of the latest petition he was making to the courts. That petition, along our report to the IAPA General Assembly, resulted in more open discussion of his plight in Argentina and around the world. Pressure from the Israelis and other governments led to another Supreme Court ruling in 1979 that the military junta had no right to keep him under detention. A week later he was freed from his 30 months of hell on earth, stripped of his Argentine citizenship (which apparently had not actually taken place earlier) and permitted to emigrate to Israel. An attempt to overthrow the government by one of the displeased right-wing military factions followed his release.

Somehow our report to the General Assembly made its way into his hands, and he wrote an effusive thank-you letter to me. In it he was especially grateful to Raúl Kraiselburd, because he had believed that no important Argentine editors had come to his defense. I gave the letter to Raúl when he and Cecilia visited our home in Kansas.

Jacobo and I exchanged letters after that, and he came to California to address and thank the IAPA in the fall of 1980. In a letter in April that year he asked me whether he should write a book. I responded that at the very least he should produce a personal account of his experiences and views. Before the year was over he published *Prisoner Without a Name, Cell Without a Number*, which was widely acclaimed around the world and was still in print 25 years later.

Few Argentines at the time knew about the terrible secret world Timerman revealed in the book, and those who did either supported its aims or were uncertain what to do about it. There was great hypocrisy about it.

In a review of the book for *The Manhattan Mercury*, I wrote that Timerman was the Alfred Dreyfus of our generation. While the book relates the cruel reality of Argentina's horrifying secret world, Timerman's overriding theme is that dark periods like the Holocaust and the Argentine Dirty War should be understood not so much for the number of victims as for the magnitude of the silence. Moderates fail to speak out, he says, for fear of damaging moderate forces in the government or other sectors of society. He explains how a crusade against insurgency and violence, which he himself welcomed in 1976, can lead to fear and indifference and finally silence. Just as silence in Nazi Germany overcame the most advanced nation in Europe, a similar paranoia overcame the most advanced nation in Latin America.

In my decades of working on delicate press freedom issues, I don't think I ever worried more about our safety than when we received the death threat the day Nacho Lozano and I interviewed Timerman. Already on edge about what we'd read and heard about Argentina's "Dirty War," Karen and I had developed a case of nerves from our very arrival in Buenos Aires. The taxi driver we engaged from the airport pulled off the main road without explanation and began a route through back streets. Given what we had heard about disappearances and kidnappings, we became very concerned. Eventually he pulled into a gas station and filled his tank.

Other experiences did little to calm our nerves. Our IAPA colleagues Jorge and Bunty Fascetto organized a buffet for us to meet several of the leading editors and publishers, who briefed us on the situation that some of them said was improving. That was reassuring. Then, while we were having breakfast the next morning at the Plaza Hotel, one of the participants from the previous evening, Julio Rajneri, sought us out to tell us what we had heard was mostly untrue. This courageous politician-editor from Rio Negro then detailed what was going on at the naval facility in La Plata, where many of the victims were initially housed, and other details of the secret dark world run by Gen. Harguindeguy. He told us about a reporter's recent disappearance which strongly implicated local authorities in Rio Negro. "If I publish the facts of that case as I know them," he whispered, "I will disappear."

We would hear apologists, including the editors of the largest circulation Spanish language newspaper in the world, *Clarín*. Like some of their colleagues at the regional dailies, they did not publish stories on kidnappings or subversive activities. Disappearances are so commonplace, they are not news, *Clarín*'s editors told us. "They're like fender-benders in your country," said one. Other editors and publishers said they didn't publish accounts of violence because they agreed with the government's campaign against terrorism, and they were "going to cooperate."

Timerman was always a controversial figure in Argentina. He was widely regarded as an opportunist with a significant ego. He founded several innovative publications prior to starting *La Opinión* in 1971, and he had always had close ties with the military. He supported two military takeovers before backing the 1976 coup. In fact, the overthrow of democratically elected Arturo Frondizi, with whom he was closely allied, was the only military takeover after the fall of Juan Perón in 1955 that he didn't support.

Controversy around him, especially within the military, mushroomed when it came to light that *La Opinión* had received significant financial help from a wealthy Jewish financier named David Graiver. Graiver was killed in the suspicious crash of a private jet in Mexico just four months after the 1976 coup, and after his death came proof that he had served as a banker, making regular interest payments, for a portion of the $60 million obtained in business executive kidnappings by the leftist Montoneros. This revelation cast a shadow over Timerman, despite the fact that Graiver's assistance to the guerrillas came only after the founding of *La Opinión*. Earlier Graiver had backed *Nuevo Hombre*, the magazine of the Revolutionary Workers Party from which emerged another guerrilla group, the ERP (Ejército Revolucionario del Pueblo).

Graiver and Timerman each owned 45 percent of the stock in *La Opinión*, with a neutral third person holding the balance. Graiver put up most of the capital. However, Graiver's interest remained silent until after his death. Even top executives at *La Opinión* were unaware of it. Whether Timerman kept it secret as a matter of ego so both his staff and readers thought of him as the sole owner, or because knowledge of Graiver's involvement would compromise the daily, will probably never be known. What is clear is that Timerman did not even mention Graiver in his book, *Prisoner Without a Name, Cell Without and Number*, despite the fact that the book's principal point is that he was a victim of anti-Semitism.

Timerman's principal interrogator under torture had been Ramón Camps, the same colonel who had led the investigation in the kidnapping of young David Kraiselburd. Camps focused throughout the sessions on Timerman's connections to Graiver. For years, I have believed Timerman was kidnapped and held primarily because of his involvement with Graiver, whose links to the Montoneros were known to the military by then, and not solely because he was Jewish. He didn't care to address this issue in the book, apparently, because he wanted to portray himself as a victim of anti-Semitism.

The connection to Graiver also probably explains why he was so problematic for the anti-Semitic security thugs who took him. The authorities were unable in military court to prove Timerman had any connection to the terrorists, but they undoubtedly thought they had discovered the great Marxist-Jewish conspiracy for which they were searching.

Timerman did play a role in the human rights battles, but an examination of the record makes clear he was not the crusader he portrays himself to be in his book. He crusaded against the kidnappings and murders by guerrillas before the coup, but went public about human rights violations afterward only when his own newspaper's personnel were kidnapped and murdered.

Bob Cox, the remarkable editor of the *Buenos Aires Herald*, told me later when the book was published in English that Timerman's ego let him believe he played the roles he describes. He published more *habeas corpus* pleas brought by families seeking the whereabouts of disappeared relatives than most, Cox said, and was an opponent of violence. But he usually did so after an important case had appeared in the *Herald*, and he could see that Cox had not disappeared (which he did eventually for a brief period). "We all could have done better," Cox lamented. "We wanted to do better, but we had to protect our newspapers."

Timerman was not alone in his sympathy for the military leaders who launched the March 1976 coup against the three-year rule of the popularly elected Perón government. Terrorism had become so rampant the country was approaching a state of anarchy. This reality has largely been ignored in subsequent accounts of the "Dirty War." The Montoneros exulted in killing and atrocious acts of indiscriminate bombings which claimed many lives. In some cases the murders were ordered simply to test recruits. The atrocities, of course, allowed the military to justify in the eyes of the vast majority of Argentines their even worse atrocities.

Kidnappings, nightly shootouts, bombings, beatings and general terrorism were rampant before the coup, perpetrated by both the right and the left. Guerrillas controlled certain geographic regions, including territory not far from Buenos Aires. They had become so strong that for short periods they could take over wealthy neighborhoods in the capital city itself. Officials in business and industry were being assassinated simply because of their positions. Kidnappings had generated enormous sums for the terrorists, estimated at from $200 to $600 million. The publisher of an important regional daily told me of moving her family members into the newspaper's plant for several months because security could not be maintained at their private residence. The court system virtually collapsed as judges feared for their own lives. In most of the 60 interviews Ignacio Lozano and I conducted, we were told the country would have succumbed to the guerrillas had the military not intervened.

But according to Máximo Gainza, editor in chief of *La Prensa*, then Argentina's most influential newspaper, when the capital city's publishers were called to sit across from the coup leaders for a briefing on what would be permitted in newspapers, Timerman came into the room with the military and sat with them rather than the other publishers. Gainza believed Timerman had a role in drafting the order outlining material about subversives that could not be published, and perhaps an even more important role. Timerman himself told us he was not opposed to the coup, but rather what came later. In fact, when Timerman's own graphics director was snatched off the street and vanished without a trace, he took action. He began running a box each day on the front page recording the number of days since his colleague had disappeared. Within two weeks Timerman himself disappeared.

After his release, Timerman was welcomed by Israel and had instant celebrity. There, too, he became controversial with a book attacking Israel's 1982 incursion into Lebanon. He eventually returned to Argentina, where the democratic government of Raúl Alfonsín, now unable to restore *La Opinión* to him, compensated him with $4 million in cash, which he used to acquire the struggling *La Razón*. His attempt to convert it into a new version of *La Opinión* was a failure. He later moved to Uruguay where he died in 1999.

Máximo Gainza, a good friend who later also became president of IAPA, was less controversial but no less courageous. Despite orders to keep secret the government's decree restricting news about subversives and how they were dealt with, he published the order on the front page of *La Prensa*. He told us doing so was the only way his readers would understand why certain important issues would not appear in his pages.

Later, after thousands of terrorists and others suspected of links to terrorists had disappeared, Gainza agreed to publish a paid advertisement in May 1978, listing 2,500 persons missing since the military junta took power. And just weeks after Ignacio Lozano and I made our report on the Argentine nightmare to IAPA's 34th General Assembly in Miami, Gainza's newspaper took the bold step of becoming the first major Buenos Aires newspaper to speak out. It published an opinion piece titled "The Need to Explain the Cases of the Disappeared."

Maxi was told after he published the piece that one of the military leaders said to others in a meeting, "This Gainza, if he wants to know where the disappeared are, we're going to make him disappear." Fortunately, some of the others were Maxi's friends and defended him. "If not, they would have made me disappear," he told an interviewer.

Because of either fear or complicity, many other publishers did not cross this line. In some cases they feared undermining moderate elements in the government who wanted a return to democracy. In the case of Buenos Aires' three largest newspapers, *Clarín*, *La Razón* and *La Nación*, the hesitation clearly stemmed from a serious conflict of interest.

Their conflict sprang from David Graiver's death and government takeover of his property, which included a substantial interest in Papel Prensa, the major national newsprint producer then under construction. The military junta arranged for the three dailies to acquire 75 percent of Papel Prensa, with the government holding the balance. They paid a fraction of the true value.

The newsprint plant cost $180 million and had a capacity to supply 80 percent of the needs of Argentina's newspapers. Each of the three newspapers contributed $8 million toward the start-up, but the bulk of the funding came from the government via liberal credit. While in some instances the owners undoubtedly sympathized with the government's policies, after the deal none could afford to antagonize their official banker.

The raw truth is that the great majority of publishers and editors and writers were afraid to take risks. Some supported the government campaign, known as "The Process" (*El Proceso*). Many acknowledged to us that they probably could publish without running afoul of the government, but they didn't want trouble. Official reprisal was not the only thing to fear. Para-official reprisals by elements in the military were routine. This was government hoodlumism. And, of course, the guerrillas could still be a threat.

The rules of the game were unclear. No one was sure who was responsible for many of the disappearances and deaths. The atmosphere was not unlike totalitarianism, although less well organized. It was as if Argentines were living out a novel by Franz Kafka. People died, people disappeared, then reappeared. The editor of the country's leading financial journal, Julián Delgado, disappeared along with his car shortly before we arrived. No trace of either was ever found. If victims were lucky, midnight kidnappings by persons dressed in civilian clothes would result in arrests acknowledged later by authorities. Yet in many cases no such acknowledgment came, and the police wouldn't investigate.

Reproducing commentaries on Argentina published abroad could get a newspaper closed, as did speculation about the ambitions of junta members. Denouncing the junta for human rights violations resulted in kidnapping and disappearance. Several knowledgeable journalists said their suspicion was that such responses were orchestrated not by junta members themselves, but by lower-ranking military officers acting on their own. Although Gen. Harguindeguy later would contend all military leaders were in agreement, these sources believed the top military leaders were unable to control their inferiors, and the country was in effect being run not by one authority but by the equivalent of seven or eight governments.

Three days after we left Argentina, Horacio Agulla, publisher of the weekly *Confirmado,* was shot and killed as he was parking his car in an upper-class Buenos Aires neighborhood. He was a supporter of the moderate elements within the military government and had recently spoken out in his weekly against the hardliners in the armed forces. His assassination was viewed as an effort to obstruct the moderates in their promise to begin dialogue with the democratic political sectors.

Most newspapers simply ignored the kidnappings. Máximo Gainza courageously published the list of 2,500 persons in *La Prensa* who had disappeared, including hundreds not previously known to have disappeared. At least three other Buenos Aires dailies had rejected the ad. Raúl Kraiselburd and Julio Rajneri routinely published disappearances, but they were somewhat less at risk because their dailies were regional, in La Plata and Rio Negro. They were not without risk. The provincial government cut off official advertising valued at $100,000 a year to Raúl's daily, and his reporters were barred from official functions. Inspectors combed his building at one point for evidence of minor building-regulation infringements.

The most notable exception was Bob Cox and his *Buenos Aires Herald,* the bold little daily published in English. Of the many heroes of the Latin American press I have known, Bob is the most admirable. A British citizen, he risked his life repeatedly by standing up in his adopted country, almost alone, against the violence of the left and the right. He received death threats from both, yet continued on for six years until the threats also came against his family. His newspaper carried the most complete coverage of human rights violations after the coup despite the official prohibition. It was the only paper willing to go to press routinely without official police information on such crimes. Police sources, at least in Buenos Aires, largely dried up in such cases. When a bomb went off in the *Herald* building, the only Buenos Aires paper to cover the incident was the *Herald* itself. The publisher of one capital city paper told our mission that he had withdrawn his four-man bureau from the police station because it simply was unable to confirm anything.

Cox managed to get around the military government's embargo on all but "official" news about kidnap victims (*desaparecidos*) by publishing *habeas corpus* petitions, which he reasoned indeed were official notices. The result was readers came to understand the enormity of the *desaparecido* phenomenon.

Cox's poignant editorials kept before his readers reminders of important fellow countrymen who had disappeared. He would also occasionally criticize journalistic colleagues for not printing stories about kidnappings. Later, victims like María Consuelo Castaño Blanco, who disappeared for nearly four years, would recount how their lives were saved by Cox courageously making a public issue of their cases. She did so later in a book, *Más Que Humanos.*

In her gripping account, Castaño Blanco explains exactly in detail how Bob's heroic work saved her life. She disappeared just two months before Bob and Maud had to begin plans for their own escape from the country. Her neighbors informed her family, who turned to Bob. He interviewed them two days after her disappearance and published their story on the front page the next morning. The Inter American Human Rights Commission happened to be in Buenos Aires and saw the story. The next day at noon the commissioners met with President Videla, and he intervened as she was about to be killed. She was saved by minutes, she writes.

While Cox was somewhat insulated because his newspaper was published in English—it had been permitted greater freedoms even during the dictatorship of Juan Perón in the 1950s—he was not immune from reprisal. In 1977 he was arrested and held for two days under a charge of violating a security law by publishing a front page story about a press conference held in Rome by Argentine extremists. Gen. Harguindeguy told his colleagues in the government he had to take measures against Cox to prevent other dailies from thinking they might do something similar. Bob said later he was relieved to have been officially arrested, because he knew he was not to be killed as thousands of others had been. His arrest resulted in one of the few instances where the other newspapers cried out in protest. The British and U.S. embassies also came emphatically to his defense.

Maud Cox, Bob's Argentine wife, relates details of his arrest in her book, *Salvados del Infierno* (*Saved from Hell*):

On April 23rd, Betty, Bob's secretary called. "Don't get worried Maud, I've got good and bad news for you. Bob has been arrested but he hasn't disappeared. I assure you that he's in jail. They came with proper identification."

Incidentally, the night before, we had been to a reception at the British Embassy. The Charge d'Affaires, John Shakespeare, looked surprised to see us.

"Bob, I have your telephone number and address right beside my bed." And he embraced us.

We later found out that they knew all along that the government was planning an attack on Bob.

When I heard Betty's message, I lost control. Hysterically, I ran to the breakfast room where my father and the children were. My father shook me. "You can't be like this! How can you allow yourself to be distressed for nothing?" I gained my composure. I thought of the cell, Bob's asthma, the humiliation, and I feared torture. The telephone never stopped ringing. Klein (Walter Klein, a friend in the government) called to tell me not to worry because Harguindeguy had arranged, in Klein's presence, that they allow me to see him.

I dressed and went to the Federal Police Building. He was held incommunicado and was to receive visits from no one. I got back home and called Klein.

"Did you see him?" he said.

"No. There are no orders from the minister to allow me to see Bob. They haven't even let the British Consul see him."

From then on, I never believed what was said. I understood the game.

Pressure from abroad forced the government to bring a judge in on a Saturday. During his forty-eight hours in prison, Bob was incarcerated in five different cells, having been transferred from a hole in the police station, to three other cells, and ending up in "The Sheraton"–given this name by its inhabitants because, at "The Sheraton," those with money could purchase their own food and do their own cooking.

The newspapers announced that Bob's sentence would be from eight to twelve years in jail. I went to the trial, but before entering the room, I managed to see Bob. He got me to calm down and said he was prepared for whatever happened. He had been incommunicado and wasn't aware of what was said in the outside world.

The judge let Bob out on bail. I was waiting in the back room when he came in, chaperoned by two police officers.

"They've set me free but I must first stop by the police station to sign some papers," said Bob.

"I'm going with you."

"That isn't necessary, Madam . . ." said one of the policemen, ". . . he only has to sign . . ."

"Fine," I interrupted, "and what if you decide to snatch him on the street right after you've set him free?"

"Calm down, Madam, this time we won't."

With those few words, they gave themselves away.

Incredibly, just a week later, Bob took the enormous risk of publishing an editorial supporting Jacobo Timerman, who had been kidnapped by the authorities two weeks earlier. In it he blasted the other dailies for failing to come to Timerman's defense. He also continued publishing *habeas corpus* petitions of the victims' families. "If we reported a case within 24 hours," he would say later, "we were going to see the person alive again."

Bob Cox kept up his crusade on behalf of the disappeared through late 1979, when his youngest son, 10-year-old Peter, received a letter threatening the family. Timerman had been permitted to emigrate to Israel just weeks before, and reaction inside the government was harsh, nearly bringing down the Junta. This threat apparently was a concession to the hard-liners because Bob had campaigned for Timerman's release. By that time 70 Argentine journalists had disappeared in just four years. A total of 93 disappeared between 1976 and 1983. Such threats had to be taken seriously.

Earlier that year someone had tampered with the lug nuts on a rear wheel of Bob's car, and a wheel flew off as he and his family returned to Buenos Aires from vacation. Had traffic not been slow, they might all have been killed. Afterwards, Bob told Maud he had been warned of an attack and advised to take different routes to and from work.

On another occasion that year two men in leather jackets who identified themselves as police officers came to the Cox home saying they needed to see Bob because he didn't have his documents in order. Fortunately, Bob was not home, but they went on to ask about the children—what time they went to and from school, what they did afterwards, etc. A week earlier, Bob had been warned that his name was on a death list. After the officers' visit, Bob immediately left for the United States, and the rest of the family moved in with friends.

In the United States, Bob appealed for help from Argentina's ambassador, a cousin of President Videla. The president said Bob had to be persuaded to return, and the result was full-time protection for the Cox family. Bob, who told Maud he still had a lot of work to do in Argentina, returned.

Early in November students in the school attended by the Cox children were sent home because of a bomb threat. In the mail that day came the letter addressed to Peter, but using his formal name Ignacio Peter. When Peter began reading the handwritten letter, he turned pale. It referred to confidential plans the family had made for Christmas, to a confidential offer Bob had received to work in Paris on the *International Herald Tribune*, to various properties the family owned as well as how they could all die fighting for human rights. It was signed "Montoneros," but Bob knew it was a threat from the intelligence service and believed it was intended to destabilize the government.

Bob took the letter to Minister of Interior Harguindeguy, but he refused to investigate. When Maud heard this, she immediately said: "We must leave." They began making plans to do so. A couple of days before their intended departure Maud was confronted on the street by men traveling in the notorious green Ford Falcon, the car of choice for official kidnappers. She believes by acting nonchalant she led them to think they had targeted the wrong person.

On the 16th of December 1979, the Cox family left Argentina for London and later settled in Charleston, South Carolina, where Bob writes editorials for *The Post and Courier*, which was the home paper of Peter Manigault, who owned the *Buenos Aires Herald.*

Bob and Maud returned to Argentina in 1983 to observe the October elections that would restore democracy. My wife Karen and I were on the airplane with them to Buenos Aires from Lima, where we had all attended the IAPA annual meeting. The plane made a stop in Santiago where, when we got off, Maud and Bob realized another passenger disembarking with us was Gen. Guillermo Suárez Mason, who had been in charge of the terror in Buenos Aires province and had played a role in Bob's arrest. He was taking advantage of the moment to return from exile.

Maud and Bob nearly didn't get back on the airplane. She would later inscribe her memoir to Karen and me, "For being with us in Buenos Aires and remembering your glance (that helped me) on the plane to B.A." Suarez Mason was later convicted of Dirty War crimes. Because of our close friendships with the Coxes and Kraiselburds through the years, I have been unforgiving in my encounters with former guerrillas or the Dirty War authors. One of Argentina's leading journalists today, Horacio Verbitsky, has played an admirable role in uncovering corruption, exposing military crimes and duplicity as well as taking the lead on important freedom of expression issues. But in the '70s he was a spokesman for the Montoneros, and he has never apologized for that role. He even said in an interview in 2001 that the murder of former de facto president Eugenio Aramburu, which was the starting point of Montonero terrorism, was a mistake because instead of being at the beginning of a revolutionary process, it should have been at the end "like the Cuban revolution." Even today, as Bob Cox wrote recently in the *Buenos Aires Herald* about Verbitsky, he "tells some of the truth some of the time"

As a member of the Cabot Board, I joined Bob Cox in opposing Verbitsky's candidacy for a Maria Moors Cabot Prize, and I remain suspicious of his journalism. He played a key role in the founding of the alternative daily in Buenos Aires, *Página 12*, which after democracy was restored became the darling of the foreign press. It was often quoted as the authoritative source about the country despite its very limited circulation. Its reputation suffered, however, when its original editor revealed it was founded with $1 million from the remnants of one of the two guerrilla movements, the somewhat less vicious Marxist-Leninist Ejército Revolucionario del Pueblo (ERP).

With the election of Nestor Kirchner to the presidency in 2003, the former Montoneros made something of a comeback, albeit peaceful. Kirchner, himself on the fringe of their movement as a law student at the University of La Plata, appointed a number of ex-Montoneros to important positions.

Through Horacio Verbitsky, he also has funneled government support to *Página 12*. Interestingly, he appointed Jacobo Timerman's son, Hector, his consul in New York.

After his election, Kirchner's wife Cristina Fernendéz sought and was elected to the Senate from Buenos Aires province. Raúl Kraiselburd's paper in the province's capital city, La Plata, was critical of both Kirchner and his wife. As a result, clearly in concert with the president, Horacio Timerman attacked Raúl from New York in a letter to *La Nación*, alleging that he had supported the military government and done nothing for its victims. What irony!

In 2018, 40 years after Nacho Lozano and I reported the challenges of Argentina's Dirty War to IAPA's 34th General Assembly in Miami, I was honored with a tribute at the society's 74th General Assembly in Salta, Argentina.

The executive of the Argentine newspaper association, Carlos Jornet, who is also the publisher of the Córdoba daily, *La Voz del Interior*, offered the following immediately after President of Argentina Mauricio Macri delivered his address to the assembly:

> We offer a tribute in the name of all Argentine journalists to Ed Seaton on this anniversary of his visit during the military dictatorship. It was a very key factor in revealing what was occurring in Argentina while the only version reaching the outside world was from the military government.
>
> He traveled with Ignacio Lozano to Buenos Aires to see up close the situation and in the report presented in October of that year they denounced a "totalitarian atmosphere," "self-censorship," takeover of media by military authorities and kidnapping of journalists.
>
> Valliant gestures like those of Ed Seaton and of IAPA in general . . . were keys to revealing the horror that was being lived in Argentina and how our colleagues around the world came to see the reality.
>
> Muchas gracias, then, in the name of journalism of Argentina.

2. Chile
Money, Lives at Stake

The very first IAPA meeting my wife Karen and I attended was the 1972 General Assembly in Santiago, Chile. We had lived in Ecuador in 1965–66 and IAPA seemed a good means for pursuing our fascination with Latin America. Now that I had settled, apparently permanently, back home in Kansas in the newspaper business, this made sense to us.

We were so intrigued by what happened at the Chile meeting we became hooked with the organization and didn't miss another general assembly for 42 years. IAPA assemblies were held in Santiago again in 1987, 2000 and 2014. The latter we had to miss because of a head injury I suffered on a tennis court.

In 1972, we were young and naïve and didn't have a clue about the motives of the IAPA members who orchestrated that Chile meeting, although we did know something about the situation in Chile. When I applied for my Fulbright scholarship in 1965, I asked to go to Chile to study the fascinating but tense political situation there. I got Ecuador instead.

Today it is obvious that our first IAPA meeting was part of the larger effort to pressure to topple the government of President Salvador Allende, the first democratically elected socialist head of state in the Western Hemisphere. His eventual overthrow and death interrupted Chile's 150-year-old democracy and led to 17 years of harsh authoritarian rule under General Augusto Pinochet.

What we didn't know then was that Agustín Edwards, perhaps the richest man in Chile who owned the leading daily newspaper, *El Mercurio*, had recently served as IAPA president (1969) and undoubtedly was behind the decision to hold the meeting in his country.

No discussion of the Chilean press can be complete without a careful examination of Edwards, "Dooney" as he was known to friends. He is often accused by the left of orchestrating the overthrow of Allende with the help of the CIA. Later, he and his wife suffered through five agonizing months negotiating the release of their kidnapped 33-year-old middle son. And until his 2017 death at age 89 he was the patriarch of Chile's press. At the time of our meeting, he was living with his family in Connecticut, where he had taken refuge in 1969 shortly before Allende was elected. He had become vice president of Pepsico, a company headed by President Richard Nixon's close friend Donald M. Kendall. Karen and I would through the years come to know Dooney, his wife and two of their sons.

Today, details of Dooney's involvement in the Allende coup are well documented. Perhaps the most accurate account is a 2014 book by Jack Devine, *Good Hunting: An American Spymaster's Story.* At the time of the coup Devine was a clandestine CIA officer in Chile. He later served as Acting Director and Associate Director of all agency operations outside the United States.

"I can say with conviction that the CIA did not plot with the Chilean military to overthrow Allende in 1973," Devine writes. "It is important to set this straight for history: the CIA should not be blamed for bad outcomes it did not produce." What it did do, according the Devine, was help launch an ill-conceived earlier coup attempt ordered by President Nixon to keep Allende from taking office in September, 1970.

Dooney played an important role in that 1970 attempt. On the day before the September 4 Chilean election he carried his view to the U.S. ambassador, Edward Korry: He "had plowed all his profits for years into new industries and modernization, and would be ruined if Allende won," according to one account. The ambassador gave him no satisfaction, so he promptly flew to Washington where Don Kendall arranged for him to meet with Henry Kissinger, the national security advisor, and John Mitchell, the attorney general. Kissinger had Dooney meet at Washington's Madison Hotel with Richard Helms, the CIA director, to provide "whatever insight he might have" on Allende, according to Kissinger's memoir.

Documents declassified 30 years later as well as subsequent confirmations reveal that Edwards pushed for a covert operation to prevent Allende from assuming the presidency. He briefed Helms on why the opposition lost the election as well as a possible "constitutional solution" initially pursued by the U.S. embassy, to bribe Chilean congressmen to ratify the runner-up instead of Allende. They also discussed "Timing for Possible Military Action."

That same afternoon Nixon ordered Helms to foment military action to prevent Allende from taking office. The CIA director's handwritten notes summarized the president's directive: "1-in-10 chance, perhaps, but save Chile! . . . Not concerned risks involved . . . $10,000,000 available, more if necessary. Full-time job—best men we have." Helms later told a Congressional committee, "I have this impression that the president called this meeting where I have my handwritten notes because of Edwards' presence in Washington and what . . . Edwards was saying about conditions in Chile."

Despite pessimism on the part of the CIA officers in Chile, the upshot was that on October 22 a group of retired Chilean military officers tried to initiate a coup by kidnapping the Army commander, General René Schneider, who was stridently opposed to military intervention in politics. Schneider ended up being killed by the kidnappers and the country immediately rallied to Salvador Allende.

After that fiasco, according to Devine, Nixon changed policy to end any coup plotting and enhanced support for Allende's opposition. The intent was to avoid offering Allende's supporters an excuse to exploit anti-American feelings that would increase his international standing and domestic support. CIA strategy, Devine writes, was thus limited and also aimed to prevent Allende from crushing the institutions of democracy—including the media, political parties and labor groups. This strategy would include activities intended to destabilize the country. CIA operatives had strict orders to contact the military solely for intelligence gathering and not for fomenting coups. They did, however, help create the climate for the eventual coup. Freedom of the press became the principal focus of the Nixon policy toward Allende.

Central to this strategy was Dooney Edwards' newspaper, *El Mercurio*. Dooney feared the Allende government might expropriate his newspaper empire, which included several Santiago and regional dailies as well as *El Mercurio*. IAPA's 1972 general assembly undoubtedly played a role, albeit minor and perhaps unknowingly, in that effort.

Devine personally handled the CIA relationship with *El Mercurio* but had no contact with the news side, nor did he play a role in what was printed. It dealt with the business side and pushed an agenda of continued press freedom. The news editors on their own pushed an emphasis opposing Allende economic policies including the seizures of private property, illegal and violent activities by Allende supporters and possible economic collapse.

After his arrival in 1971, Devine says, the government blocked *El Mecurio's* access to newsprint, orchestrated cutbacks in its advertising, fomented labor unrest and threatened to shut down the daily. The paper continued publishing over the course of two years with the aid of $2 million from the CIA, an amount equivalent to more than $11 million in today's dollars. "Assistance provided to *El Mercurio* has enabled that independent newspaper to survive as an effective spokesman for Chilean democracy and against the UP (Allende) government," the CIA said in a Secret/Eyes Only memo.

In June of 1973, three months before the coup, *El Mercurio* ran an editorial claiming Allende had ceased to function as a constitutional president. Allende's response was to order the newspaper closed for six days, but an appeals court reversed the order saying under the libel law the government did not have standing to suspend the paper. Subsequently, the CIA stated that "the Santiago Station's propaganda project," in which *El Mercurio* was the dominant actor, "played a significant role in setting the stage for the military coup of 11 September 1973."

As in the United States, September 11 is an historic date in Chile—but for entirely Chilean reasons. Official Chilean investigations have revealed that the Pinochet regime murdered more the 2,200 people for political reasons and imprisoned more than 38,000, many of them tortured. Twelve hundred were executed in just the three months following the coup.

My attendance at the 1972 IAPA meeting in Santiago was memorable for many reasons. With my interest in Latin America I was fascinated by the country-by-country review of press freedom in the hemisphere. But events surrounding the meeting itself especially got my attention.

For one, American activist Angela Davis, who had been sent to Chile expressly to confront the IAPA at that time, publicly threatened to lead a rally of thousands to get us out of our hotel and the country—within 48 hours.

Perhaps most striking to me was the protest Allende supporters waged outside our hotel and the anti-IAPA graffiti they plastered on the outside walls and fences. That was the case until the last day of the assembly when the new IAPA president, a Costa Rican, replaced the incumbent IAPA president from the United States. A friend of the new president came to the hotel to tell him an emissary of Allende had conveyed a surprising message: "An IAPA mission headed by a Costa Rican was fine with the president." Allende agreed to meet the IAPA delegation the next day at 10 a.m. at his home.

"We arrived punctually," our new IAPA president later reported, "and they sat us down in a spacious room in his residence whose patio doors opened out to a central courtyard where officials scurried about—Cuban agents that Fidel Castro had sent to watch over him (Allende), armed police and other members of the various branches of the armed forces. Finally, President Allende appeared, walking briskly, on his shoulders an elegant Spanish cape and at his side his military aides."

The results of a "lengthy, cordial and interesting chat" were that the threatened newsprint mill was not closed down, *El Mercurio* was not denied newsprint, Angela Davis failed to get us out and the graffiti and protesters were entirely gone the next morning.

Our new president, Rodrigo Madrigal Nieto, and his colleagues had managed to persuade the Chilean leader that our purpose was entirely supporting press freedom and not to overthrow his government. As we prepared to depart Chile, anti-government protests had become widespread, perhaps as the result of our presence. Conditions were not unlike those a year later that led to the coup against Allende. Housewives throughout the city were banging pots and pans, doctors were protesting, teamsters were barricading roads and spreading nails and other obstacles to inhibit traffic. We thought for a while we would be unable to get to the airport, but a savvy taxi driver managed to find a way.

One poignant memory is of a strikingly good-looking young mother who was working at a convention booth for a U.S. newspaper press manufacturer. She was the daughter of a formerly wealthy copper-mine owner whose property had been confiscated by the government. We had dinner with her with the press manufacturer as host. As we were leaving the table, she put all the left-over bread, butter, sugar, powdered creamer and candy and anything else left on the table into her purse. She was essentially destitute, she told us, and she needed whatever she could scrounge for her baby.

Our next encounter up close with the Chile issue was the following year at the subsequent IAPA general assembly held in Boston. It took place just weeks after the September 11 coup. The Chilean newspaper representatives, led by Dooney Edwards, tried to make the case that IAPA should remain silent about the events in their country. They likened the situation to that of a critically wounded person in intensive care who needs a period to recover. At the time, of course, many observers believed the military would soon convene elections and return the country to civilian control.

I still have a copy of the special edition of *El Mercurio* distributed in Boston with the headline "Acción Militar Impide Golpe Marxista" (Military action impedes Marxist coup). It makes the case that the Communists had been about to launch a coup of their own and offers extensive coverage including photos of arms caches and other supplies supposedly at their disposal. The coup was planned for September 17, the newspaper reported.

A number of key U.S. members of the IAPA were adamant that the coup had to be condemned. They were appalled by the reports of possible mass killings and violence. Led by *Time* magazine publisher Andrew Heiskell, who had participated in the session with Allende the previous year, they became quite agitated, and the debate turned ugly. Ultimately, a somewhat soft condemnation was passed by the general assembly.

Five years later, in August 1978, I was joined on a fact-finding mission to Santiago by a young Brazilian newspaperman, Julio C.F. de Mesquita, son of the editor of *O Estado* of São Paulo. We were assigned by the then IAPA president to assess the state of the press under the Pinochet dictatorship. A mission three years earlier had reported only pro-government publications remained, including few besides *El Mercurio.*

I wrote the report, which began: "The IAPA's recent mission to Chile found a substantially improved environment for the press of that country compared to the situation reported by the association's previous special mission in 1975. But the Chilean press still is not free."

A state of siege had been lifted the previous March and remaining political prisoners had been released. Publications were now covering the news and expressing opinions, I said, but arbitrary government measures from time to time served as bold reminders there were no guarantees. The government had warned the previous month the relaxation of restraints was not a return to complete freedom.

Shortly before we arrived came a stark illustration of exactly what that meant. The afternoon daily owned by the Edwards family, *La Segunda*, had been closed down for publishing an interview with a Christian Democrat party official. The official had referred to the military government as a "dictatorship" and indirectly suggested President Pinochet was responsible for the death of former Ambassador Orlando Letelier, who had been assassinated two years earlier in Washington, D.C.

We gathered from local editors a list of subjects which could be trouble. The list was confirmed for us by the government's communications director. Among clearly dangerous topics:

- A personal attack on the president.
- Promoting or inciting terrorism, subversion or Marxism.
- Charging government involvement in disappearance of subversives or terrorists.
- Criticizing the military or the national honor.
- Revealing division or dissension within the military.
- Jeopardizing national security.
- Promoting a political party or inciting a strike.
- Pornography.

Two Catholic Church periodicals, *Solidaridad* and *Mensaje*, were the most outspoken on these topics. The former had been founded by the church in 1976 because of the absence of coverage on political prisoners, the unemployed and other sensitive issues like torture. *Mensaje*, a Jesuit magazine, had been the only publication to push the limits before 1976, although often only indirectly.

At the time of our visit, the mainstream publications were probing the limits. The big daily *La Tercera* was extensively covering labor problems, once considered off-limits, and the *El Mercurio* group was carrying interviews and analyses that would not have run a year earlier. Every month or so, according to the editors, a telephone call would come from the government admonishing the publication or advising that certain information should not be used. But these calls were framed more as requests than prohibitions. On the other hand, by the time of our visit extremely harsh criticism of the government on the wire services could be published.

A major concern for us was the prohibition of starting new publications without government permission, Edict 107. Nearly all publications not supporting the government had been shut down shortly after the military coup, and in 1976 the government issued Edict 107 to prevent the courageous editor and staff of a weekly news magazine, *Ercilla*, from starting a new publication. According to the editor, Emilio Filippi, his magazine had at government urging been purchased by economic interests favorable to the government.

Filippi's group, who did not support the government, made application under Edict 107. After several false starts and enormous quantities of red tape, but with strong support from the IAPA, they received approval almost a year later to publish *Hoy*. Two other publications had previously received permission to exist. The government's communications director assured our mission that Edict 107 would be repealed. He also revealed to us that the list of prohibited foreign correspondents had been eliminated. That list at one time included some of the major publications and news agencies of the world.

We also had the privilege of a briefing on the press freedom provisions of a new constitution which had been promised since the outset of the military government. No Chilean reporter, editor or publisher knew the details of the proposal at the time they were revealed to us by the president of the constitutional study commission, Enrique Ortúzar Escobar. He told us the provisions would be similar to the 1925 constitution, except to prevent the media from falling into the hands of those who wanted to promote non-democratic government. Courts would be permitted to prohibit publication or broadcast of information or opinions "that violate morality, public order, national security or the private lives of individuals." Media "against the institutional order" as determined by a special independent tribunal would be prohibited.

After our departure from Chile, Ortúzar wrote a detailed account of the proposal which was published exclusively by *El Mercurio*. The new constitution was eventually approved two years later in a controversial and tightly controlled plebiscite on the seventh anniversary of the coup, September 11, 1980. It has since been amended more than a dozen times, especially after Pinochet stepped down in 1990 as the result of a 1988 plebiscite that rejected him for a second eight-year term.

Given these experiences, I was intensely interested at IAPA's 1987 general assembly in Santiago, nine years after our 1978 mission, when Captain General Augusto Pinochet Ugarte, President of the Republic of Chile (as he was listed in the official program), inaugurated the meeting with a lengthy speech. He arrived for the formal ceremony in full military dress and began his remarks by sternly banging his hand on the sensitive microphone, which set a bizarre confrontational tone. This apparently was in response to comments IAPA's president, Alejandro Miró Quesada Garland, had just given, where he skillfully made the case for press freedom while the Chilean dictator was forced to listen.

That session was followed by a panel of leading journalists and politicians titled "The Role of the Press in Transition to Democracy." Among the speakers was Ricardo Lagos, a socialist who later would be elected president of the country. This to me seemed to be the beginning of the campaigning that led to the "No" vote the next October.

On the 1978 visit I also played a minor role in the highly contentious and visible case of the murder of Orlando Letelier, the former Chilean ambassador who was assassinated on an Embassy Row street in Washington, D.C. Julio Mesquita and I met for background with the Chilean foreign minister, Hernán Cubillos, who had been on the IAPA board of directors when he was editor of the magazine *Qué Pasa*. He had previously worked for the *El Mercurio* group including as president of its advisory board. He was well-known to all of us who regularly attended IAPA meetings.

Hernán was helpful in advising us on our mission, but what especially stood out later to me was a message he asked me to convey to the U.S. ambassador about the Letelier case. At the time considerable tension existed between Santiago and Washington because U.S. authorities were convinced the murder had been ordered by high Chilean officials and carried out by Michael Townley, a US expatriate who worked for Chilean intelligence. At the time Townley had been extradited to the U.S. and the month we were in Chile he was indicted for the murder. In the air was whether he would cooperate with the U.S. to the extent of implicating the head of the Chilean intelligence service and even General Pinochet.

Townley had been turned over to the United States after President Jimmy Carter himself pressured the Chilean government to do so. A deal had been struck for Townley's expulsion from Chile on condition he could testify about the Letelier case but not reveal other activities of the Chilean Intelligence Service. Now the Chileans wanted the case to be handled strictly judiciary to judiciary without more political pressure.

Hernán asked me to reassure the U.S. ambassador that this approach would result in cooperation, and that is what occurred. At the trial Townley, still loyal to Chile and having made a plea bargain, confessed and identified the five actual hit men, three of whom were subsequently convicted (although Pinochet's government later refused extradition for two of them). General Manuel Contreras, head of the intelligence service (secret police), also was indicted, but as a result of the "agreement" I had conveyed word of to the U.S. embassy, his case was handled as a petition of extradition and not, as with Townley, a political-diplomatic issue.

Contreras was arrested and confined to a hospital in Santiago. But the independence of Chilean courts, which had been assured, was a fiction, and they denied his extradition because, they said, the evidence from Townley was "tainted" by his plea bargain. Shortly afterward, Contreras publically accused Hernán Cubillos of "jeopardizing the honor of the nation." Not long after his plea bargain, Townley was freed under the U.S. Witness Protection Program.

In 2015 the Obama administration released classified U.S. State Department cables to Chile summarizing a series of informant reports, one of which said General Contreras asserted "he authorized the assassination of Letelier" on "direct orders from Pinochet."

I have long believed that in a minor way I aided in a resolution of the Letelier case and exposure of those guilty including General Contraras (not Pinochet). But I was also a party to preventing Contreras from facing U.S. justice or further implicating the government in the murder. In the end, the Townley confession and plea bargain agreement were a way to prosecute him while shielding the Chilean government.

The saga of the Edwards family in Chile cannot be complete without recounting the horrific events experienced by Cristián Edwards, Dooney's third son.

As Salvador Allende came to power, Dooney moved his family to the United States. Cristián attended the private Choate School in Connecticut, earned a degree from Amherst College in 1979 and later a master's in business administration in 1985 from the Wharton School at the University of Pennsylvania. He worked for Pepsico, Inc. and then after graduate school for General Reinsurance Corp.

While by this time he had lived the bulk of his life in the United States, speaking English like a native, he decided to return to Chile in April, 1990. A promising executive, he was given charge of Edwards' regional daily newspapers and viewed by many as the natural successor of Dooney.

But on September 9, 1991, his new life took a harrowing turn. As he was getting into his car, he was kidnapped by the leading Marxist insurgent group, Frente Patriótico Manuel Rodriguez, known by its acronym FPMR. He was held for 145 days in "*la caja*," what amounted to a closet constructed in a private home's bedroom. *La caja* was six feet by nine feet without windows, with a bare light bulb and a chemical toilet. The walls were covered with egg cartons to muffle sound. For five months Cristián didn't see the face of another person. He captors watched him through special lenses. Strident music played constantly and he could communicate only by written note. He believed his guards intended to drive him crazy.

The FPMR had an extensive history of assassination and kidnap. In 1986, also in early September near an anniversary of the September 11 coup, it attempted unsuccessfully to assassinate General Pinochet. The dictator suffered only minor injuries when his car was bombed, but five of his body guards were killed and 11 wounded. In 1987, FPMR simultaneously assaulted the offices of the Associated Press and eight radio stations in Santiago, killing a security guard.

In 1990 after civilian rule returned, it bombed a restaurant in the seaside resort Viña del Mar, wounding three sailors from the U.S. aircraft carrier Abraham Lincoln. Five other people were injured. Then, in April 1991 the group killed Senator Jaime Guzmán, a close ally of General Pinochet. The kidnapping of Cristián Edwards was planned shortly thereafter, but the timetable was upset when Cristián left on a trip to the United States

According to an extensive prize-winning report produced in 2009 by the Chilean Center for Investigative Journalism (Centro de Investigación Periodística), the FPMR undertook his kidnapping on the belief it would receive a multi-million dollar ransom. It needed funds to continue its activities. Now it acted virtually on another anniversary of the September 11 coup.

The morning after the kidnapping a note was discovered in *El Mercurio*'s office saying Cristián "was captive" and asking to "negotiate his life." It used language seen in previous FPMR kidnappings. The note warned against going public. For two weeks the news media maintained the silence, then the family consented to disclosure. The story was a blockbuster.

Dooney appointed an advisory committee the week of the kidnapping. The chairman was Juan Pablo Illanes, editor of *El Mercurio*, whom I have known well for many years through IAPA. It included a lawyer, a business man and a former agent of British intelligence with experience in Chile negotiating with kidnappers. Later Dooney added a well-known priest who after some halting attempts became an intermediator with the kidnappers. To confirm his role in negotiations *El Mercurio* ran a photo of him with Dooney shaking hands. Just weeks after the kidnapping became public, I had the opportunity at the IAPA General Assembly in Sao Paulo, Brazil, to discuss the situation with Felipe Edwards, Dooney's youngest son. Felipe and his older brother Augustín (Gus) had become our good friends over the years through the twice-a-year meetings of the association.

We produced a statement of support there and I also followed that up with a statement I drafted for the American Society of Newspaper Editors. As released in early November, the latter stated:

> The board of directors of the American Society of Newspaper Editors deplores the kidnapping of Cristián Edwards del Río, manager of the regional newspapers of the El Mercurio group, who begins a third month in captivity Saturday, November 9.
>
> Mr. Edwards was last seen September 9 leaving his office in Santiago, Chile.
>
> The only news about him to emerge was a note of unclear origin.
>
> The ASNE board stands solidly with the members of the Edwards family and expresses its deepest concern at this unconscionable act. It petitions the government of Chile to do all within its power to solve this abhorrent situation.

Dooney and his advisors used classified ads in *El Mercurio* to offer a ransom—17 ads in all beginning with an offer of $420,000. The kidnappers wanted $8 million. The first ran November 3 under "Antiques and Objects of Art" saying "I buy old icons (*iconos vedas*), best prices. Please call 6981417." Three days later an ad read "I buy old icons. Perfect condition, cash payment, $420,000."

A response from the kidnappers was indignant, characterizing the offer as "miserable." Two weeks later the offer was $520,000 and at the end of November $595,000. Meanwhile, Cristián Edwards, it was later learned, offered to pay the kidnappers with his own money he had in the U.S. Later, he would communicate to his father he would reimburse whatever had to be paid.

The next offer was $650,000 but required a photograph as proof of life. The reply was that there would be no photo and the offer had to be in MILLIONS, not thousands. It warned of Cristián's deteriorating condition. Later in December the offer was $700,000, which resulted in a reply with a photo containing a copy of a current daily newspaper. The message said the demand had lowered to $1.5 million.

Another offer January 4 published under "Musical Instruments," as suggested by the kidnappers, said "I buy Irish bagpipes, I pay cash $740,000." Finally on the 19th an ad under music instruments said simply "I buy Irish bagpipes, I have a special offer. Call Monday 6981417." The special offer was $1 million and was accepted.

A first attempt January 29 by the priest and Dooney's chauffeur to deliver the ransom under precise instructions from the kidnappers turned out to be a trial run to assure they were not being followed by police. A second try, after a lengthy drive around Santiago, was successful. The chauffeur and priest were directed to a soda fountain where they found a copy of the previous day's *El Mercurio* wrapped around a photo of Cristián with final directions. Eventually a man emerged from the shadows to take the cash, which was in $100 bills.

In fact, at the time of the release authorities believed they had identified the house were Cristián was held. Among other signs, agents had observed vastly more garbage coming from the house than the two residents would normally accumulate by themselves. The night after the ransom was paid a party was observed at the house.

Cristián was taken from *la caja* after five months and put in a tent where he spent his last hours as a prisoner. Music was again blasted and he was given a dose of sedatives. He then was hooded, wrapped in a sleeping bag, put in a car and dropped into a field. He was told not to move. Eventually he got up, walked toward some lights and eventually ran into a taxi driver who loaned him money to call his parents. Within a year several of the kidnappers were arrested. Only two served their full sentences. One was released for health reasons. Two escaped in a helicopter from prison. One of them was caught in another kidnapping in Brazil. The other remains free along with three who were never caught.

Cristián soon left Chile and after counseling took a position in the United States with *The New York Times*. He didn't care to talk about his experience. He eventually became president of The Times News Services and Syndicate Division. In that position he routinely corresponded with me about my Kansas newspaper's relationship with *The Times*. I still recall a conversation in Panamá in 2005 with Dooney and the publisher of *The Times*, Arthur Sulzberger Jr., when Dooney casually asked Arthur when he was going to let Cristián come back to work in Chile. Arthur light-heartedly responded: "When you pay him as much as I do."

Cristián returned to Chile after 18 years in 2009 to take an administrative position again with *El Mercurio*. He is now executive vice president of *El Mercurio* and the apparent successor to Dooney.

3. Paraguay
Steel and Nerve

Using money he'd made selling a business in Brazil, Paraguayan entrepreneur Aldo Zuccolillo started his Asunción newspaper in 1967. He said at the time he had in mind "*un gran diario.*" But at the inaugural ceremony, with the county's long-serving dictator Gen. Alfredo Stroessner present, he elaborated: "*un gran diario, al servicio de un gran gobierno*"—a great daily at the service of a great government. Although he declared the newspaper would "assess with objectivity" the Stroessner government, in its early years it was one of Stroessner's staunchest advocates. I recall at an IAPA meeting five years later in Santiago, Chile, his pleading the case for the Paraguayan regime on the grounds it was "democracy without communism."

This came as no surprise to insiders. After all, as Aldo acknowledges even today, he started his paper, *ABC Color*, because the major newspaper in Asunción refused to accept advertising from his family's hardware business, Ferretería Americana. "That was the spark that ignited the powder keg," he recently explained in his typically colorful language answering my question about the founding. "It was in 1965, and a daily called *La Tribuna* had a monopoly on the market because it had put all the other dailies out of business. I was the general manager of my father's hardware business and wanted to place a pre-paid advertisement which they wouldn't publish. That's when the idea occurred to me to found a daily." He continued:

La Tribuna didn't really publish the news and carried only international news on its front page. In those years I had a girlfriend who lived near La Tribuna's plant, and when I'd drop her off in the afternoon, I'd see newspaper boys living abandoned and unprotected on the street. This newspaper, owned by a very powerful family, used scare tactics. From this perception as well as the rejection of our ad arose the idea of starting a newspaper. That's the true story.

What was a surprise is that over time Acero ("Steel"), as he is known famil-iarly because of his hardware business, came to prize freedom of expression and built *ABC Color* into the leading independent daily in Paraguay. For years he was best known around Asunción as a businessman, former star athlete and eligible bachelor with family connections to the regime. The newspaper's name was suggested by one of his hardware store employees, and his first managing editor quit, accusing Acero of knowing more about nuts and bolts than newspapers.

I have always maintained that Acero's exposure to IAPA helped him realize the role an independent newspaper could play. After a few years defending Gen. Stroessner and his cronies, he began to absorb at our meetings the im-portance of independent journalism. Eventually, his newspaper became Stro-essner's most important foe. Although it didn't directly confront the dictator, it became thorough and provocative. It attacked corruption, arbitrary behav-ior and the politicization of the military. And it defended human rights.

Acero's family was closely linked to Stroessner. In 1974 his nephew, Hugo Fernando Zuccolillo, married Stroessner's daughter, María Olivia. Conrado Papalardo, the brother of Zuccolillo's wife, was Stroessner's protocol chief. His brother Antonio was named the dictator's ambassador to Great Britain in 1980, and another brother, Julio César, was also an ally of Stroessner.

Into the 1970s Zuccolillo's allegiance to Stroessner continued unabated. He was fervently anti-Marxist and a strong advocate of free trade and laissez-faire capitalism. He initially opposed President Jimmy Carter's defense of human rights and published justifications for abuses not only in Paraguay but Argen-tina and Chile. While lamentable, he said, they were necessary under the cir-cumstances. President Stroessner attended the tenth anniversary celebration of *ABC Color* in 1977.

This posture began to change in 1978 as the Carter policies brought to light the level of human rights abuses. Robert E. White, who became President Car-ter's ambassador to Paraguay in late 1977, told a Manhattan, Kan., meeting of the Kansas Paraguay Partners I attended that Zuccolillo was the key to the po-litical opening that took place while he served there from 1977 to 1980. While *ABC Color* never attacked or directly challenged Stroessner or asked how offi-cials in government or the military could afford their mansions and luxury se-dans, it was breathtakingly audacious by Paraguayan standards. Acero would later say what changed his view was the rampant corruption that grew around the regime. His newspaper attacked the corruption, the politicization of the military and arbitrary government behavior.

It also began to defend human rights by publishing the U.S. State Department's annual report on human rights in Paraguay, and it defended poor farmers forced from their lands.

Stroessner first came after others at the newspaper. He had taken power in a 1954 coup and governed under an almost continual state of siege, a modified form of martial law. Renewed every 90 days for nearly 35 years, it enabled him to pressure his critics with a variety of methods. Because of the isolation of Paraguay and the limited international communication then, he could rule arbitrarily in ways not possible today. Only six months after the paper was founded in 1967, the paper's news editor was jailed for eight days, sent to the jungle and then held for months in a police station cell. Over the next 17 years its journalists were jailed 32 times until Stroessner finally shut *ABC Color* down permanently on March 22, 1984. Zuccilillo was in jail at the time—his second confinement by Stroessner.

Among those receiving the most attention from the dictator was Alcibiades Gonzalez del Valle, the paper's lead investigative reporter, columnist and the general secretary of the journalists union. In one poll he was identified as Paraguay's most "credible" journalist. The country's most illustrious writer, he was known as the Jack Anderson of Paraguay. I became involved in his case as a result of a visit he made to the United States in May 1980 on a one-month U.S. State Department-sponsored tour. The timing was between two of his detentions in Paraguay. My wife Karen and I had the interesting privilege of serving as his hosts for a two-day visit to Manhattan, Kansas. He included Kansas in his itinerary because he wanted to thank those of us in the state who had campaigned for his release from jail the previous December. We Kansans had taken an interest due to the Kansas-Paraguay match in the Partners of the Americas program.

Soon after he arrived in the United States he learned another warrant had been issued for his arrest for activities against the state. He told us he wasn't entirely clear about the charge, but he expected to be arrested at the airport upon his return. He speculated the warrant was the result of a recent column castigating a judge for releasing an accused murderer on a technicality. This would prove true. He had called for the prosecution of a well-connected sports figure who under the influence of alcohol fired a revolver at two youths standing on a street corner, killing one. The government had refused to take testimony from the dead youth's companion because he was one month short of the "legal" age of 18 when the case came to trial. "He witnessed a crime, but his words are worthless," Alcibiades had written, "What good are such formalities to a 17-year-old boy murdered in cold blood?" Ascibiades was attacked for the column by the government daily which claimed he had violated Law 209. Among other things, the law prohibited the "preaching of disobedience of the law."

His jailing the previous year had been without charge. He spent 44 days in jail that time as a result of a satirical column which appeared in *ABC Color* the day before his arrest. The column had referred to a French minister who committed suicide when his honesty was questioned. Alcibiades wrote such a wave of conscience would be a catastrophe for Paraguay because "there wouldn't be enough room in our cemeteries, and our casket-makers would be unable to meet the demand . . ."

He told me the regime's handling of him on the earlier occasion was cruelly devious. He was not badly treated, but his wife was not able to see him and was fed rumors of torture and hospitalization by the police. Since then she had insisted he be more cautious.

That arrest was the first in three or four years—a period in which the Paraguayan press had much wider latitude as a result of the Carter human rights policy. Alcibiades explained that efforts to develop an independent press had begun a decade earlier under the leadership of Zuccolillo and *ABC Color*, but the movement was cautious and slow until the previous three years. He suspected the new crackdown resulted from the departure at the end of 1979 of U.S. Ambassador Robert White, who was moved to El Salvador and had not yet been replaced.

Because of the increased independence the press had enjoyed, Alcibiades believed the new threat against him while he was in the United States might represent a turning point toward a reversal unless it could be made an international issue. Uncontested, he said, his arrest undoubtedly would discourage other independent journalists and produce additional self-censorship. He asked me, as he had others on this U.S. visit, to fuel the protest, which I did through the IAPA as well as several Kansas politicians. I took him to Topeka to meet with Gov. John Carlin, who later wrote a letter to Stroessner protesting Alcibiades' eventual new arrest upon his return, as did Sen. Nancy Landon

Kassebaum. Both leaned on the relationship in the Partners program between Kansas and Paraguay.

Even in the less restrictive situation, known limits and self-censorship were ever present. Publishing a wire story even slightly critical of Stroessner would bring closure, Alcibiades assured me. Somewhat less obvious but also dangerous were favorable accounts of Cuba or Russia and negative stories on the United States. A slightly favorable wire story about Cuba would bring a telephone call from the government.

Facing three years in prison, Alcibiades nonetheless returned home from the United States to confront the government. Reporters and photographers were waiting for him at the airport, but nothing happened. I had worked with officials in the United States to make them aware of what might occur, and the day after he returned, the officer in charge of the U.S. State Department's Paraguay desk told me the United States had made its interest known in a strong way with the Paraguayan government because of the fact that the arrest warrant had been issued while he was a guest of the U.S. government. The Paraguayan attorney general had intervened, I was told, apparently at United States' urging.

Before he left, Alcibiades told me that he intended to present himself to police the day after arriving if he were not arrested at the airport, and he did so. He was taken to the National Penitentiary, where he was held incommunicado. But pressure resulting from reports of his arrest both in Paraguay and more importantly internationally led to his release from solitary confinement and, after two months, his complete release and return to work for *ABC Color*. His trial was not reopened despite his insistence that it be; and he believed, as a pretext, the possibility of its reopening was used to deny return of his passport.

Pressure for his release was mounted not only by the Kansas governor and senator, my fellow Kansans and the IAPA but also, and perhaps more importantly, by attention from *The New York Times*, columnist Jack Anderson and others who had been alerted by two New York–based journalists. Michael Massing, executive editor of the *Columbia Journalism Review*—a national professional monthly—and Laurie Nadel, a CBS News writer, had met Alcibiades on his last U.S. stop, in New York City. Their success mobilizing the New York press for him led them to enlist other prominent journalists in founding the highly successful and today well-funded Committee to Protect Journalists, which is the premier U.S. advocate for journalists in jeopardy worldwide.

While in prison Alcibiades sent me a handwritten letter in Spanish, translated as:

My dear friend,

As expected, I am writing you from jail. In spite of this situation, I am happy to have become better acquainted with your country and to have dealt with such wonderful people like you.

As to my "legal proceedings," they are following the "normal" course. Quotation marks are necessary because such procedures are a farce in my country. Everyone laughs and cries at the same time about them.

The main purpose of this letter is to express my sincere gratitude for all you did while I was lucky enough to be in that beautiful and friendly city of Manhattan (Kan.). Also for what you have done when I was in prison for having committed the grave "crime" of thinking. Please extend these thanks to my journalistic colleagues and friends whom I will never forget.

I am among criminals, thieves and other common delinquents, but with a clear conscience because all I did was to fulfill the mission of all journalists who think and who feel that social justice is the top priority for a country. In addition to the satisfaction of having fulfilled my obligation, it is reassuring to know I can count on such good and distinguished friends like you.

Please extend my thanks to the rest of the leadership of the Inter American Press Association not only for what they did for me personally but also as an expression of solidarity with the movement which I and other journalists represent in favor of freedom of expression and opposed to all injustice. My thanks also to your newspaper staff.

Please send my greetings to your distinguished wife who I remember fondly. To you I reiterate my gratitude.

A strong embrace,

Alcibiades.

Two years later in an interview he again thanked his friends in Kansas for his release and humane treatment while in prison: "Tell them," he said. "I can't find the words to thank them. Out of my private problem came a happy discovery: that we're not alone in our struggle in our anxiety to have a country where everyone is sheltered by the law and by respect for human rights. But tell them the struggle has been good for us. It strengthens us, it tests our democratic convictions. Peace is a shroud, a burial cloth like the one we've been wrapped in for the past 28 years. If not we, at least our children will come to know the peace that comes from living and sharing together."

Two-and-a-half decades later, in 2006, Alcibiades González del Valle was recognized by the Committee to Protect Journalists as one of 16 "Faces of Freedom" from every corner of the world whose "lifetime contributions have had a lasting effect on the press freedom movement of the past 25 years."

The next time I would see Alcibiades was when I participated in an IAPA mission to Paraguay after *ABC Color* was closed in 1984. By then he was banned by the courts from the practice of journalism in Paraguay. He again had been arrested the previous September as part of a crackdown on the newspaper. Two months earlier Stroessner had finally decided to jail the paper's owner, Acero Zuccolillo, despite his wealth, reputation and close personal connections to the regime. The excuse was that he published remarks of a female lawyer critical of the Paraguay Supreme Court, which was prohibited. Zuccolillo had refused to reveal his source for the lawyer's remarks, which had been made in a closed hearing.

Zuccolillo's jailing came in the context of the sweep by the government through the academic, labor and journalistic sectors including the closing of the principal opposition radio station, Radio Nandutí. He was released after two weeks. Other staffers of *ABC Color* also had been jailed—the presidential palace reporter, the wire editor, a city editor and a news editor. Then, in March of 1984 Zuccolillo again was jailed, this time for refusing to divulge the identity of his reporter responsible for an interview with an opposition leader after Stroessner allowed exiled opposition leaders back in the country. And this time Stroessner also shut down the paper the 22nd of that month.

Two weeks before the closure *ABC* referred to Stroessner (using his name) as bearing sole responsibility for the corporatist, autocratic, dictatorial state. At least one prominent Paraguayan journalist would later maintain Zuccolillo did so to provoke closure, believing it would force a popular and military reaction producing a change.

The charge was sweeping: *ABC Color*'s editors had "a permanent desire to subvert public order, putting in danger the peace of the Republic and the stability of institutions, which includes the daily sermon of opinions of a seditious nature, either in editorials or serving as the permanent spokesman for the ir-regular political groups without legal or institutional support, thus promoting a state of confusion, or restlessness in public opinion and causing social alarm ..." The government cited Article 71 of the Paraguayan constitution: "Freedom of thought and of opinion are guaranteed on equal terms to all inhabitants of the republic. It is forbidden to preach hatred or class struggle among Paraguay-ans, or to defend crime or violence. The law may be criticized freely, but no one may proclaim disobedience to its provisions." The resolution of closure said that ABC "preached hatred" and "class struggle among Paraguayans." The resolution was signed by the Interior (Domestic Security) Minister.

As a result, at IAPA's April mid-year meeting in Jamaica, in my capacity as vice chairman of IAPA's executive committee and due to my Kansas connec-tion to Paraguay, I persuaded the board to instruct the executive committee to hold its next meeting, which would be in June, in Asunción. Acero was released a week after Stroessner closed his paper and therefore would be able to assist with this attempt to pressure the Paraguayan government. We would include in the trip a subsequent visit to Uruguay, where the military govern-ment was cracking down again.

My first-person newspaper article about our mission would be picked up by the trade magazine *Editor & Publisher* and later entered into the *Congres-sional Record* by Senator Kassebaum, who was a member of the Senate Foreign Relations Committee. It was included in support of a resolution that con-demned the closing of *ABC Color*. My piece reads:

> Meet A. Zuccolillo: Uncompromising, determined, courageous. A newspaper publisher forbidden to roll his press in Kansas' sisterland to the south, Paraguay.
>
> Now, say hello to A. Stroessner: Tough, bold, cunning. The longest ruling dictator in Latin America—and one of the most durable in the world—who three months ago shut down Paraguay's leading daily, Zuccolillo's.
>
> These two strikingly similar personalities are locked in a struggle of power and principle that is gaining worldwide attention and recently brought this writer face-to-face with both of them.
>
> The executive committee of the Inter American Press Association (IAPA) was mounting an on-site campaign on behalf of Aldo Zuccolillo's

newspaper, and as the committee's vice chairman I was the nominal
leader of the 16-member delegation. The committee chairman was unable
to participate.

The case has more than passing interest to Kansans because Paraguay
is matched with Kansas in the Partners of the Americas program.

One of the newspaper's editor-reporters, Ricardo Caballero Aquino,
is a K-State graduate. Its most illustrious writer, Alcibiades Gonzalez
Delvalle—known as the Jack Anderson of Paraguay—visited Manhattan
in 1980. He currently is banned by law from the practice of journalism in
Paraguay.

Most assessments we heard were pessimistic. Reopening the
newspaper, we were told, was a dead issue in Paraguay. Zuccolillo had
pushed too far in his struggle for an independent newspaper.

His paper had more circulation than the other three dailies put
together, it was monopolizing advertising, was disrupting national life,
and was even in violation of the constitution.

Despite Zuccolillo's appearing to be a virulent anti-communist to
outsiders, the government party branded him a subversive.

Our only hope, we concluded, was to change the mind of President
Alfredo Stroessner himself. We therefore went to a great deal of trouble to
arrange a meeting with him personally, but upon departure from home
we had no response.

An official at the Paraguayan embassy in Washington told us the
president had never been known to reply to requests for meetings
made by cable from abroad. A personal visit to the presidency would be
necessary, he said.

We were apprehensive. We could see ourselves in Asunción being told
we should have asked earlier for the interview. But upon arrival, we made
the formal request in person.

To our delight, the response was positive.

We would be permitted interviews with President Stroessner and
other high-ranking figures in the government. We immediately sat down
with Zuccolillo to map out strategy.

Most interviews with Stroessner turn into a monologue by the
president, we were told, so we drafted a three-page letter to present to
him as insurance that our message would not be lost.

Our delegation, which included five Americans, two Brazilians, two Nicaraguans, five Argentines, an exiled Cuban and a Mexican—all representing daily newspapers—listened intently as Zuccolillo reminded us of the two recent stints in jail he'd endured as Stroessner pressured him before deciding finally to close the newspaper.

We determined we should not dwell with the president on restoring press freedom to Paraguay, since even before *ABC*'s closing freedom of the press as other non-communist countries know it did not exist.

In fact, Stroessner has controlled this fiefdom with martial law by renewing every 90 days (for 30 years!) a suspension of civil liberties. We would push a re-opening of the newspaper and the peoples' right to information, we determined, and avoid a confrontation on civil liberties.

Meanwhile—unknown to us—the president's political party, the Colorados, were papering the city with posters and banners attacking our organization. They had previously launched vicious attacks over the party radio station.

We woke the next morning to a view outside our hotel of three-feet-high red banners with large white letters stretching across the major downtown streets.

Perhaps the most telling of them was the one that said, 'Primero La Ley. Después La S.I.P.' (First the law, Then the Inter American Press Association.) In other words, law and order comes ahead of civil liberties in Paraguay.

The posters were everywhere:

> Free Press, Yes
> Libertinism, No
> Fatherland, Yes
> I.A.P.A., No.

Or

> The I.A.P.A. Does Not Defend
> Freedom of the Press
> It Only Defends the
> Interests of Owners

The scene was set. Our group divided up according to assignments. Three met with the Minister of Justice. Three carried our message to the Interior Minister, head of domestic security. Others interviewed the local bishop and made calls on the pro-government newspapers and broadcasters.

My assignment, along with the president of IAPA, Horacio Aguirre, was to meet with Stroessner himself.

Our experience, later recounted with front page color photos and stories in all three government-oriented dailies, began with a flourish.

Greeted at the palace gate by the president's secretary of information, we were ushered into a session with the heads of each branch of the military. Also present was the minister of justice, who earlier had seen our colleagues.

His message was that the publisher himself, Zuccolillo, had not actually asked the government to re-open the paper. Later, we realized this was an invitation to negotiate the re-opening, with perhaps the key trading stock being Zucolillo's resignation as editor and publisher.

Ten minutes into the conversation an aide invited us into the president's office, which was lined on one side by still and television photojournalists. The shutters popped and we shook hands with Gen. Alfredo Stroessner, one of the world's most hated, yet misunderstood, chiefs of state.

The president then ushered us into a huge conference room, probably the cabinet chamber, adjoining his office.

We asked the information secretary, who joined us at the end of the mammoth table as the only other participant, how long we would have with the president.

He did not answer.

We hoped for the best and began the discussion of the re-opening of a newspaper.

The conversation was cordial and without acrimony.

At 71, Stroessner is a husky six-footer who appears the picture of health. He lives unostentatiously and is known to rise before dawn for a workday that often runs from 4:30 a.m. to midnight.

Despite his reputation abroad, in Paraguay he appears genuinely popular and apparently can be seen driving about unaccompanied by bodyguards.

There are reasons for this, of course. Growth the past decade has averaged nearly 10% per year, due largely to a massive hydroelectric dam project financed by Brazil. Asunción is more prosperous than Managua or Port-au-Prince, Haiti. The tragic poverty so evident to travelers to Mexico, for example, is not seen even in the countryside.

Interestingly, the most miserable housing on the 900 miles of roadway between Asunción and Montevideo, Uruguay, is just across the border in Argentina, Latin America's most developed country.

But while to many of his countrymen Stroessner is a benevolent dictator and author of prosperity, others—like Zuccolillo and González Delvalle—have seen the dark side, which can include widespread arrests without charge, exile, torture and even death.

Since seizing power in a coup d'etat in 1954, General Stroessner has maintained a balance between coercion and tolerance.

So long as it does not become unruly or threatening, opposition is tolerated within the facade of a republican system with an elected congress and re-election every fifth year of Stroessner himself as president. Martial law persists, however, through periods of relative liberalization that alternate unpredictably with crackdowns.

The closing March 22 of *ABC Color* seems to mark such a reversal. Earlier this year, at the urging of the new popular president of Argentina, Raúl Alfonsín, Stroessner permitted most of the exiled opposition living in Argentina to return home.

It was *ABC*'s coverage of their activities and comments, he told us, that led him to close the newspaper. The "irregular opposition" have a right to their own newspaper, he said, but Zuccolillo was providing them one free.

We countered these statements with responses about the value of an independent source of news for economic, political and social development. We pointed out that in a democracy information and criticism should not be confused with subversion.

We also spoke of Paraguay's image in the Western democracies and explained that many foreign governments had hoped the return of he opposition signaled a permanent liberalization.

We alluded to aid that would come to Paraguay if world opinion of his regime improved. This point, we believe, may be especially significant in view of the end of the construction phase of the hydroelectric project with Brazil. Stroessner now has hopes of a similar project with Argentina.

The president spoke with pride of Paraguay's prosperity. He described the stability he'd brought to the country after decades of a revolving-door presidency. He talked of Nicaragua, where his friend Anastasio Somoza fell to the Sandinista revolution. Somoza later took refuge in Paraguay but was assassinated on an Asunción street by Sandinista-hired gunmen. The attitude of our Nicaraguan colleagues, who now oppose the Sandinistas, interested him.

Our conversations evolved to nearly an hour's length, so finally we asked the general what we could tell our 1,200 member publications throughout the hemisphere about the future of *ABC Color.*

He hedged.

He alluded to the obstacle of the constitutional suit brought by Zuccolillo despite his earlier agreeing with us that, regardless of how the suit came about, re-opening the paper rests in the hands of the executive.

In the end, he said neither yes nor no. He left the door open to a re-appearance.

We were not satisfied, but we were encouraged. We resolved to continue the campaign.

Since returning home, we have solicited editorials of support from many of America's major dailies, which will be appearing in the next few weeks.

We arranged for more pressure from Argentina, and we are mailing a request for support to all of our 1,200 member publications in both North and South America.

Stroessner has the power, we have only principle. We marshal our forces in the court of international opinion, which is our only battlefield. Our only weapon is public arousal.

We look forward to the next issue of *ABC Color.* We know only one thing it will contain. Zuccolillo told a University audience of more than a thousand persons the evening of our interview he'd already written the lead editorial for the next edition. He said it was too long to read, so he'd just give the title:

"*Como siempre.*"

"(As always.)"

In the *Congressional Record* my article was the lead piece along with editorials and columns about our visit from *The New York Times, The Wash-*

ington Post, Chicago Tribune, Miami Herald and *Wichita Eagle-Beacon.* After Sen. Kassebaum entered them as exhibits, and speeches in support were made by Senators Claiborne Pell, David Durenberger and Chris Dodd, the Senate passed the concurrent resolution she sponsored condemning the closing of *ABC Color* and urging the Paraguayan government to permit it to reopen and to guarantee freedom of the press.

One detail I thought a bit too racy for my article. Among the numerous attacks by Stroessner's supporters on Zuccolillo and us was a slick broadside promoting a contest, supposedly underwritten by Zuccolillo's hardware business, to identify a nude fisherman shown from the rear in a large full-color photograph. The fisherman with no clothes on obviously was Zuccolillo. He told us he had been fishing in a remote area and got so hot he disrobed. The supposed silly prizes were a fishing reel for first, a pole for second, and for third "a bag of Paraguayan sugar re-imported from Bolivia."

After the session with Stroessner, three of us and Zuccolillo participated in an emotion-charged forum on press freedom at Asunción's Catholic University and received a standing ovation from an audience of 1,000. I spoke about our interview with the president. Also speaking, in addition to powerful remarks from Zuccolillo, were Raúl Kraiselburd of Argentina and Pedro Joaquín Chamorro Barrios of Nicaragua.

From the Catholic University we planned to march a few blocks with the crowd from the forum to the offices of Radio Ñandutí, the feisty radio station that also had been closed by the government. As we approached our destination, we were confronted by numerous policemen with raised billy clubs, who prevented us from going further. After a half hour of standoff including catcalls and threats, our crowd dispersed. Those of us unaccustomed to the ways of dictatorships were relieved to return safely to our hotel.

About our mission, the Paraguay/Uruguay desk officer at the U.S. Department of State wrote me:

> Congratulations on what can only be described as a very successful
> visit to Paraguay. Your group impressed the embassy as well as the
> Paraguayan officials. Your concern about *ABC Color* appears to have
> been heard by those who count. I also received very good feedback on
> IAPA's visit to Uruguay. We hope that your goal of encouraging greater

freedom of the press will be fully realized in both of the countries you visited.

Two months after returning home I received a letter from Acero suggesting I invite President Reagan to speak out in behalf of *ABC Color,* preferably at the upcoming IAPA general assembly that October in Los Angeles. Based on his suggestion, I checked with several sources in Washington about that possibility. What I learned was that the State Department was nervous about either Reagan or Secretary of State George Shultz becoming involved because of what Stroessner's government described as Zuccolillo's refusal to discuss the issue of a re-opening with them. Sources at the State Department told me that so long as Stroessner's government could legitimately make that claim, they would be putting the entire weight of the U.S. government behind one man and his newspaper against his government and that man was unwilling even to discuss the problem with the government.

I urged Acero in my reply to at least open discussion with the government and told him I would try to get United Nations Ambassador Jean Kirkpatrick to mention his case in her scheduled talk to the IAPA general assembly. Ultimately, she sent a substitute, Assistant Secretary of State Thomas Enders, who did mention the case in his remarks, but without effect on Stroessner. *ABC Color* would remain shuttered another five years until the dictatorship was overthrown.

The next year, 1985, I helped organize a panel, Latin American "Publishers Under Fire," at the annual meeting of the U.S. publishers' organization, the American Newspaper Publishers' Association (ANPA). The panelists were Pedro Joaquín Chamorro Barrios of Nicaragua, Raúl Kraiselburd of Argentina, and Zuccolillo. In his statement Acero reviewed his history and the challenging obstacles he faced in Paraguay and the "negative aspect" of the present political situation, but also another aspect he viewed as positive and "an indication of the democratic aptitude of the Paraguayan people."

The "very fact of the closure gives me hope," he said. "I see that the newspaper was shut down because the people trusted it and made it into the main daily of the country. It merited such trust because it never printed a lie and because it chose not to capitulate before corruption; rather, it confronted it."

Upon his return to Asunción, Acero wrote me thanking me for my help in getting the case of *ABC Color* before the U.S. publishers and then added, "I take advantage of this opportunity to send you a Paraguayan (embroidered) shirt and a blouse for Karen. She spoke highly of the one I wore at ANPA, and it occurred to me that you two are very deserving of the right to a garment—produced from cloth woven by the hands of a rural Paraguayan woman—given the permanent aid and moral support you offer to all Paraguayans."

Less than a month after he spoke at ANPA, law students from the National University in Asunción organized a demonstrations calling for the reopening of *ABC Color*. Some 500 demonstrated at the closed offices of the newspaper after 2,000 had tried to protest at the law school and their gathering was broken up by police.

Also in 1985 I joined others in nominating Acero for Columbia University's prestigious Maria Moors Cabot Prize, which he was awarded that October. At the ceremony he was described as a "journalist in forced unemployment." The press release on the occasion said "Throughout its 17-year existence, *ABC Color* struggled against government attacks and harassment. Threats, insults, humiliations and pressure of every kind were brought to bear against the paper's journalists. . . . Members of the staff went to jail 37 times during those years; Mr. Zuccolillo himself was jailed twice. The paper's continual exposure of human rights violations and government corruption won it the Pedro Joaquín Chamorro award from the Inter American Press Association, but also finally cost it its existence last year. Despite protest from around the world, the newspaper remains closed."

Returning to Paraguay from the ceremonies in New York, Acero was again arrested when he arrived at the Asunción airport. He was taken to the capital's police headquarters for a meeting with the police chief, who showed him a copy of the speech he had just given in New York and said, if he is not happy with the government and peace "which reign" in Paraguay, he could leave the country. He was then set free, although subsequently he was viciously attacked by the state sponsored radio, which congratulated him for receiving an award from the "association of homosexual Latin American journalists" and suggested he might also have AIDS.

After being named chairman of the IAPA executive committee at the 1985 general assembly and in hopes of further raising his international stature, I also nominated Acero for the prestigious Golden Pen award, a press freedom prize presented annually by FIEJ (now WAN), the worldwide publishers' organization. It is given annually to focus attention on individuals who may be in danger and could benefit from international exposure. However, a deserving editor from the Philippines won instead.

Our efforts to make *ABC Color* an international issue bore fruit when a Washington-based organization, the International Human Law Rights Group, advocated for it at the Inter American Commission on Human Rights and in a confidential proceeding at UNESCO. The commission resolved for *ABC Color*, finding Paraguay was violating the American Declaration on Human Rights, but Stroessner's government ignored this 1984 ruling. Paraguay responded to the law group's initial petition to UNESCO by setting forth its justification for the closure. The government participated in additional hearings, which were before the Committee on Conventions and Recommendations, and optimism emerged at one point that the newspaper might resume publication if it made clear it would respect the laws. Ultimately this effort, too, failed.

Knowing of these developments and on the advice of the World Press Freedom Committee, I pushed a campaign by IAPA at the Geneva-based United Nations Commission on Human Rights. We had voice there because our association held, despite objections of Cuba and the Soviet bloc, official "consultative" status within the United Nations system. We decided to bring to the commission the cases of both *ABC Color* and Nicaragua's *La Prensa*, which had been closed by the Sandinistas, because we thought we had a better chance of success in both cases if we were fighting both rightwing and leftwing authoritarians.

In March 1987, the IAPA president, Alejandro Miró Quesada Garland, presented our case in Geneva. I drafted his speech in which we urged the commission to include press freedom abuses within its portfolio, which it was not doing at the time. I argued that limiting the press undermined the commission's ability to protect other human rights, and I used the Paraguayan and Nicaraguan cases to illustrate the point. We urged the commission to condemn restrictions throughout the world.

Don Alejandro was resolute in his appearance there. He was required to wait days beyond his originally scheduled appearance, but finally got the opportunity to speak. While it would be several years before the commission began speaking out on press restrictions, our efforts kept the issue of the closures of *ABC Color* and *La Prensa* on the world stage.

On April 9, 1987, after three decades save brief interims, Gen. Stroessner lifted the state of siege, apparently in anticipation of elections scheduled for the next February. Although arbitrary arrests continued, some opposition leaders returned. They called the improved situation a "lukewarm opening" without the re-opening of *ABC Color.*

In the fall General Stroessner again agreed to meet with an IAPA delegation about the closure. I headed the delegation which included Raúl Kraiselburd and Bill Landrey, vice chairman of the IAPA executive committee and chairman of its freedom of press committee, respectively. We were accompanied by Lea Browning of the Human Rights Law Group with which we were then collaborating. We agreed ahead that our approach would be that there could not be credible elections without an independent press. We held preliminary meetings with the president of the Supreme Court Luis María Argaña (who in 1999 would be murdered as he was about to succeed to the presidency of Paraguay), the minister of interior (domestic security) and the attorney general.

Our session November 11 with President Stroessner was brief, only about 15 minutes. I found him much more reticent than three years earlier. He apparently was suffering from some sort of skin ailment. We were told ahead of time he would not shake hands, and he didn't. In our conversation we made our point about a free press being required for credible elections and also expressed our disapproval of a right of reply law that had been promulgated the previous month. He listened but had little to say beyond thanking us for coming. He gave us no assurances that *ABC Color* could re-open. From Asunción we travelled by van with Acero and his wife Graciela to Santiago, Chile, where we gave a report on our Paraguay visit to the IAPA general assembly.

The 1988 elections were held in Paraguay February 14. The government announced that 90 percent of the citizens had voted and 88 percent voted for President Stroessner. Nothing had changed. I decided our best hope of pressuring the Paraguayan president was to bring the entire IAPA membership to Asunción for the 1989 Midyear Meeting the next April. Based on the reception our executive committee had received in 1984, I anticipated a likely fierce and even vile government and official party response to our presence, but I also knew Stroessner wanted to sell his so-called "democracy" and therefore would not prevent us from coming.

There was a lot of opposition initially within the IAPA leadership to the meeting in Paraguay, but in Santiago I was elected to the ladder (second vice president) leading to the presidency in two years. This gave me additional clout, and Acero was very much in favor of the idea. After getting approval from the IAPA executive committee, we therefore set out, with significant support from the IAPA staff, to mount a major conference in hostile territory.

The pressure brought by the upcoming 1989 IAPA Midyear Meeting in Asunción cannot take credit for the violent overthrow of Stroessner by Gen. Andrés Rodriguez just weeks before our meeting, although it may have played a role. The overthrow resulted primarily from a struggle within the Paraguayan power structure. But Rodriquez' immediate decision after the February 3 coup to permit a political opening including the immediate re-opening of *ABC Color* and other media undoubtedly is linked to past international pressures, particularly that of the IAPA.

Aldo Zuccolillo's first message after the initial run of 80,000 copies had been distributed was one of gratitude for the steady support of journalists from throughout the Americas. "IAPA made the difference," he commented. "The benefits that flow from freedom of the press again will be enjoyed by the people of Paraguay." Later, speaking to IAPA's Asunción meeting in April—a virtual celebration—he stated eloquently: "Without the powerful help of this institution, that maintained permanently the memory of this daily and the liberty of Paraguayan journalists, we would have been hidden here, overcome by a powerful dictatorship. I thank you with all my heart."

Elections were held three months after the coup and General Rodriguez became president.

In succeeding years I have kept regular contact with Acero and his family. In fact my niece, as a favor to me and my wife, lived briefly with them in Asunción. I would also come in contact with other well-known Paraguayans including one who played the key role in revelation of the atrocities of those years not only in Paraguay but also in Argentina, Chile, Uruguay, Bolivia and Brazil.

Martín Almada came to Manhattan, Kansas, in 2000 to learn English. He would stay three years as a visiting professor at Kansas State University. During this time he would receive the Right Livelihood Award of $50,000, an alternative Nobel Prize awarded the day before the Nobel ceremony. He was cited for his role in the discovery of the Archive of Terror, the records of Operación Cóndor, the campaign of political repression, assassination and intelligence operations conducted in the 1970s and 1980s by the right-wing dictatorships in the Southern Cone. While living in Kansas he was routinely invited as a coveted speaker to human rights conferences throughout the world.

His story is surreal. He was a teacher and a fervent Stroessner (Colorado) Party activist who earned Paraguay's first PhD in education while studying on a government scholarship at the University of La Plata in Argentina. He returned to Paraguay in 1974, took a job running a small private school and was asked to be a consultant for the government. But on November 24 that year police came to his home and arrested him. He was interrogated and subjected to savage torture for 30 days because a car-bomb attempt had been made on President Stroessner's life by young Paraguayans Martín had studied with in La Plata. He was put on display before a large group of officers including foreigners he later described as a "Condór tribunal."

Those involved in the attempt on Stroessner later confirmed Martín was innocent. Meanwhile, his wife Celestina was put under house arrest at the school. For ten days the police called her by telephone and forced her to listen to Martín's cries and shouting. They told her he died. Under the strain, she collapsed and died herself in December of a heart attack.

After three years, Martín was released as a result of international pressure. He went into exile with his mother and children in Panamá, where he wrote *Paraguay: The Forgotten Jail, the Country in Exile*, a sobering account of torture and corruption in his native country that gained attention for human rights around the world.

He then made his way to Paris where he obtained a position with UNESCO as an education specialist. He remained in that position until the fall of Stroessner in 1989, when he returned to Paraguay, one of the first exiles to return. Rather than wanting retribution, he was bent on documenting what had happened to him and especially to learn how Celestina died. He petitioned the courts in 1992 using a new constitution's "habeas data" provision, under which a citizen can have access to any public document about himself or herself. He sought the records related to his case as well as the death of his wife. It was the first use of the new provision.

Martín found a sympathetic judge who ordered the police to release the records, but the police claimed the records were destroyed in the chaos of the coup. He then went to the press and made his case public. Eventually, a policeman came forward saying he knew of some documents that had been hidden at the "Department of Production," an obscure police facility outside Asunción.

After alerting a group of reporters and television cameramen and using a map drawn by the policeman, Martin and the judge went to the facility. With some necessary persuasion by the judge, they were permitted to enter and follow the map to a second-floor room in the rear of the complex of buildings. The press watching, they broke the formidable padlock on the door. Inside they found nearly three tons of documents. When later microfilmed, the complete archive contained 593,000 document pages. Acting on another tip, they discovered additional documents buried in the courtyard, including scores of identification cards of prisoners who had been executed.

Among the discoveries were hundreds of ringed archive binders, bound chronological volumes, quantities of surveillance tapes and photographs and rap sheets of thousands of prisoners, both Paraguayan and foreign, many of whom were on the lists of disappeared. Included were Martín's own rap sheet as well as interrogation reports and other documents on his case.

Most important, they found correspondence with security forces from Chile, Bolivia, Argentina, Uruguay, Brazil and the United States. Eventually, these included the invitation from Chile to Paraguay to attend the founding meeting of Cóndor, documents on prisoner exchanges and various phases of the operation.

A journalist friend of mine on the faculty at Columbia University, who served with me on the Cabot Board, John Dinges, published a book in 2004 on the operation, *The Cóndor Years: How Pinochet and His Allies Brought Terrorism to Three Continents.* In it, he writes: "Almada's discovery is by far the largest collection of previously secret security force documents from any of the Cóndor countries. The Paraguayan Archive forms a major part of the documentary backbone of this book." Earlier, when I inquired about Martín while he was living in Kansas, Dinges wrote me: "If it hadn't been for Martín, the archive might never have been discovered and made public."

When Martín received the "Alternative Nobel Prize" in the Swedish Parliament in 2002, the prize committee said "the 'Archive of Terror' has proved the most important collection of documents of state terror ever recovered. It is important not just for Paraguay but for the whole of Latin America and, indeed, for the world." The award, the Right Livelihood Award, is given "to honor and support those offering practical and exemplary answers to the crucial problems facing the world today."

BBC, the British broadcast network, aired a special on Martín and the Archive. Martín, now back in Paraguay, continues to work with Kansas State University including on environmental issues and on exchange agreements. An effort by Kansas-Paraguay Partners is underway to bring a copy of the Archive of Terror to KSU.

In 2009 I had the opportunity at a dinner at the presidential residence in Asunción to visit with Paraguay's new president, the former bishop Fernando Lugo. It was an elegant dinner for the IAPA executive committee in conjunction with a midyear meeting on the 20th anniversary of the earlier IAPA meeting in Asunción immediately after the fall of Stroessner. The moment I mentioned I know Martín Almada, President Lugo lighted up and expressed at length his profound admiration for my friend. He also was very aware of the Kansas-Paraguay connection.

Over many years I have continued my interest in Paraguay. I've celebrated victories like the 1997 court victory that upheld a constitutional right to criticize public figures. I worked against legislation limiting press freedom. At one point I collaborated with one of the country's presidents in hopes of organizing a conference on journalism ethics.

The latter grew out of the visit to Manhattan, Kansas, and Kansas State University by President Juan Carlos Wasmosy in 1995. He had succeeded General Rodriguez to become the second freely elected head of state. Because of my history, KSU's president had asked me to entertain Wasmosy and his entourage at the big football game between Kansas' two major universities, KSU and Kansas University. They joined me in our skybox at the stadium.

I'm certain they enjoyed the lunch more than the game, which was not their brand of football. Nonetheless, I was thrilled to have a freely elected president of Paraguay as my guest after so many years fighting the country's dictatorship.

There was one rather curious link to the past in the experience. Among the delegation was Conrado Pappalardo. He is Graciela Zuccolillo's brother and the long-time protocol chief for Alfredo Stroessner I'd dealt with in my visits to the dictator. Now he was a member of congress.

4. Uruguay
Mouthpiece Becomes Press Advocate

Uruguay's military response to the 1970's leftist violence was restrained compared to nearby Argentina and Chile. "Only" 200 Uruguayans were kidnapped and killed by security forces during the military rule initiated by President Juan María Bordaberry. In March 1972, six weeks after his inauguration, Bordaberry suspended the constitution and individual liberties and allowed the military to begin crushing the guerrillas, who called themselves Tupamaros.

Attacks in 1970 and 1971 by the guerrillas had precipitated great unrest. A U.S. CIA instructor had been kidnapped and executed. The Brazilian counsel was kidnapped and released for a $250,000 ransom. The British ambassador was kidnapped. Undoubtedly the most disturbing event for the military was the machine-gun killing of four Army soldiers guarding the home of the commander-in-chief of the Army. President Bordaberry served as constitutional president until mid-1973, then headed a civilian-military dictatorship. He abolished the Congress, suspended the constitution and acquiesced in press censorship and political repression.

The press office of the president from 1972–1975 was headed by Danilo Arbilla Frachia, who would later become a prominent defender of press freedom in the hemisphere and president of the Inter American Press Association. Like many others in the Southern Cone, he believed those circumstances and Castro-like takeovers required harsh answers.

Later, I participated on many missions with Danilo, although for years I was unaware of his role in the dictatorship. He served Bordaberry until the end of 1975 and later maintained his role was not political, "We had no kind of political participation—it was a technical position." He also has described the repression of the period as "not all bad."

There is no doubt things got worse after Danillo left the dictatorship. Eventually Bordaberry was convicted of orchestrating at least a dozen assassinations including the murder of two legislators. Those murders took place in 1976 after Danilo had resigned. A month after the legislators' deaths, Bordaberry proposed a new, corporatist constitution that would have banned the political parties and codified a continuing military role. That proposal went further than the military was prepared to go, and he was forced to resign. The military rule lasted until early 1985.

During Danilo's tenure heading the press office, 14 media outlets were closed permanently and 159 closed temporarily. Dozens of journalists and media executives were jailed. Three of them died in jail, allegedly as a result of torture. Years later Danilo described the dictatorship as the most totalitarian in the Southern Cone, especially in 1975–76. He said there was no voice raised in protest outside the country.

Only later did he realize that IAPA was the one voice denouncing the dictatorships in Latin America. "Thanks to the IAPA, denunciations about press freedom in Uruguay went around the world," he said. After he himself was detained—and released in part as the result of an IAPA mission to Uruguay—he joined the association in 1978. I was a member of that mission.

Since then, Danilo has been an admirable and effective advocate of press freedom and democracy. His columns on the subject are published by many Latin American newspapers, especially those affiliated with IAPA. He also is controversial. As he told an interviewer in 1999, "Those who know me know I am a very polemical person and not very diplomatic. I do not try to ingratiate myself with anybody, but to defend what I believe in—rightly or wrongly—with such passion that I am hardly a vote-catcher. Anyone in the IAPA will confirm this."

5. Bolivia
History Turns Tragic

Bolivia's media have not received the attention they deserve either from IAPA or me, but they are not entirely ignored. Representation at our semi-annual meetings is sporadic, although the newspaper of the Jorge Carrasco family periodically is represented.

El Diario, founded in 1910 by the Carrasco family in La Paz, the capital, is the dean of Bolivian newspapers—the oldest and most prestigious. In 1971, during the populist fervor of the socialist military government of Juan José Torres, workers took over the newspaper and converted it to a cooperative. This was similar to what occurred shortly after to Peruvian dailies under the leftist military government of Juan Velasco Alvarado.

The Hugo Banzer government eventually returned the newspaper to the Carrasco family. *El Diario* is currently represented at IAPA by Jorge Carrasco Guzmán, who serves the society as freedom of press regional vice president for Bolivia. He and his brother Antonio now run the daily. I knew their father Jorge Carrasco Johnsen when he attended IAPA meetings in the late 1990s. He became IAPA's regional vice president in 1999. His history turned tragic three years later.

In January 2002, he organized with his wife Maria Teresa Guzman de Carrasco, who edited the newspaper's magazine, a successful forum on IAPA's Declaration of Chapúltepec. Bolivian President Jorge Quiroga and other officials attended along with several IAPA officers. Three months later his wife was killed in in a dynamite blast attacking his car. She had been driven in his vehicle rather than her own from the office so he could stay late. He was dissatisfied with the front page layout. Her death had the earmarks of other deaths of journalists in Latin America. Jorge's sons believe, even today, the bomb was intended to stop *El Diario*'s investigation into official corruption. "The bomb had my name on it," Jorge declared at the time.

The IAPA and other press freedom groups took up the case and demanded answers. Argentine reporter Jorge Elias conducted IAPA's investigation. A month after the murder, Jorge Carrasco himself was arrested. Five people confessed to roles in the crime. His longtime chauffeur testified Jorge had offered him $10,000 to commit the murder. He said Jorge suspected his wife of 27 years was unfaithful. He remained IAPA's regional vice president until October of that year. Adding a soap-opera element, a Bolivian shaman claimed Jorge hired him to conjure something that would throw police off the trail.

While Jorge's sons called the trial "a mockery," Jorge's sisters and daughter believed he was guilty. They suspected he was behind another recent explosion at one of the sister's homes. There were family rifts about money going back a decade.

Jorge was convicted and sentenced to 30 years without parole.

On January 18, 2016, he died.

NORTHERN SOUTH AMERICA

6. Colombia
Do Not Enter

Of my many experiences in Latin America, one I thought might rank as the most significant, at least in my own country, turned out to be the most controversial. Motivated by the treatment of two highly-respected Colombian journalists who were denied entry into the United States in 1986, I worked with Kansas Senator Nancy Kassebaum to push legislation that reformed McCarthy-era immigration law.

More than a decade later our reform was blamed by some critics for allowing the 9/11 hijackers to enter the country. Ultimately, we were cleared of responsibility by the chairman of the 9/11 Commission that investigated the terrorist attacks.

The McCarran-Walter Immigration Act of 1952, passed over President Harry Truman's veto, had kept thousands of foreigners out of the country because of their beliefs—among them Gabriel García Márquez, Csezlaw Milosz and Pablo Neruda, all recipients of the Nobel Prize for Literature. My focus was on Patricia Lara, a political-affairs columnist for the leading daily in Bogotá, *El Tiempo*, and Olga Behar, a correspondent for the Colombian publication *Zona*. Both today are highly esteemed journalists and book authors. In October 1986 Lara, later married to Colombia's attorney general, was expelled from the United States, and just days later Behar was detained upon entry as well, although eventually she was permitted to remain in the country.

Patricia Lara had been invited to attend the Maria Moors Cabot Awards banquet at Columbia University, her alma mater. Upon arriving at Kennedy Airport, she was taken into custody by agents of the Immigration and Naturalization Service (INS) because her name was in their "lookout" book, which listed 350,000 names of people considered a risk to the security of the United States. Under federal law, people listed in the book could then be denied entry into the country.

Normally, when an alien is found to be excludable from entry into the United States, the case is referred to an immigration judge for hearing in an exclusion proceeding. The alien can bring an attorney and respond to the evidence. However, at that time hearings could be refused aliens who were found excludable because they sought entry "solely, principally or *incidentally* (emphasis added) to engage in activities which would be prejudicial to the public interest, or would endanger the welfare, safety, or security of the United States," or who were excludable as members of communist or anarchist organizations. This denial was limited to cases in which the decision was based on confidential information that was "not disclosable without prejudice to the public interest, safety or security."

The U.S. Supreme Court had upheld this approach, saying "Whatever the procedure authorized by Congress is, it is due process as far as an alien denied entry is concerned." The Court also upheld language authorizing the Attorney General to detain, and hold in custody without hearing or appeal, aliens "likely to engage in activities adverse to the national security or the national safety."

Three days after Patricia Lara was detained, the State Department revoked the valid non-immigrant visa she had received in Paris the previous year. She had used that visa to enter the United States six months earlier without incident. After a week's detention she was sent back to Colombia.

Her first night in detention was at the airport's Viscount Hotel. She was then transferred to a processing center where she was "required to disrobe and shower in the view of an unknown INS detention officer and she was visually examined by the officer," according to a lawsuit brought later on her behalf. Her possessions were taken and she was made to wear a yellow jumpsuit. That night she was locked in a room along with two other women who said they had been convicted of crimes. "The toilet facilities in the room were not enclosed and were in full view of anyone present in the room. During that period she did not sleep and was afraid for her safety," the lawsuit stated. She was not permitted visitors until two days after her detention, and after each visit she was "physically strip-searched by an unknown INS detention officer."

On the third day she was transferred to a maximum security federal prison in New York. She was kept away from the general prison population in a locked cell with a female prisoner who stated she was serving a sentence for selling heroin. She was not allowed a hearing and was told her detention was based on "information of a confidential nature, the disclosure of which would be prejudicial to the public interest, safety or security of the United States."

While she believed her treatment stemmed from her published criticism of U.S. policy in Central America, a later Freedom of Information request indicated her "lookout" book listing more likely was linked to a book she had written about the motivation behind the M-19 guerrilla movement in Colombia. The FOI disclosure revealed an English translation of the book had been provided to INS by the CIA—a translation she had not known about before. Subsequent statements by officials further cited her M-19 connections.

Just two weeks after Lara was stopped, Olga Behar was detained upon her arrival in Miami. She was coming from Madrid and planned to spend only one day in Miami visiting her sister. Her name was also in the security "lookout" book. A year earlier she, too, had published a book about her country—an uncompromising account, today in its eleventh edition, on the four decades of political violence that had wracked Colombia.

She was held overnight in an airport hotel and the next morning permitted without explanation to remain in the county. Her case was later elaborated upon in a telex from Deputy U.S. Attorney General Arnold Burns to me in my capacity as chairman of the IAPA Executive Committee. I had written to U.S. Attorney General Ed Meese asking for a meeting to discuss both cases. In denying a meeting, Meese's top deputy provided the following explanation: "When it was determined that information contained in the classified source material was not sufficient to preclude Ms. Behar's admission, she was admitted and her name was subsequently removed from the lookout system."

Oddly, despite this assurance, three years later Olga Behar was denied a student visa she needed to begin graduate studies on a fellowship at the University of Southern California. She was told when she applied at the consulate in Mexico City that her name was still in the "lookout" book. Consular officials said they had been instructed by Washington to approve her visa only after the U.S. embassy in Bogotá cleared it. Again, this time as first vice president of IAPA and after our successful reform of the immigration act, I protested to the Justice Department saying, "It would indeed be ironic if a person whose earlier difficulties led to the Section 901 limitation on the McCarran-Walter Act were to become the subject of litigation and a *cause célèbre* involving that act." A few days later I received notification from then acting deputy attorney general, Edward Dennis Jr., that the matter had been resolved and she had her visa.

On Patricia Lara, Deputy Attorney General Burns' telex to me said she never should have been issued a visa. "Fortunately," he continued, "information concerning her support for and membership in a known terrorist organization was made available to the Immigration and Naturalization Service in time to ensure that she not be permitted to enter this country. Patricia Lara's exclusion from the United States was not based upon her political ideology, as you appear to believe. Rather, she was prevented from entering this country because of her membership in and support for the M-19, a Colombian terrorist organization. Ms. Lara's employment as a journalist provides an excellent cover for her other less admirable activities. Further explanation is not possible because the source material is classified."

This U.S. government characterization came despite protests of her deportation by the Colombian government and of her editor at *El Tiempo* as well as other important Colombian editors and journalists. *El Tiempo*'s managing editor, Francisco Santos, a friend of mine who later served as his nation's vice president in the Alvaro Uribe government, strongly objected to the INS treatment of her. She had been a columnist for his paper for five years. "I do not see how they can paint a picture of her as a Communist or as a terrorist," he said. "She is a wealthy capitalist who inherited a fortune from her father and runs a private business, as well as participates in politics and journalism."

Both 1986 cases received extensive media coverage, especially Patricia Lara's. CBS Television's widely popular and highly rated *60 Minutes* broadcast a segment on her case within a month of her ordeal. Elliott Abrams, the U.S. Assistant Secretary of State for Latin American Affairs, told an interviewer on the program that she was a member of the M-19 guerrilla organization, and that her involvement in "terrorist activities" was the reason she was denied entry to the United States and subsequently deported.

"She is involved in terrorist activities. She is a member of the M-19 terrorist organization in Colombia. She is an active liaison between that terrorist organization . . . and the Cuban secret police," Abrams said. He claimed she served on one of the guerrilla group's "ruling committees," and that her being a journalist was a "cover." In reply, Lara issued a statement through her attorney. She said she had "never been a member of the M-19. I am a journalist who began writing about M-19 at a time when they wanted a dialogue with the Colombian government, which they later obtained in the peace process of 1984."

That peace process came to nothing in 1985 when the M-19 killed 11 justices of the Supreme Court. "I have a clear conscience," she continued. "Violence has no place in a democracy. In the just-published edition of my book on the

M-19, I condemn the assault on the Palace of Justice and the breaking of the truce . . ." She also said she had worked for several months in 1983 as a radio correspondent in Cuba where she made a few friends.

She later explained that she had been a full-time journalist until 1982 when her father, who became wealthy through his association with International Harvester, died. "I am an only child, and a widow," she said, "so since then I have taken on the responsibility of running the family business. Now I am a businesswoman as well as a journalist." Among the family's assets were a 2,500-acre farm near Bogotá, a shopping mall and condominium apartments. She had 65 full-time employees. Three family members had been victims of kidnappings, two ending in death.

Shortly after Patricia Lara was expelled, I issued in my capacity as chairman of the IAPA executive committee, along with IAPA's president, a cable of protest to U.S. Secretary of State George Shultz. "In the name of more than 1,300 newspapers from 33 countries of the hemisphere, members of the Inter American Press Association," we said, "we must strongly protest the inexplicable treatment accorded by your government to Colombian journalist Patricia Lara. Ms. Lara is an accredited reporter for the daily newspaper *El Tiempo* of Bogotá, a longtime IAPA member universally respected for its defense of democratic principles and freedom of the press both in its own country and throughout the hemisphere. We express our unqualified support for our member *El Tiempo* and its reporter, and urgently request that she and her newspaper be advised of the specific charges which led to her expulsion from a country with a long history of respect for justice and freedom of thought and expression."

After her expulsion, I sent the letter requesting the meeting with Attorney General Meese seeking explanation and to discuss improvements in the INS procedures. I was joined in my request by seven U.S. professional journalism organizations including the American Society of Newspaper Editors (ASNE). The telex response from Deputy Attorney General Burns came after a delay of nearly three months. Regarding the INS procedures, he basically said there was nothing wrong with them and that no mistakes had been made and that, therefore, no meeting with the Attorney General was necessary.

After discussion with other members of the IAPA leadership, we concluded the response had been inadequate, did not satisfy our real concern that journalists and others could be excluded from the United States without ever being told the reason for exclusion or the evidence supporting it, without facing their accusers and all the while being detained without right of appeal. We determined our most appropriate and effective response would be to seek revision of those sections of the McCarran-Walter Act that permitted such occurrences. Working toward that end with efforts already underway in the Congress, we believed, we also would be increasing pressure on the executive branch to overhaul its procedures. We also decided that given ASNE's considerable clout with Congress we would ask the U.S. editors' society to take the lead in the effort. I persuaded ASNE to endorse a change in the law at its April 1987 meeting in San Francisco.

We knew the executive branch could overhaul the procedures it was using without a change in the law. Guidelines existed for how names were entered into the "Lookout" system, but I also had learned from a friend, Doris Meissner, who had recently been acting commissioner of the INS, that the guidelines were not rigorously enforced and review, once the names were in the "Lookout" book, was "virtually nonexistent." She gave me a number of recommendations for improving the procedure, which we pushed in our joint effort. But the successful approach was via legislation. We ultimately joined a statutory reform initiative sponsored by Sen. Pat Moynihan and pushed by Rep. Barney Frank, both Democrats.

At the time Sen. Moynihan's problem was no Republican co-sponsor in the Senate. I contacted Kansas Senator Nancy Kassebaum, who served on the Senate Foreign Relations Committee with Moynihan, urging her to support his proposed revisions to the McCarran-Walter Act as an amendment to the State Department Authorization Bill. She agreed to support them, and I worked with her and her staff to come up with language acceptable to the committee. The result was adopted by the committee in May 1987 and subsequently by the full Senate. Unfortunately, the revisions were not in the House version of the bill. Our challenge then was to get the conference committee of the two congressional chambers to accept our version. I wrote personally to each member of the conference committee in my ASNE capacity as vice chairman of its international committee noting the ASNE board strongly endorsed the changes and explaining why. I received responses, including from the chairman of the House Foreign Affairs Committee Dante Fascell, who supported us.

The problem boiled down to objections from the House conferees led by Chairman Peter Rodino and Romano Mazzoli that immigration reform should be handled by the Judiciary Committee. Fortunately, I had previously contacted Rep. Barney Frank, a member of the House Judiciary Committee and the prime sponsor of its comprehensive immigration reform proposal. He had written me in early November that he supported our effort and "would do all I can to fight for the inclusion of (our reform) in the final version of the authorization bill." He explained that the final version might not preserve our exact language, but that he was hopeful for something close to it. On December 3 the conference committee approved the 1988–89 authorization bill including our reform with minor modifications. Among others who supported the bill was Senator Jesse Helms, the staunchly anti-Communist Republican from North Carolina, who was chairman of the Foreign Relations Committee. The House and Senate approved the Conference Report December 14.

The bill provided that "no alien may be denied a visa or excluded from admission in the United States . . . or subject to deportation because of any past, current, or expected beliefs, statements or associations which, if engaged in by a U.S. citizen in the United States, would be protected under the Constitution of the United States." The federal government would continue to be able to use foreign policy and national security concerns to exclude people other than on the basis of their ideology. Exceptions included applicants linked to "terrorist" acts and activities as well as those who are "official" representatives of "totalitarian states." Also exempted were persons who assisted in persecutions by Nazis, labor organizers from totalitarian countries and member of the Palestine Liberation Army. Several of the exceptions were necessary to obtain majority support for the bill.

Now the question was: Would President Ronald Reagan sign the bill? Fortunately, I had had the exchange with Deputy Attorney General Arnold Burns. He told me we would not get a meeting with Attorney General Ed Meese, but he did acknowledge that the exclusion grounds based on ideology in current law raised more questions than other exclusion grounds. And he also said, "The Department of Justice, although appreciative of your concerns, is not in a position at this time to either support or oppose the passage of the Department of State Authorization Bill containing the amendment in question."

I also managed to have a conversation on the issue the previous spring with Assistant Secretary of State for Inter-American Affairs Elliott Abrams when he spoke at the University of Kansas in Lawrence. Abrams had previously served as Assistant Secretary for Human Rights, so I had hopes he would support us. He told me he favored a reasonable change in the McCarren-Walter Act to eliminate ideology as a basis for denying visas, and in a letter following up our Kansas meeting, I urged him to push for support of our revisions by the administration.

In his June response Abrams reiterated the administration's commitment to protecting the free exchange of political ideas, but said our amendment added "complication and uncertainty to the already tangled structure of the visa laws." He noted that the House and Senate Judiciary committees planned hearings on a comprehensive immigration reform later in the year. "The State Department plans to participate in this effort, but sees no need for interim measures," he concluded.

I have no idea what discussion, if any, occurred at the White House, but eight days after the Conference Committee approved the bill, President Reagan signed it into law. It went into effect January 1, 1988.

I was extremely proud of what we had accomplished. I wrote a piece for my newspaper, *The Manhattan Mercury*, later published in a number of other newspapers and the ASNE magazine, extolling the new law. "With the new year," I wrote, "U.S. law no longer seeks to protect us from people like Gabriel Garcia Marquez, Csezlaw Milosz and Pablo Neruda. All are recipients of the Nobel Prize for Literature and, like hundreds of other well-known but controversial foreign politicians, authors, academics, journalists and artists, they at one time have been denied visas to enter our country because of their political beliefs." I went on to explain the new provisions, then added, "For 35 years we had exposed our nation to needless ridicule abroad and denied our own citizens the benefit of views outside our mainstream. The old law, Mexico's grand man of letters Carlos Fuentes said three years ago, 'endangers the Republic, mocks Democracy, demoralizes the true friends of the United States, and offers undeserved aces to the Soviet Union . . . ' Now Americans again can take pride in living up to our political ideal of an open society tolerant of divergent views.

"That such a contradiction with our fundamental beliefs could have existed so long is nearly inconceivable . . .

"Thought-policing is simply unworthy of a country that thinks of itself as free. It mocks what we say we are. If we are to be an open society, unafraid of all ideas, criticism can only strengthen us. We have to preserve our internal security, but this can be done without eroding our principles. We have been at odds with the American tradition of pluralism and tolerance for dissent, and this law was a clear insult to the public's intelligence . . .

"In revising this unfortunate law, Congress paid a marvelous tribute to the Constitution in its bicentennial year. Ideological protectionism is simply not the American way. It damaged our reputation and injured First Amendment rights here at home."

For those of us battling for press freedom around the world, this battle was worth fighting. As I had said in an earlier piece, "If reporters coming to the United States can be denied admission because of ideology without even a hearing, how in good conscience can we protest the detention of U.S. reporters in the Soviet Union, their exclusion from Latin American, Asian and African countries or abuses of the local press in other nations?"

Senator Kassebaum sent me a framed copy of the revision on which she wrote: "Thanks Ed. Appreciate your assistance with this legislation. Nancy Landon Kassebaum." Her general counsel, Dan Bolen, who had been extremely helpful, wrote in a separate note that "Our efforts can be attributed to your interest in this legislation."

But not everyone was happy. State Department officials contended the revision, which came to be known as "Section 901," would provoke a legal nightmare because every plaintiff denied a visa would charge he or she was excluded for an invalid reason. Popular radio commentator Paul Harvey told his vast audience: "There are people who would have Western societies commit suicide, and we are doing it with this new law . . . ."

Nonetheless, Section 901 proved a resounding success for more than a decade. It stopped the paranoiac practice of barring certain people from the country for fear of what they might say. It was originally enacted for a period of one year, but was extended for another two years later in 1988, although at the same time its application was narrowed to protect only temporary visitors. In 1990 Congress made Section 901 permanent as part of a comprehensive reform of the McCarran-Walter Act. The reform incorporated the standard embodied in Section 901, completely eliminating the ideological grounds for excluding visitors, and significantly curtailing the use of such criteria for permanent immigrants. It did expand government authority to exclude visitors who have "engaged in terrorism" or whose entry in the view of the State Department would harm U.S. foreign policy. It also required the purging of the "lookout list" of foreigners no longer excludable under the standard.

In 1996 the Republican-controlled Congress expanded the government's authority to prevent entry into the country with two bills, both signed into law by President Clinton, that added specific references to "representatives" and "members" of terrorist organizations as being excludable, and also established "incitement" to acts of terrorism as a ground for exclusion.

Then came September 11, 2001, and the devastating attacks on the World Trade Center twin towers in New York and the Pentagon in Washington, D.C. More than 3,000 were killed and the blame game began.

Admiral R. James Woolsey, who had been Director of the CIA in the Clinton administration, wrote in reviewing a book about 9/11 in the Wall Street Journal that with the Section 901 reform Congress had made it "illegal to deny visas to members of terrorists groups," and described the reform as one of the underlying causes of 9/11.

Woolsey was reviewing a 2003 book by Gerald Posner, *Why America Slept: The Failure to Prevent 9/11*. Posner, a former lawyer and award-winning author, is a frequent commentator on television and in the printed press. His book on Lee Harvey Oswald and the Kennedy assassination was one of three finalists for the 1994 Pulitzer Prize when I served on the Pulitzer Board. He had to be taken seriously.

In his 9/11 book he, too, states that under our reform "membership in a terrorist organization was no longer sufficient to deny a visa." A visa could only be denied, he wrote, "if the government could prove the applicant had committed an act of terrorism." He does point out that individuals suspected of foreign intelligence connections could be denied entry, but this "loophole" could only work if the CIA and FBI shared information, which they did not in many instances.

While Posner's description of the reform accurately characterized limitations in the original language, it did not take into account the 1996 revision which added specific references to "representatives" and "members" of terrorist organizations as being excludable, which was the law of the land leading up to and including 9/11. Admiral Woolsey's assertion that it was illegal to deny visas to members of terrorist organizations is simply an over-simplification of the original limitation; he also ignored the 1996 revision.

The blame game might have ended there, but it was kept alive by the man whom Rep. Barney Frank defeated in his 2004 re-election. Chuck Morse, a conservative talk-radio host, repeated the accusations in that campaign and eventually in his 2005 book: *Barney Frank and the Law of Unintended Consequences: How the Frank Amendment Helped Terrorists Get Legal Visas.* In the book Morse quotes Jessica M. Vaughan, the policy director of a respected Washington research institute, the Center for Immigration Studies, to the effect that immigration officials were told they couldn't even consider political opinions when issuing visas as a result of our reform: "The person," she said, "practically has to come out and say, 'Yeah, I was going to blow up whatever.' And that might not be enough if they didn't do it."

In his book Morse asserts that "the nineteen al Queda affiliated hijackers ... would be the beneficiaries of the new law." He continued his push to make the congressman shoulder blame for 9/11 in a second run against Frank in a 2006, this time with a write-in campaign.

I was not personally a subject of these assertions, but needless to say, I began wondering whether I, too, might get blamed for 9/11. Fortunately, Barney Frank issued a strong response to the allegations. He pointed to the 9/11 Commission Report released in the summer of 2004 that made clear the law at the time was not the problem.

The preface to the Commission's staff report on terrorist travel states clearly: "This introduction summarizes many of the key facts of the hijackers' entry into the United States. In it, we endeavor to dispel the myth that their entry into the United States was 'clean and legal.' It was not. Three hijackers carried passports with indicators of Islamic extremism linked to al Queda; two others carried passports manipulated in a fraudulent manner. It is likely that several more hijackers carried passports with similar fraudulent manipulation. Two hijackers lied on their visa applications. Once in the United States, two hijackers violated the terms of their visas. One overstayed his visa."

In his statement Congressman Frank elaborated: "While one of the conspirators, Zacarias Moussaoui, was intercepted and detained when he tried to enter this country, the final Commission report states that, under the law in effect at the time, as many as 15 of the 19 murderers could have been excluded at the border, and suggested that all of them might have been, though it did not have enough information about the other four."

When Commission Chairman Thomas Kean testified before the House Select Committee on Homeland Security after release of the Report, Congressman Frank asked him, according to the text of a Federal News Service account:

"I take it, from reading your report, that you don't find the problem is in the definition statutory of who can be excluded but rather in the failure to use the definition appropriately. Am I reading that accurately?

Chairman Kean: "I think you're reading that accurately. I mean, we had a wonderful example of an immigration official in Orlando, Florida, who simply asked a couple of questions. A lot of these people just automatically granted access, even though they had . . ."

Congressman Frank: ". . . can I just say that the key point is here— under the statutes as they now exist, these people were excludable [*inaudible*] procedures . . ."

Mr. Keen: "That's exactly right."

Congressman Frank: "It's not that the statute allows that people should be . . ."

Mr. Keen: "No, they were excludable, and they were not excluded, but what I'm saying there was at least one case of a very alert customs agent who simply started asking questions, and that was probably the twentieth hijacker who was excluded because of a good civil servant who was doing his job."

Personally, I felt a great relief. Of course, after 9/11 the Patriot Act restored an ideological exclusion clause. Section 411 of the act authorized the designation of terrorist organizations for immigration purposes, known as the "Terrorist Exclusion List (TEL)."

It added Section 212(a)(3)(B) to the Immigration and Naturalization Act describing visa ineligibilities related to terrorism. This provision renders ineligible for a U.S. visa anyone who engages in terrorist activities, belongs to a terrorist organization or endorses terrorist activities. An immigrant can be excluded if his or her advocacy is determined to undermine anti-terrorist efforts.

While the Patriot Act focuses specifically on terrorism and in that way is narrower than the pre-Section 901 law, its provisions are even broader when it comes to terrorists and persons believed to aid them. Still, many authors and controversial journalists like Gabriel Garcia Márquez, while he was alive, or Patricia Lara have received visas under it.

Another highly visible project in which I took a part with Colombian journalist colleagues and a worldwide group of communications executives was raising funds to keep alive one of Colombia's most distinguished newspapers, *El Espectador,* a determined critic of the drug cartels. It was the nation's second largest daily with circulation of 200,000, staff of 1,200 and for many years the publishing outlet for literary luminaries like Garcia Márquez. The newspapers of Colombia, with *El Espectador* leading, had become the backbone of the war against drug traffickers—maintaining its momentum by pressing government and other institutions to carry on with the battle.

The government launched a war against the cartels in August, 1989. Given the threat of extradition to the United States for trial, the self-styled "Extraditables" issued a communiqué August 23 declaring "all-out war on the journalists who have attacked and insulted us." The next day two bombs were defused in Medellín at the Caracól and RCN radio stations.

Then, on September 2, just a month before I became president of the Inter American Press Association, the drug cartel headed by Pablo Escobar, in the name of "the Extraditables," set off a powerful truck bomb outside the *El Espectador*'s plant that killed one employee and wounded at least 83 others. The 220 pounds of dynamite, which left a 10-foot crater, also blew out all the huge glass panels that served as walls and damaged the presses and electronic editing system. Estimates of damage exceeded $2.5 million.

In addition to the bombing in Bogotá, a bomb also destroyed the resort home on the Caribbean Island of El Rosario of the Cano family, owners of the newspaper. A month later three additional employees, including the newspaper's circulation and advertising directors in Medellín, were shot and killed. Less than three years earlier Escobar's organization had assassinated the paper's editor, Guillermo Cano.

After the bombing the drug lords who claimed responsibility said they would be back to "finish the job" if the newspaper continued to distribute in Medellín, Escobar's hometown.

Newspaper industry reaction was swift. *El Espectador* did not back down and within three weeks of the IAPA's early October General Assembly in Mexico, the U.S. publishers' organization and others had joined IAPA with a goal of raising $2.5 million to get the newspaper back on its feet. Alvah Chapman, of the Knight Ridder media group which included *The Miami Herald,* spearheaded the fundraising. He had recently been chairman of the American Newspaper Publishers Association (ANPA). In his solicitation letter, he wrote: "We cannot allow the drug lords to win this one—it is contrary to our national interest. We must take a stand and send a clear message—'you cannot have *El Espectador*.' With your generous support, we can win this fight by helping *El Espectador* to continue publishing with the courage and veracity that have been its hallmark for the past 102 years."

He went on to emphasize the urgency, pointing out the newspaper would not survive more than two months without substantial assistance. He sought leadership gifts in the $150,000 to $250,000 range and said they would be channeled through the ANPA Foundation and the IAPA Foundation. Frank Bennack, CEO of The Hearst Corporation, and Punch Sulzberger, CEO of The New York Times Company, had already made such commitments, he said, and he believed the Knight Foundation and Knight Ridder would soon make comparable gifts. The money was to be used to fund a long-term interest-free loan, for eventual repayment to the IAPA Foundation's press freedom emergency fund for use in similar future cases in the hemisphere.

In a press release Chapman noted the possible "demise" of the daily and then was quoted: "El Espectador has been a special target of the cocaine barons because of the extraordinary courage of its publisher, Luis Gabriel Cano, his family and staff. The newspaper has continued its condemnation of drug traffickers despite the 1986 assassination of its publisher, Guillermo Cano, brother of Luis." He also singled out in the release United States Information Director Bruce Gelb for "his major efforts in publicizing the plight of the newspaper." Gelb had made phone calls to a number of leading publishers in the U.S. and abroad.

Alvah Chapman at the same time corresponded with U.S. President George H. W. Bush informing him of the narco-traffickers' attacks against the Colombian press, including *El Espectador*. In an immediate "Dear Alvah" response the President wrote his friend saying "These criminal acts point out again that the drug problem threatens not only individuals, but also governments and other institutions vital to a democracy. Your effort to support *El Espectador* therefore is an endeavor worthy of the support of all who cherish a free press. I strongly endorse your efforts."

As a result, later that month I organized a four-city tour of leading Colombian editors to the United States to raise the funds. President Bush met with them at the White House. Included were Luis Cano of *El Espectador*, Juan Manuel Santos of *El Tiempo*, Alvaro Lloreda of *El País*, Cali, and Alejandro Galvis, of *La Vanguardia Liberal*, Bucaramanga. Lloreda was president of the

Colombian Association of Dailies and I had appointed Santos vice president for Colombia of IAPA's freedom of the press committee. He would later be elected president of Colombia in 2010 and 2014.

In the previous eight years fifty Colombian journalists had been murdered, eight since the government war on the cartels that began in August. A second daily, Alejandro Galvis' Bucaramanga newspaper was 80 percent destroyed by a bomb on October 16. Four of his employees were killed in the blast.

We were able to arrange the meeting with President Bush in the Roosevelt Room of the White House with help from his press secretary, Marlin Fitzwater. Marlin had worked at my newspaper when he was a student at Kansas State University, which undoubtedly helped our cause. The session was essentially a previously arranged interview for ten other journalists from countries the President was soon to visit in a forthcoming trip to Central and South America. My group was an add-on, but Luis Cano was given the first question.

We knew ahead that time for our questions would be limited, so Juan Manuel Santos, a graduate of the University of Kansas who had recently been a Nieman Fellow at Harvard, drafted a statement to leave behind with the President. With advice from the others, he wrote it in longhand and I provided some light editing and typed it for him. I still have his handwritten statement, which today probably is a collector's item.

In the interview, a transcript of which was made available by the White House, the Colombian editors called on the United States to address more forcefully the issue of drug consumption and distribution. They also asked about U.S. views on a possible dialogue between the Colombian government and the cartels and raised the need for economic support, "a type of Marshall Plan." While such support did not come under the Bush administration, the Clinton and subsequent administrations did initiate such a multi-billion-dollar project called Plan Colombia that has provided $10 billion in assistance, mostly military.

The leave-behind document written by Juan Manuel Santos set out these points in more detail and called for more credit from private banks and multilateral organizations as well as better access to U.S. markets, especially for coffee. In advocating a "Marshall Plan-type program," it noted, "The total U.S. aid this year including military equipment, $87 million, doesn't even buy the cocaine that the Colombian government has confiscated in the last week."

"We also think much more could be done to control (a) the flow of chemical raw materials used in the production of cocaine, (b) the flow of weapons to the drug traffickers and (c) the money laundering," the letter noted. It also asked President Bush to encourage other countries to get involved with the war, and concluded that "we would greatly appreciate your personal support with private foundations and other institutions that could help us (the newspapers) in our struggle to survive."

That same day I took the Colombians to a luncheon with top executives at the headquarters of *USA Today* and then a meeting at the U.S. Capitol with the Senate Foreign Relations Committee. The latter was organized at my request by Kansas Senator Nancy Landon Kassebaum, a committee member. Those attending, at least briefly, in addition to Sen. Kassebaum were Senators Dick Lugar, Chris Dodd, Richard Cohen, Joe Biden, Alan Cranston, Bob Dole, Jesse Helms, Frank Murkowitz, Claiborne Pell and Warren Rudman.

The Senate session was one of solidarity. As I wrote in a thank-you letter to Senator Kassebaum about her guests, "Theirs is a fight most of us simply would not undertake. The support they received from you and your fellow senators will encourage them to continue with this difficult struggle."

That evening we boarded an Eastern Airlines flight to Atlanta, and on subsequent days to Dallas and Los Angeles. One interesting detail in view of today's tight airport security is that I purchased all the Colombians' tickets in the last name "Seaton," Luis Seaton, Juan Manuel Seaton and Alejandro Seaton. (Alvaro Llorado did not participate in the remainder of the tour.)

Doing this today would be impossible and unthinkable, but I was extremely concerned about the safety of my Colombian colleagues. The lives of these men were at stake constantly. The Cano family, for example, travelled at all times under armed guard in Colombia. Luis's bodyguards carried submachine guns and other weapons and travelled both in his car and another vehicle accompanying it. The others took similar precautions.

We were questioned about the last names only once. An American Airlines agent did a double-take in Dallas as we were checking in for our flight to Los Angeles. I explained to her who my companions were and the risks they were under. She said she had heard of Pablo Escobar and let us board the airplane.

The visits in all four cities were facilitated by editor friends of mine from the American Society of Newspaper Editors. In each case we met with editorial boards. *Los Angeles Times* publisher Dave Laventhol organized a luncheon attended by publishers and editors of several other California newspapers. Virtually everyone we met made donations. Dallas Morning News publisher Burl Osborne also wrote letters to industry suppliers, in many cases successfully, asking them to waive fees and extend credit to *El Espectador*.

As a result of our tour, the diligent work of Alvah Chapman, the support of President Bush and many others, I was able to report to the IAPA executive committee in January, less that three months after we started, that through the generosity of donors in the U.S., Australia, Canada and Japan we had nearly $2.7 million in cash and pledges for the fund. The money was forwarded to El Espectador as a no-interest loan.

Later that year I received this personal note from President Bush:

Dear Mr. Seaton:

Alvah Chapman tells me that you were most helpful in the all-out fundraising effort on behalf of El Espectador in Colombia.

This magnificent support will send a strong message to the narco-terrorists that they cannot prevail.

I know Alvah, who did a superb job in heading up this effort, joins me in thanking you for your generous response.

Sincerely,

[Signed] George Bush

Subsequently, I had the privilege of working with courageous Colombian colleagues on several other occasions. As president of IAPA I was joined in a mission in early January 1990 to Guatemala and Panama by Francisco "Pacho" Santos. The two of us went to Guatemala to protest pressures on the media, especially from the defense minister, Héctor Gramajo, which appeared to be leading to physical attacks on reporters and media facilities.

Then we met several other IAPA members in Panamá, which had just been invaded by U.S. forces to overturn the dictatorship of General Manuel Noriega. There we investigated the closing down by the U.S. forces of pro-Noriega radio stations. Among memorable activities there, we visited Noriega's home, still set for Christmas celebrations. A voodoo altar and vast book collection on military history were also there.

On this mission Pacho Santos, 28, was a stand-in for his cousin Juan Manuel Santos. Later that year, in September, Pacho was kidnapped off the street by Pablo Escobar's cartel and held hostage for eight months. He and eight others were released only after a decree from the Colombian congress prevented extraditions of Escobar and others to the U.S. Nobel laureate Gabriel García Márquez in 1996 published an account of Pacho's ordeal, *News of a Kidnapping.*

Later, because of his highly public push for peace, Pacho's name appeared in 2000 on an assassination list of the left-wing rebel army, FARC (Fuerzas Armadas Revolucionarias de Colombia). This time he fled for Spain where he became assistant to the publisher of Madrid's *El País.* He wrote a weekly column for *El Tiempo* until he returned to Colombia in 2002 to become the vice presidential candidate on the ticket of Álvaro Uribe. They were elected and he served as Colombia's vice president from 2002 until 2010, when his cousin Juan Manuel succeeded Uribe. I would see Pacho only once while he was in office, when IAPA met in Cartagena in 2007. I would also see Juan Manuel as president a couple of times and exchange numerous emails with him regarding a possible lecture at Kansas State University.

Juan Manuel had twice entered government previously but returned to *El Tiempo.* On the occasion of Pacho's decision to run for office, the two senior Santos decided that family members entering government would no longer be welcome back at their newspaper. This was undoubtedly a difficult decision. The senior Santos were brothers married to sisters, so the generation of Pacho and Juan Manuel were, in a sense, double cousins.

In President Uribe's second term Juan Manuel was appointed minister of defense. In that capacity he oversaw the most decisive blows against the FARC including the dramatic rescue of Colombia's most famous kidnap victim, Ingrid Betancourt. She was rescued using a ruse of transferring the hostages to FARC headquarters. Three American Northrop Gruman contractors were among those released. Juan Manuel parlayed his renown from that event into a successful run for the presidency.

In 1991 Juan Manuel helped me organize a visit to Colombia for editors from the American Society of Newspaper Editors as part of a trip around South America. He arranged interviews with top officials including President Cesár Gaviria. By the time of our visit in late 1991 he had decided to become President Gaviria's minister for foreign trade, so he asked another cousin, Pacho's brother Rafael Santos, to take over. Rafael and Pacho had both been members of ASNE for several years, and I had often seen them at conventions.

Among memorable moments on that visit was a reception at the home of the father of Pacho and Rafael, Hernando Santos, *El Tiempo*'s editor-in-chief. Among the guests was Ernesto Samper, who would succeed President Gaviria. Some of the ASNE members including me were accompanied by our wives. Hernando presented each of the wives with stunning, authentic pre-Columbian pottery statues.

Another memory I have about Hernando, whom I had known for a least a decade, was his role at IAPA's 1980 general assembly in San Diego. For a program segment focused on violence and newspaper ethics, I had written a hypothetical exercise based loosely on the takeover earlier of an embassy in Bogotá by the M-19 guerrillas. Appropriately, Hernando was to play the role of a newspaper owner. As the plot unfolded and several other IAPA members played their roles as judges, reporters and so forth, the moderator finally turned to Hernando asking him whether he would publish the troubling story. Hernando abruptly declined to answer, saying only, "This is too real."

Eventually I would also work closely with another of the cousins, Hernando's nephew Enrique. He served as IAPA president in 2008–09 and later played a key role in setting up peace talks between his brother's government and FARC leaders in Havana. He also was the target of an assassination plot by the FARC, in 2009. Ten FARC guerrillas were arrested for conspiring to kill him over the Holy Week vacation period while he was IAPA president.

In 2016 Columbian President Juan Manuel Santos was awarded the Nobel Peace Prize for brokering a peace agreement with the FARC guerrillas.

7. Venezuela
Dictocracy

My first encounter with Hugo Chávez was at Venezuela's Miraflores presidential palace July 9, 1992. I say encounter because I didn't meet him personally on that occasion. Rather, I watched as Venezuelan President Carlos Andrés Pérez (CAP) pointed out pockmarks on the building and bullet holes in his office windows to a small group of IAPA colleagues and me. They were put there five months earlier in an attempted coup by Chávez, the 37-year-old charismatic lieutenant colonel, and his followers.

The damaged windows had yet to be replaced, perhaps left as a reminder. Lt. Col. Chávez had surrendered on condition he could speak to the country on television. The speech was permitted and would thrust him into the national spotlight and eventual victory—after two years in prison—in the 1998 presidential election. He called the failed coup a temporary setback in his "Bolivarian Revolution." He announced in his speech the revolution would institute a socialist state advancing the needs of the people.

Our IAPA group was in Venezuela to address several challenges confronting local media. Most important of these were proposed constitutional reforms that would require news reports to be "truthful and timely" (*veraz y oportuna*), the breakup of so-called media monopolies; and the establishment of a right-of-reply and correction. We also looked into charges against Rafael Poleo, the crusading publisher of *ZETA*, a feisty magazine, who had taken refuge in the United States.

In a cordial meeting, President Pérez told us he disagreed with the proposed constitutional reforms, although he criticized some media attacks against him as excessive. The Congress was against him, he said, and attacks by its members on the media were related to opposition to him. The president, a popular chief executive in the 1970s when he nationalized the oil industry and Venezuela prospered, had won office again in 1989. Facing falling oil prices this time, he ordered austerity measures including spending cuts and higher gasoline prices. These immediately triggered a chaotic episode called the "Caracazo" in which hundreds of lives were lost.

By 1970 Venezuela was the richest country in Latin America and one of the 20 richest in the world. Twenty years later, it was still second. But discontent had grown and the Chávez 1992 attack was the first of two coup attempts which culminated in Pérez' impeachment and removal in 1993 on corruption charges. Key allegations were about a secretive fund used to pay for bodyguards for my friend Violeta Chamorro, the president of Nicaragua.

Hugo Chávez was elected president in a landslide 1998 election and served until his death 14 years later. He won decisively every election, including two constitutional reforms, except a 2007 referendum on a broad constitutional amendment that would have eliminated term limits for the president. A year and a half later he cast that issue as a plebiscite on his rule and won 54.3 percent of the vote. He was re-elected in 2012 for another term before his 2013 death.

His 1998 success resulted from a promise to crack down on corruption and raise the minimum wage. During his various terms, unemployment fell by half, the domestic economy doubled, poverty was nearly halved and infant mortality dropped by a third. Income inequality dropped to one of the lowest levels in the hemisphere. A tenfold increase in the price of oil was, of course, the key driver of the improvements, which were wildly popular with the poor.

In his early years as president he spouted leftist rhetoric but sought to get along with the United States and compromise with his opponents in Venezuela. "Don't pay attention to what he says," the U.S. ambassador at the time advised, "pay attention to what he does."

He called honest elections nearly every year using a touch-screen system he introduced with thumbprint recognition and printed receipts. Jimmy Carter described the system of the "the best in the world" where he had monitored elections.

Just after he won the December 1998 election and before his inauguration our IAPA leadership had an opportunity for a brief private meeting with him at the National Press Club in Washington. He was there for a public appearance. He assured us of his support for press freedom and we thought he almost sounded like a latter-day Thomas Jefferson.

The next week, however, he visited Beijing. There he was Mao Zedong reincarnate. We knew then battles with Hugo Chavez were just beginning.

While the new president routinely used his Sunday radio program, "Aló Presidente," to accuse publishers and journalists of being "enemies of the revolution, "no journalists in his first three years had been prosecuted and no media outlets had been shut down. A constitutional rewrite in 1999 consolidated his power over the National Assembly and the courts.

The new constitution established the principle that "every person has the right to timely, truthful and impartial information without censorship," and the Supreme Court ruled the Right of Reply was mandatory for the private press but exempted the president's weekly broadcast program. It required publishing or broadcasting responses to media stories.

"Freedom of the press is alive and well and kicking every day," Minister of Communication and Information Andres Izarra said. "Everyone says whatever they want every day without the government messing with them." Izarra was educated as a journalist in the United States and had worked for the Spanish language programs on CNN and NBC.

That media environment changed dramatically in April 2002 when Chávez was briefly ousted from office by his opponents in the military and civilian society. The attempted coup marked the turning point for him. After the coup attempt, which he believed the U.S. supported despite a Congressional investigation concluding the contrary, he declared the "anti-imperialist" character of his revolution and became a strident and vocal critic of President Bush and U.S. policy. His domestic program also took a sharp turn to the left with a series of social "missions" including admitting 20,000 Cuban doctors and health workers. "I came to the conclusion above all after the coup . . . that any attempt to reach an agreement with the forces of the old regime here, the old order, would be in vain," he later told a biographer.

The National Assembly enacted a Telecommunications Act effective immediately. It empowered the government, at its discretion, to close down radio and television programs it regarded as contrary to the revolution. Media owners were urged by the Assembly to adopt a Code of Ethics to govern their conduct.

The Venezuelan media had been among Latin America's most prosperous, best trained and equipped and was respected for high quality. After 1998 owners and their editors began siding with the opposition to Chávez, slanting stores and reporting unfounded speculation, rumors and unchecked facts. As one prominent journalist, Alonso Moleiro, put it: "Reporters bought the argument that you have to put journalistic standards aside, that if we don't get rid of Chávez, we will have communism and Fidelismo."

In March and April of 2002 television gave blanket coverage to opposition marches, but pro-Chávez marches were not covered at all. On April 11 a huge march was called to support a national strike and the four major channels coordinated wall-to-wall live coverage including on-air pleas for people to participate. Half a million joined the march toward Miraflores, demanding Chávez resign. A faction of the military took the president into custody and installed a business leader as new president.

Coverage of Chávez supporters was nil, but the new military-installed government soon began to collapse and a major military unit declared support for Chávez's return. Eventually 19 people were killed among pro- and anti-Chávez demonstrators. Chávez survived, but the turmoil continued for two years until a recall referendum in August, 2004. Instead of forcing him out of office it was a victory for the president. His approval ratings surged to 70 percent. During these tumultuous months the major press and broadcast media were seen as leaders of the opposition.

With 63 percent of the votes in the 2006 presidential election Chávez's agenda moved another step to the left. He now defined his goal as "21st Century Socialism." Included was nationalizing companies in key sectors such as telecommunications and electricity, and refusing to renew the license of the RCN television network. A six-day work week was adopted, as were pensions for housewives and rigid pro-government education.

He also began ruling by decree on many issues. He initiated another rewrite of the constitution to allow his re-election. "I have to continue until 2030," he declared. In essence, he had dismantled the country's democratic institutions one by one. He consolidated power more quickly. He persecuted rivals and levied draconian restrictions on industry.

He was a military man with an authoritarian streak and an indelible suspicion of a free press, summarized the brainy editor Teodoro Petkoff of *Tal Cual*, a newspaper which remained independent of the opposition. "He has one foot in democracy, one foot in authoritarianism. But he is going to maintain that ambiguity, that unstable equilibrium," he commented.

The mainstream media had stumbled. As Andrés Cañizalez, a respected Venezuelan columnist and head of the Institute for Press and Society, a widely respected organization defending press freedom in the Andean region, stated: "For media organizations to take a political position is not necessarily bad journalism. But here you had the convergence in the media of two things: grave journalistic errors—to the extreme of silencing information on the most important news events—and taking political positions to the extreme of advocating a nondemocratic, insurrection path. They lost the guiding star of democratic discourse."

I went to Caracas several times during the Chávez years in support of Venezuelan colleagues and media including attending the IAPA mid-year meeting there in 2008. I even organized with my Washington Post editor friend, Milton Coleman, a fact-finding visit there that same year for a 21-member delegation from the American Society of Newspaper Editors (ASNE). I wrote reviews for magazines of books about Chávez and Simón Bolívar, his supposed intellectual mentor.

In the early years I tried to persuade the Venezuelans to lower their rhetoric about the "regime" and the "dictator." I even recall a conversation in Washington in 2001 with Andrés Mata, the owner of the biggest Venezuelan daily, who told me he agreed and thought the better course was to "get along and go along" with Chávez. That, of course, did not occur.

By late 2007 IAPA had sent 10 missions to Caracas during Chávez' tenure. Most were delegations of officers. I went on these in 2003 and 2007. On the former we called on the government to comply with protective orders to guarantee the safety of reporters and media attacked by government supporters. The orders had been issued the previous year by the Human Rights Commission of the Organization of American States (OAS).

We also criticized government curbs on U.S. dollar purchases needed to import newsprint. A government spokesman told us press freedom was stronger than during previous administrations. He also said he hoped Congress would soon pass legislation that would regulate radio and television content.

I had plans to participate in a second mission that year but just before departing home my wife Karen suffered a heart attack that required surgery to put a stent in one of her coronary arteries, which was 95 percent blocked. I did not go.

A group from the International Press Institute jointed our mission. Our IAPA colleagues had requested the mission to observe the four-day signature collection required to trigger a recall election. The process obtained more than the required 2.2 million signatures and led to the recall vote, which took place in August 2004. President Chávez survived with 58 percent voting "No."

The National Electoral Council promised our delegation it would ensure the free practice of journalism and not allow any abuse of freedom of expression and of the press. Specifically, it would not allow protest rallies or the president himself to use television networks to undermine the electoral process. The IAPA representatives were led by my good friend Jack Fuller of the Chicago Tribune, who was then president. The IPI delegation was led by its president Jorge Fascetto, a good friend from Argentina who had previously had been IAPA president.

Jack reported that the foreign minister called our members, among other things, a bunch of Citizen Kanes who represent the ultra-right wing of the hemisphere. He called IAPA an indelible stain. Wrote Jack, "I guess that means we are in addition to Citizen Kanes, men of la mancha," tilting at windmills.

I pointed out to Jack in an email that "the indelible stain" had previously soiled the administration. We had spoken out a few years earlier on behalf of José Vicente Rangel when he was being persecuted by Carlos Andres Perez. Rangel was now Hugo Chavez' vice president.

A mission in late May 2007 led by IAPA President Rafael Molina of the Dominican Republic went to Caracas at the time President Chávez planned to shut down the country's No.1 television network, Radio Caracas Television (RCTV), which was also the most important voice independent of government. Chavez said a few months earlier he did not intend to renew its broadcast license, because it had violated the communications law by supporting the 2002 coup attempt.

The IAPA delegation joined the network staff at their TV studios during an emotional meeting May 27 in which the transmission equipment was switched off one second after midnight, ending 53 years of uninterrupted broadcast. Two days earlier the Supreme Court authorized a new government channel, TVes, to use RCTV's equipment on the same frequency.

The licenses of other channels critical of Chávez at the time of the coup were left untouched. Most of these, including the other most important network, Venevisión, had changed editorial policy to stop criticizing the government.

According to RCTV's chief executive officer, Marcel Granier, its transmitters and equipment were worth $130 million. It had annual revenue of $250 million and a staff of 3,000 employees.

Even before IAPA's press conference at the end of the mission was over, where our leaders characterized the developments as "undemocratic," a spokeswoman for the Communications Ministry called on news outlets to refrain from reporting our statements. She cited recent legislation that enabled the government to shut down media for 72 hours if coverage incited people to violent protests. She said coverage of our position could allow viewers, readers or listeners to think the Chávez government was "tyrannical."

Knowing the situation was worsening, I joined pressing for Caracas as the site of the next Midyear meeting. I had pushed in earlier years in similarly difficult situations in Nicaragua and Paraguay with good outcomes. In response, immediately after our October 2007 annual General Assembly in Miami, the Venezuelan congress approved a measure asking Chávez to declare members of IAPA "unwelcome" ("*no grata*") in the country.

A resolution of the General Assembly had called for a mission to assess the viability of holding the Midyear in Caracas. I participated. IAPA President Earl Maucker of the South Florida *Sun-Sentinel* headed the nine-member group.

A week before we arrived in Caracas President Chávez spoke out against IAPA at the 12th Ibero-American Summit in Chile. He accused us and other similar groups of provoking him so he would throw us out. He also said the IAPA was part of a "real media dictatorship."

We were concerned about our mission's safety as well as our plan for the Midyear, but we went forward. We encountered no violent incidents nor any attempt to scare or demonstrate against us, although no one from the government agreed to meet with us.

At a final press conference we expressed "deep concern at the instability of press freedom in general" and warned of the limited debate and public awareness and transparency surrounding the upcoming constitutional reform proposed referendum. The December 2 election was a Yes-or-No vote on a 69-article change to the 1999 Constitution, including measures we believed raised concern of undermining freedom of the press. It was narrowly defeated, giving President Chávez his only electoral loss.

While at our press conference we confidently confirmed our intention to hold our next membership meeting the following March, in truth our president said privately we'd wait for a decision until after the referendum vote. If the "Yes" were to win, the view was holding the meeting anywhere in Venezuela was problematic. If the "No" won, we'd take a look at holding the meeting in Caracas itself. Meanwhile, Plan B was to hold the meeting in Panama City.

With the "No" victory we went forward with the Caracas meeting as an opportunity to encourage improvements for the media. At the meeting we saluted the electoral decision and denounced restrictions, especially on television. The one remaining critical television operation still on the air, Globovisión, was under mounting pressure. A 24-hour news network, its owners had to leave the country in 2010 for their own safety. Later, it was sold in 2013 to a businessman with connections to the government.

Government supporters staged protests outside our meeting hotel, but there was no violence. A few blocks away an "alternative" assembly of Latin American journalists was held under the heading "Latin American Meeting Against Media Terrorism." (Encuentro Contra el Terrorismo Mediático.) A government media executive described that full-house meeting, supported and promoted by the government, as "an act of rebellion against the IAPA." Another official called for taking control of the School (Colegio) of Journalists and the Press Workers Union, which had joined the opposition.

The meeting also provided an opportunity to join Milton Coleman, deputy managing editor of the Washington Post, in planning the fact-finding visit to Caracas in May for members of the American Society of Newspaper Editors (ASNE). Milton was on the ladder to be president of ASNE in 2010 and a year later would be president of IAPA.

Most importantly, we met with Andrés Izarra, the Minister of Communication. In 2002 he had resigned as the production manager at the RCTV for what he termed ethical conflicts when the network aired extensive coverage of the coup attempt. He was a key promoter of the Radio and Television Social Responsibility Law, known by the opposition as the Gag Law, and he helped launch TeleSUR, the Venezuela-based, multi-state funded socialist answer to CNN. He was its president from 2005 to 2011.

He knew Milton from his service in 2003 as the press attaché for the Venezuelan embassy in Washington, and we received a cordial welcome. He helped us set up a possible meeting with President Chávez as well as other highlights for the ASNE visit. He also, interestingly, handed Milton a letter of protest to be delivered to Washington Post's Jackson Diehl, who wrote most of its editorials about Venezuela.

At the March meeting I also met opposition leader Leopoldo López, the charismatic mayor of the Chacao Municipality where our Midyear was taking place. He agreed to meet our ASNE members when they visited, which he did. Later, as a result of his political activities, he was barred from running for office and eventually sentenced to 13 years in prison. Subsequently, after imprisonment he was granted a change to house arrest, and at this writing in 2018 he is one of the most celebrated human-rights victims in the world. Many believe he will be president of Venezuela one day.

In May Milton and I led the ASNE trip. The following is what I wrote for the ASNE's magazine, *The American Editor*:

Like to get in the middle of a hot news story?

How about this: Interpol releases a report validating documents that implicate Venezuela in aiding terrorists in Colombia. And on that day, you get to spend five hours with the president of Venezuela—one of the most important figures in the Western Hemisphere—to hear his response.

That was the scenario for ASNE's fact-finding trip to Venezuela, a Latin American country that sells half its oil to the United States—ten to twelve percent of U.S. consumption. It is a sharply divided democracy flirting with authoritarianism, building a worrisome military force and promoting its socialism throughout Latin America. It apparently also is sponsoring terrorism in the neighborhood—a troubling issue we watched unfold before our eyes.

President Hugo Chavez, who famously branded George W. Bush "the devil" in a United Nations speech, is our hemisphere's new Fidel Castro. He has charisma and the loquacious public speaking style of the former Cuban leader, and one-on-one, like Castro, can be charming and a gifted storyteller—as our 21-member delegation would learn. But he differs from Castro because he holds more-or-less legitimate elections and perhaps most importantly, he has oil—lots of it. He even acknowledged a loss in an election last December that would have eliminated term limits for the president.

We began our five-day visit in mid-May with a briefing by U.S. Ambassador Patrick Duddy and his top staff at the Embassy Residence in Caracas, enjoyed an evening in a Venezuelan publisher's home with two leading opposition politicians, met with pro- and anti-regime business leaders, listened to a pollster and commiserated with newspaper and television executives about harassment and press freedom struggles, including the chairman of Venezuela's oldest and largest television network that the government took off the air a year ago. We learned

that poverty remains entrenched despite the enormous windfall in
oil revenues, inflation is high and foreign investment falling as a
consequence of aggressive, although compensated, nationalizations.

But let's back up to where the Chavez government began jerking
us around. Three days before the trip, we were ready to cancel because
Venezuela's Washington embassy still had not issued us visas, which
it said were required, despite having had our passports for nearly two
months. Then came word we could go without visas, and the passports
were returned—the day before our departure. We were later to conclude
this episode was not intended to discourage our visit as we thought, but
more likely a matter of the incompetence, inefficiency or confusion—you
choose the word—in Caracas that virtually everyone acknowledges is
rampant. After that, subsequent failed promises and delays should not
have come as surprises.

When a president exercises nearly absolute control over the congress,
the courts and his administration, very little of importance takes place
without his approval, and Chavez apparently hadn't made up his mind
about us. Upon arrival in Caracas, despite much advance work by
ASNE secretary and delegation taskmaster Milton Coleman as well as
others including Venezuelan friends, the only confirmed appointment
we had with a government official was Information Minister Andrés
Izarra. Even this interview was temporarily put off because the president
wanted him elsewhere. Ultimately, it took place as originally scheduled.
It was a useful meeting that provided a window into the success of the
government's expansive welfare programs in education, health care and
food distribution as well as its efforts to address one of the highest crime
rates in Latin America.

We had been promised meetings with other ministers, but none
were materializing—or so it appeared. We were told weeks earlier that
President Chavez would not be available. So we thought we would
spend our remaining time interviewing the opposition and going on
show-and-tell visits arranged by the Information Ministry. The latter
were worthwhile and included a model health care facility, one of many
throughout the country staffed in part by 30,000 Cuban doctors; a textile
cooperative and two remarkable cultural sites. The first of these was
Teatro Teresa Carreño, a magnificent state-of-the-art concert hall where

we watched the National Philharmonic Orchestra practice two modern (dissonant) pieces. Then we were totally thrilled by hundreds of young musicians at the Monte Alban music school, including the Venezuelan National Youth Orchestra, which has played to sold-out audiences and rave reviews in New York, Los Angeles, Boston and around the world. It has been featured on CBS' 60 Minutes and is the flagship ensemble of Venezuela's world-renowned music education network. With more than 1,000 schools nationwide, "El Sistema" has trained more than 600,000 young Venezuelans the past 30 years. Their enthusiasm and technical skill, from pre-schoolers whose feet dangled from their chairs to precocious adolescents, opened our eyes. The visiting conductor of the National Philharmonic, Germán Cáceres from El Salvador, characterized the Venezuelan system as "the best youth program in the world."

Back on the bus we were preparing for a final day of visits with opposition leaders and a tour of the Contemporary Art Museum when we received a call inviting us to a surprise presidential press conference for foreign journalists at noon the next day.

All was forgiven. We were to see Hugo Chavez. Be at Miraflores, the presidential palace, two hours ahead, we were told. We began canceling other appointments, including the museum. These press conferences can be all-day affairs, we were told, and our last day was to teach us a lot about time and priorities in Chavez's Venezuela.

The next morning on our way to Miraflores came a call saying the press conference had been delayed until 2 p.m. We had time to kill, so we headed for the art museum—now unexpected and five hours earlier than our original appointment. The museum director had celebrated a birthday the night before and had to be rousted from bed. But we were treated to a classy tour of what is arguably Latin America's best contemporary art museum followed by exotic juice drinks and scrumptious chocolate desserts, both items of national pride. The collection has outstanding representation of modern art including more than 100 Picassos.

We arrived at Miraflores at noon and were ushered into the press conference site, filling the right-hand side of the room. At 3 p.m., an hour after the scheduled start, we were still the only press in the room and wondered if we were to be the only attendees, but finally the site began to fill. The others had been watching a press conference being conducted in

Bogotá, Colombia, by Interpol, the international police agency. President Chavez finally arrived at 4:12—more than four hours after we were told to be in place and two hours behind schedule. We would be with him the next five hours—three in the press conference and nearly two in a private audience in his private office, where he talked with us through an interpreter with family photos spread behind him.

The first hour was a Chavez soliloquy on his plans for a summit in Peru for which he would depart later that night. But the real purpose was to be a seminal moment in the Chavez presidency—his response to the Interpol report. It put him on the international hot seat and presents a problem he may not overcome because it authenticated the origin of computer files implicating Venezuela in aiding and arming guerrillas in neighboring Colombia. The laptop files contain e-mails and other records that show his government offering money and assistance in acquiring surface-to-air missiles and other weapons for the Revolutionary Armed Forces of Colombia or FARC, identified by both the U.S. and European Union as terrorists. Rather than respond to the allegations, Chavez chose to denounce Interpol and attacked the report as "the show of clowns." He described Ronald K. Noble, Interpol's secretary general, variously as "a gringo policeman," "a Dick Tracy," "a vagabond" and "a bandit." Coming off the dais, he even staged a show of his own with a dramatic pantomime demonstrating how false evidence can be planted.

A correspondent commented privately that Chavez was "loopier than usual today."

Chavez critics in the U.S. are now calling for punitive sanctions based on the FARC computer-files. Should Venezuela be declared a "state sponsor of terrorism," however, the $54 billion in bilateral trade with the U.S.—mostly oil—would be in jeopardy.

At the press conference, Chavez also threatened to "reclaim" an area in Colombia near the Venezuelan border if Colombia permits the U.S. to move a reconnaissance base now in Ecuador to Colombia.

Speaking to reporters afterward, he was asked if he plans nationalizations beyond the takeovers of big oil, the telephone company, the power company, the television network and recently a large cement company and steel mill. "Not right now, today," he answered, "but I might tomorrow."

While Chavez used blistering rhetoric at the press conference in his comments about the United States—"the empire"—he also said he wants to return to "reasonable relations like I had with Bill Clinton."

At our private audience, where we were served coffee, he was more conciliatory. As I greeted him, I said I hoped relations could improve. "I have faith that our relations will get better," he responded. He declined to state his preference in the upcoming U.S. elections, although he said he has one. "Bush has refused to sit down with me," he said.

"I would love to be able to work with the United States, regardless of ideology, on issues like health, infant mortality and food production," he said, "but if we can't do all that, we at least can talk."

"Rest assured, we will supply you oil," which he said amounts to 1.5 million barrels a day. Venezuela has the third largest oil deposits in the world.

He said his criticisms of the U.S. are not of its people, but of some of its political elite. "We are friends of the United States, but we are being ill treated," he commented. He called a possible U.S. invasion "a genuine concern" and likened it to the invasion of Iraq, which he said was for oil.

He also spun elaborate stories about his personal dealings with Fidel Castro, including a baseball contest, and his encounter with troops who intended to kill him at the time of a 2002 attempt to overthrow his government.

A full day indeed, but a memorable finale. As ASNE President Charlotte Hall e-mailed the morning after we arrived home, we were all "basking in the glow of Caracas. What a trip!"

Earlier, in one of the book reviews I had written for *IAPA News* I compared Chávez to the Venezuelan liberator Simón Boívar. Published in both English and Spanish, it read:

Hugo Chávez won Venezuela's presidency in 1998 with the promise of a "revolution" in honor of South America's liberator, Simon Bolivar. He would redress social injustice and inequality, he said, and fight for Latin American solidarity and stand up to the overbearing United States. After the election, his fellow citizens were astonished when, by decree, he renamed their country "the Bolivarian Republic of Venezuela."

Nine years later the "Bolivarian Revolution" is alive and well. Chavez' charisma and oil dollars have led to success. But what of its namesake? Is the revolution faithful to the legacy of Simon Bolivar?

John Lynch's recent biography of the Liberator is the first written in English in more than half a century, a period of revealing scholarship about Bolivar and, perhaps more importantly, the emergence of Hugo Chavez. Although Lynch mentions Chavez only in his concluding paragraph, he brands the Venezuelan president a heretic. The book offers a well-written chronicle of the evolution in Bolivar's thinking and therefore a useful means of judging the growing authoritarianism in Chavez' Venezuela. The cult of Bolivar has been invoked by Latin American military dictators in the past, but in contrast to Chavez, Lynch reports, these earlier rulers more or less respected his basic principles.

Bolivar spent two decades, from age 27 in 1810 until his death 20 years later, first winning independence from Spain for much of South America and then attempting to establish, to use his term, "republican government." In an 1819 address, he described its principles as popular sovereignty, division of powers, rule of law under an independent judiciary, civil liberty, prohibition of slavery and abolition of monarchy and privilege. He defended freedom of conscience and of speech and the press. His beliefs were from the mainstream of Western revolutionary thought since 1776. One of the richest men in Venezuela, he had studied for two years in Europe and traveled extensively, including a short visit to the young United States.

As he confronted the reality of 19th Century South America, his thinking evolved. He was a pragmatist. His first success, independence for Venezuela and founding of the First Republic, turned to failure and led to recapture of his native land by Spain. Out of failure he concluded a federal system similar to the United States, which had been the model, leads to weak and divided government. It was not viable in faction-rich Latin America. Only strong central government with a powerful executive, accountable to a legislature with financial control, could survive in such a heterogeneous society where the vast majority were either indigenous, multiracial or freed slaves. Constitutions had to conform to "the environment, character, history and resources of the people."

With his successes in liberating the former Spanish colonies, he was called upon, like George Washington, to serve as president on several occasions. As the years passed and after long experience fighting anarchy and instability, his lifelong search for a balance between tyranny and anarchy evolved toward authority. In his waning years he proposed, in a culmination of his political thinking, a draft constitution for Bolivia that envisioned a president appointed for life with the right to appoint his successor. The Bolivian Constitution preserved the separation of powers as well as civil liberties and the president was to be picked by the legislature.

But he had gone too far for his political and military allies, perhaps because they could see little possibility of becoming president if only one man held the office for life, and they turned on him. Ultimately, he was pushed in despair into exile.

So how does the eclectic blend of populism, nationalism, militarism and socialism of Hugo Chavez stack up? Chavez has consolidated power far beyond even Bolivar's final, rejected proposal. With a veneer of legitimacy through a series of elections and referenda, he has rewritten the constitution to extend the presidency and allow reelection, reorganized and taken control of the national assembly and the judiciary and, in a measure passed in February, received power to issue decrees over an 18-month period on a variety of key issues ranging from eliminating private education to redrawing territorial divisions. Under a new criminal code, showing disrespect for the president is punishable by up to 20 months in jail. A new media law imposes "administrative restrictions" on radio and television broadcasts, and he recently announced he plans to confiscate Venezuela's most important television network in late May.

Meanwhile, the price of oil, which was at less than $10 a barrel when he took office, is now over $60. Even Bolivar would find difficult halting this revolution.

Since Chávez's death in 2013, his hand-picked successor, the former bus driver Nicolás Maduro, has led Venezuela to a spiraling decline with increasing crime, inflation, poverty and hunger. The country is now one of the most impoverished countries in the hemisphere.

President Maduro has blamed an "economic war" waged by opponents.

Winning an election in April 2013, a month after Chávez's death, with 50.62 percent of the vote, he has ruled by decree since November that year. In part as a result of the attention given to imprisoned Leopoldo López's lengthy hunger strike demanding elections, President Maduro called National Assembly elections. The opposition won control. The government-controlled Supreme Tribunal as a result removed most of its power from the National Assembly. This resulted in months of protests, leading President Maduro to call for a rewrite of the constitution.

The Constituent Assembly of Venezuela was elected in a suspect election in July 2017, with the U.S. calling Maduro a "dictator" and freezing his U.S. assets and prohibiting him from entering the United States. The new assembly had power to rule over all state institutions as well as rewrite the constitution. President Maduro was reelected in a show election in 2018 which had the lowest turnout in modern Venezuelan history.

Space for the independent press grew more and more narrow. An "Anti-Hate Law" was enacted in an expedited procedure by the Constituent Assembly in 2017 that provides criminal penalties not subject to a statute of limitations for encouraging discrimination. Broadcast licenses can be suspended and broadcasters fined, and they are obligated to provide advertising space free of charge for messages promoting diversity, tolerance and mutual respect as well as preventing political violence, hatred and intolerance.

By 2014 nearly all of the critical independent press had come under government control or influence with the exceptions of the courageous *El National* and a few smaller, mostly regional publications. Even Globovisión, the critical television network under pressure for years, stopped airing live speeches of the opposition. It was repeatedly hit with large fines by the government regulator for its news coverage, including charges that its coverage of a prison riot had instigated violence. It was sold in 2013.

Two important pro-oppositions outlets were sold in 2014. *Ultimas Noticias*, one of Venezuela's highest circulation dailies, and *El Universal*, the venerable 105-year-old broadsheet. *Ultimas Noticias* was sold to an undisclosed buyer and its editorial line became friendly to the government. *El Universal* was sold to a Spanish investment firm previously unknown in Venezuela.

These and other papers had experienced increasing difficulties because the government had refused to allow them to obtain dollars needed to import newsprint. *El Universal*'s new owners announced it would now have paper to operate, and criticism of the government abated. Staff members complained about self-censorship, some reporters resigned, and the leading cartoonist was fired. A list of untouchable issues was implemented. On-line articles critical of the government were deleted.

Such straw-man transactions in which wealthy or powerful individuals use another person as a stand-in to hide their ownership have a long tradition in Venezuela. These sales had the earmarks of straw purchasers connected to people friendly to the government.

Most of the owners of opposition media had come regularly to IAPA meetings for support, and I know many of them. The owners of the RCTV network and Globovisión continue attending. The history of *El Universal*'s owners illustrates challenges Venezuelan and other media owners face even if they can survive government abuse. I knew well the owners of *El Universal*. It had always been a conservative, business-oriented daily. It had the largest reporting staff of any Venezuelan newspaper. I first met its publisher, Luis Teófilo Núñez, at the IAPA General Assembly in 1974 in Caracas where he and his wife were hosts of a spectacular dinner party at their home. My wife Karen and I at the time had never previously attended such a lavish affair.

Eventually I learned Luis was only a minority owner of the paper. It had been founded in 1909 by Andrés Avelino Mata, a well-known writer and poet, with a cofounder, Andrés Vigas. Luis Núñez's father was brought in to run the administration in 1922 while Mata oversaw the editorial side. Luis, who attended Harvard Business School, succeeded his father. Luis was elected president of IAPA in 1977 after a controversy, and he was forced to step aside temporarily due to corruption charges brought by the government of Carlos Andrés Peréz. For 70 years the Mata family had always remained in the background with the Núñez family fronting the enterprise.

In 1992 the grandson of the founder claimed his inheritance. Andrés Mata Osorio, who had lived and been educated in the United States and spoke Spanish with an American accent, took control. The transition was conflictive and Luis sold his family's stock. It was not a friendly departure.

Andrés Mata had joined the *El Universal* board of directors in 1988 after receiving a master's degree from the University of Chicago the same year. He did his undergraduate work at Princeton. I came to know Andrés when he became active in IAPA. At one point in conversation with me he characterized his view that Luis Núñez had "stolen" the newspaper. Luis stayed on as editor until

1994. He said the split was necessary after seven decades of Núñez leadership and harmony at *El Universal* between the two families, a "third party's acts" broke the relationship. "This is something I greatly regret and Andrés knows this is so. The newspaper was my life and the separation devastated me."

After Chávismo took hold, Andrés received death threats against himself and his family. He sought and received protection ordered by the Inter American Commission on Human Rights in January, 2002. Eventually he moved back to New York and kept watch over the daily through video conferences and infrequent visits to Caracas.

The business prospered significantly after Andrés took over. He sold *El Universal* in 2014 for more than $100 million.

8. Peru
Leadership and Courage

Peru has witnessed some of the very best journalism in Latin America as well as some of the worst. The late publisher of Lima's *El Comercio*, Luis Miró Quesada, had it right about Peru in his oft-quoted dictum: "Depending on how it is practiced, journalism can be the most-noble profession or the most despicable craft."

Even his distinguished daily—founded in 1839 and thereby the second oldest continuously published newspaper in the Spanish language—has had moments the current owners would just as soon forget. Like other major newspapers in the nineteenth- and early twentieth-century, *El Comercio* was born as a partisan voice serving the elite, in its case the guano-exporting interests. But its importance in Peru has never been in doubt. When it was less than a decade old in the late 1840s, a Chilean correspondent visiting Lima reported:

> Lima is an odd, one might even say a unique place; everyone here has a passion for writing . . . and whoever writes is certain to be read. . . . Do not think that gentlemen are the only ones who read here; the people, artisans, and laborers of all types save their money in order to buy an issue of *El Comercio*, and those who are too poor to purchase their own copy borrow from others. Those who do not know how to read listen, comment and discuss with the rest. Even the women join in. . . .

El Comercio's early years also included a commitment to protecting the human and civic rights of oppressed native peoples. In 1866 Lima's elite formed a Friends Society of the Indians in response to an indigenous-led uprising in the Andean highlands, where opinion against the Indians was pervasive among the landlords, regional commanders and politicians. The Society's purpose was to make the public aware of cases of abuse. Its offices were in the back room of *El Comercio*, which published articles and pamphlets.

Although I traveled in Peru as a student in the mid 1960s, my close association with *El Comercio*'s owners, the Miró Quesada family, came after their newspaper was confiscated in 1974 by the leftist military government of General Juan Velasco Alvarado. He had come to power in a 1968 coup with nationalistic ideals and a promise to revolutionize Peruvian society. Inspired by leftist intellectuals, he aimed to create a semi-corporate, neo-Marxist state similar to the Yugoslav system under Marshall Tito.

Luis Miró Quesada, guided by nationalism, initially supported the coup and its moves to expropriate the International Petroleum Company and cancel an important oil contract with a U.S. company. As early as 1970, however, *El Comerico* joined other influential dailies in outright opposition when President Velasco's government ordered the takeover of two opposition dailies. All the leading newspapers, including *El Comercio*, were confiscated in July 1974. By law all newspapers with distribution of more than 20,000 copies or that circulated in more than half of the country's departmental capitals were taken.

As these events unfolded, the IAPA executive committee met in Lima hoping to pressure Velasco Alvarado's government. Nothing was accomplished, but the meeting has long been remembered because a small earthquake occurred as the society's leaders gathered around a conference table in a Lima hotel. The moment stayed with them because a chandelier came crashing down on the table, splintering glass in all directions.

Less than two years after the confiscation, Luis Miró Quesada died at the age 95. He had spent 71 years in journalism and was a founding member of the IAPA. His 61-year-old son, Alejandro, led the fight for the return of the seven dailies. The perceptive and important guidance he provided in this most difficult period for him and his family invariably stands out in my mind.

On several occasions I listened to him recount the surreal 1974 July evening when he was at his desk in *El Comercio*'s newsroom working on the next morning's issue. An Army colonel he had long known as a friend arrived and asked to speak with him. "I'm sorry, Don Alejandro," said the colonel, "but you'll have to leave now. I am the new editor of *El Comercio*." Soldiers with rifles accompanied the colonel. Alejandro spent the next six years teaching law and working for return of his and the other dailies.

The government of General Velasco Alvarado contended the nationalization was necessary for reasons of "social interest" and so the dailies could serve as "hound dogs against the oligarchy." Newspapers were classified under the expropriation law as "social property." The intent, it stated, was that each daily would represent an organized sector of society. *El Comercio* was assigned to the farmer organizations; *La Prensa* to the labor sector; *Correo* to the professional sector (lawyers, physicians, engineers, etc.); *Ojo* to the writer, artist and intellectual community; *Ultima Hora* to the service organizations; and *Expresso* to the educational organizations.

In practice this did not occur. The military controlled the papers. The decree provided for a period of transition in which reorganization committees named by the government—and subject to government removal—were to control the papers for one year, when the various social sectors were to take over. That deadline passed without the turnover, as did the next year and a third year. Most members of the committees were not professional journalists but intellectuals who supported the revolution, and the results for Peruvian journalism were disastrous. In the first three months, more than 100 employees of the papers were dismissed. The farming sector that was to have *El Comercio* came closest to being organized to take over thanks to a recently forged Agrarian Federation. After six years, the papers lost much of their circulation and revenue. A majority of them no longer exist.

Editors interviewed at the time said they practiced self-censorship and limited news and commentary within the parameters of the revolution. "For example," one editor said, "a newspaper would not be able to call for a return to a liberal capitalist system nor could it sing the praises of a communist system as an option." Occasionally, several explained, they were cautioned not to touch on some subject, and they sometimes received "coordination" phone calls from the government.

By 1978 Peru was under the control of Velasco Alvarado's successor, General Francisco Moralez Bermudez, and sentiment was widespread that the revolutionary experiment had failed. In September that year I was appointed by IAPA president Argentina Hills to join another member of the society, Ignacio Lozano of Los Angeles' *La Opinion*, on a mission to study a new military decree laying out future ownership of the confiscated dailies. A constitutional assembly had been elected and was in session. President of the assembly was the venerable populist warhorse Víctor Raúl Haya de la Torre.

Haya de la Torre and the Miró Quesadas shared a long and bitter history. Haya, the founder of the APRA (Aprista) party, first ran for president in 1931 and his supporters believed fraud kept him from winning. Prominent among his opponents was the then publisher of *El Comercio*, Antonio Miró Quesada. In 1933 a militant Aprista assassinated the new president, and in 1935 another young Aprista assassinated Antonio Miró Quesada and his wife. They were killed near a movie theater on Lima's main square, Plaza San Martín, as they headed for an elite club. He was shot at point blank range five times and she twice. Sentiments between the Apristas and the Miró Quesadas had never healed. The family blamed Haya for the deaths, and Haya blamed the family for his political difficulties.

An ill-conceived 1978 decree, while compensating the former owners, limited them to purchasing no more than a quarter of the shares in their newspapers and restricted any individual to just five percent ownership. Another quarter of the shares were reserved for workers. The remaining 50 percent were to be offered to the public. At the time of our visit, opinions varied as to whether the decree would be accepted by the Constitutional Assembly. Virtually everyone we interviewed believed the law represented the Miró Quesada family's best chance of regaining even partial ownership. Our sources believed if a solution were left to the Constitutional Assembly controlled by the Aprists and headed by Haya de la Torre, the family had no chance. The problem was "a matter of passion against the Miró Quesada family," we were told by Enrique Zileri, publisher of Peru's leading news magazine, *Caretas.*

After we understood these troubling and difficult circumstances, we scheduled a meeting at the suggestion of Don Alejandro with Andrés Townsend Ezcurra, the number two leader of APRA and a member of the Constitutional Assembly. He had been editor-in-chief of APRA's newspaper, *Tribuna,* until it folded, and he had attended past IAPA meetings. We also took Don Alejandro's advice on how to handle our approach to Townsend.

He recommended a strategy which, as things eventually developed, proved to be a key factor in the return of *El Comercio* to the Miró Quesadas. Make it clear to Andrés Townsend, Don Alejandro suggested, that the family members who would now run the newspaper are a new generation. They had nothing to do with the old quarrels. Have him convey this message directly to Haya, he insisted. That's what we did, and Townsend passed along the message. He told us he personally believed a new law that discriminated against the Miró Quesada family would not be fair, and he was sympathetic with our position that all the papers should be returned to their owners.

Just a month later the Constitutional Assembly approved a resolution declaring the military decree incompatible with the guarantees that must surround the coming constitutional debate. More importantly, it resolved:

"There must be respect for the unlimited right of any person to establish and maintain a daily newspaper, magazine or other communications medium without any restriction to the constitutional rights of a free press, which are guaranteed by the State."

In his wisdom, Don Alejandro had brought peace, and with it, the return of the family's newspaper. The very first act of the newly re-elected president, Fernando Belaúnde Terry, the very man overthrown in 1968 by the military, was to return Lima's dailies to their legitimate owners.

When I reflect on Don Alejandro, I also recall his skillful 1987 confrontation later as IAPA president with Chilean dictator Augusto Pinochet about press freedom there. I also remember his resolute leadership in Geneva at the United Nations Commission on Human Rights. But his role in the return of *El Comercio* to his family stands above these accomplishments. With the return of *El Comercio*, Don Alejandro offered thanks to IAPA by inviting the society for a celebratory general assembly, which took place in October, 1983. I served as program chair for the meeting and worked closely with him.

The evening before the official events began he asked Karen and me to join a few other IAPA leaders for dinner at his new suburban home. He proudly showed his guests bound copies of *El Comercio*'s original 1839 issues which he kept in his upper-level library. The night's most memorable moments, however, were the drive from and return to our downtown hotel. We knew Shining Path (Sendero Luminoso) guerrillas had become a security threat in remote areas of Peru since 1980 when they announced their war on modern society by hanging dogs from lampposts in major cities, but we had not expected problems in Lima. The armed caravan that picked us up inside the hotel parking garage and whisked us to Don Alejandro's home suggested the situation in Lima was not as safe as we'd thought.

That same night guerrillas attacked a police station not far from our hotel and left two officers dead. Several of us went to a wake for the unfortunate victims the next night, where we found them, wounds apparent, lying without embalming in wooden caskets surrounded by grieving family members. The next night small round grenade-like projectiles, fortunately unarmed, were rolled into the entrance of the hotel. Security tightened quickly, with armed guards on every floor and tanks outside the building.

These events foreshadowed the wave of urban terrorism Shining Path would inflict later in the 1980s that over the course of two decades led to as many as 69,000 deaths, mostly civilians. Even today the movement persists in Peru, although its threat to take over the country ended with the capture in 1992 of its founder and leader, Abimael Guzmán, whose *nom de guerre* was "Presidente Gonzalo."

Months before our meeting in Lima eight Peruvian journalists had been hacked to death in the Ayacucho region southeast of Lima where Shining Path began. Abimael Guzmán had been a philosophy professor there. The journalists, seven from leftist publications, had traveled to Uchuraccay, a near-feudal village high in the Andes north of Ayacucho, to investigate the recent killings of seven Shining Path guerrillas. The Army had announced that peasants in a nearby community had killed the Maoist guerrillas because the guerrillas had previously executed local leaders for refusing to cooperate with Shining Path. Local peasants were finally turning against Shining Path, the Army contended.

The journalists doubted the story and set out to find the truth. For them, this could be the biggest story of their careers, and they presumed they had safety in numbers. They were mistaken. Their mutilated bodies—stoned, beaten, cut and bruised by sticks and knives—were discovered several days later. Eyes gouged, they were buried face downwards "so that their souls could go straight to hell," according to a later commission report drafted by Peru's best-known contemporary writer, Mario Vargas Llosa. The bizarre killings sent shock-waves throughout Peruvian society.

Vargas Llosa's commission supported the official contention that the peasants had mistaken the journalists for guerrillas. Two peasants were eventually tried, convicted and imprisoned, but few in Ayacucho or on the Peruvian left bought the official version. Their theory, even today, is the peasants did kill the journalists, but under orders from the Army. The events of January 26, 1983, remain clouded in mystery.

Having read about the massacre and also knowing the risks faced by journalists covering the wars at the time in Central America, I decided to organize a panel at the Lima meeting on safety for journalists. The very idea was controversial because of an international debate at the time about the risks associated with government-issued identity cards. There was widespread fear that governments with authority to grant such cards, which would give journalists official status, also could take away privileges. I had to reassure various leaders who were fighting this battle in UNESCO and elsewhere that I was simply hoping to surface, perhaps in a form to be published, common-sense ideas that might save lives.

The panel was remarkably successful in its intended purpose because the five participants were seasoned journalists. They were Arturo Salazar, the editor of Lima's *La Prensa*; Peter Eisner, Associated Press news editor for Mexico and Central America; Jim Brooke, the *Miami Herald*'s South American correspondent who would later have a distinguished career with *The New York Times*; and James Nelson Goodsell, Latin American correspondent for the Christian Science Monitor. They all had first-hand knowledge of dangerous assignments.

A tense moment during the panel occurred when the families of the eight murdered journalists confronted us protesting the absence of formal recognition of the martyrs at the general assembly as well calling for us to press for further investigations. As moderator, I explained that the panel was intended to focus attention on the fate of their dead relatives and that we would be issuing a resolution later. I met afterwards with them, and they seemed somewhat mollified.

The panelists articulated a long list of suggestions, ranging from the basic rule that no story is worth a journalist's life, to the mundane practice of carrying a white flag. We tape recorded the panel and extracted a list of more than a dozen basic rules and a score of practical suggestions. A month later *Editor & Publisher* magazine ran the list in a full-page article, based on a press release I prepared, and promoted the list on its cover. The magazine deemed not to include my 12 "Lessons from the Dead." Those ranged from the case of two journalists who died when their car hit a land mine after they ignored warnings from local residents that fighting was taking place on the road they traveled, to the cases of journalists killed trying to cross from one side of a conflict to another while waving a white flag, and the tragedy of the eight Peruvian journalists who died earlier that year near Uchuraccay.

Because we seemed to be onto something useful, we decided to circulate a reprint of the *E&P* article to a number of leading industry figures and editors for comment. We received useful suggestions from many, including Al Neuharth, William Randolph Hearst Jr. and Charles Scripps as well as from the wire services. Hearst, for example, wrote humorously in his response that his company no longer had any veteran war correspondents. "Bob Considine and Frank Conniff, both close friends of mine, had unfortunately died in bed," he said, but then he added: "One bit of advice someone gave me early after we landed in Normandy in '44, 'Keep your head down. It's better to be a live newspaper man than a dead hero.'"

With the results in hand and financial assistance from the World Press Freedom Committee (WPFC), we printed a pocket-size folder titled "Surviving Dangerous Assignments" which we distributed free to all newspapers with foreign correspondents as well as anyone who asked. It listed 41 safety guidelines as well as quotes from experienced journalists and key words and phrases in Spanish. In addition, we produced hundreds of vinyl sleeves for standard reporters' notebooks with the tips embossed on them.

It was a small thing, really, but a project I felt worthwhile. *Harper's* magazine reproduced a dozen of the guidelines in its "Readings" section. *Columbia Journalism Review* called the tips "simple, commonsensical, and chillingly matter-of-fact." Dana Bullen, WPFC executive director, called the project a "major contribution" that "totally rebuts the claims of those who say that free-press groups are not interested in the safety of journalists. Further, this practical approach will provide help—while the desire of many others to 'protect' journalists only masks their desire to license them. My hat is off to IAPA and its dedicated members for, first, having the inspiration to do this and, second, for carrying it out."

For our work, we received an "Excellence in Association Publications" award in the annual competition sponsored by *Association Trends*, the national weekly newspaper for association executives. But my greatest satisfaction came in the form of a post card from El Salvador, at the time the most dangerous country for journalists in the hemisphere, where 11 had died in the previous five years. Jim Brooke, who was then leaving the *Miami Herald* for a job with *The New York Times*, wrote that the head of the Salvador Press Association had posted the guidelines on the bulletin board at the Camino Real Hotel, home then to virtually all correspondents, and that he "hands them out to new arrivals."

Security and safety in Peru, of course, became much worse as Shining Path grew. I did not return to Peru again until I led a group of U.S. editors there in 1991, but in the interim I followed Peruvian news not only for its importance but also because I had suggested to my oldest son, Ned, that he consider writing his Harvard undergraduate honors thesis about Peru. With the insurgency at its height, Ned spent part of his 1989 summer vacation in Lima researching the impact on Peru's democratic left of the insurgency, and even today he recounts harrowing stories of steel doors with peepholes and ferocious guard dogs. He received a magna on his thesis, but he was cured of any genetic international wanderlust he may have inherited from me.

My 1991 visit, still at the height of the Shining Path violence, was part of a grand tour of Latin America I organized at the request of ASNE President Dave Lawrence, the publisher of *The Miami Herald*. I asked my friend Alejo Miro Quesada, the son of Don Alejandro who by then was running *El Comercio* on a day-to-day basis, to assist me, and he orchestrated an extraordinary five days for the American editors and accompanying spouses.

He arranged interviews with the top political, civic and journalistic leaders—except for President Fujimori, who was out of the country—that gave us an up-close look at a country seen at the time as on the verge of failing. He also joined us for a visit to Cuzco, Machu Picchu and the Upper Huallaga Valley, center of the coca growing region. He wanted us to see that tourism was possible despite the dangers. Arriving in the afternoon at Machu Picchu, we could see why he was so concerned. We had to take a specially guarded private train and were virtually the only tourists at the ancient Inca site.

The day following we flew a Russian prop plane to the Upper Huallaga, where we boarded anti-drug helicopters to view the coca fields. We didn't necessarily feel in our greatest danger there, but realized later this part of the adventure was probably the riskiest. Less than two months afterward one of the choppers was shot down, presumably by the Shining Path, as it flew to the rescue of another helicopter that had gone down accidentally. Three U.S. agents and a Peruvian policeman were killed in the attack.

Meanwhile, as a matter of prudence, our spouses went on a separate tour south from Lima to see by air the Nasca Lines, drawings on the ground that can be appreciated only from on high. Among the more than 300 drawings, created between 200 BC and 600 AD by the Nasca culture, are a gigantic hummingbird, monkey spider and lizard. The spouses' trip also had its rough spots as several of them became air sick in the single-engine plane. We met our spouses the following day in Iquitos for a short trip up the Amazon River to a fascinating jungle lodge called Explorama Inn, where we rubbed elbows literally with the fauna and flora of the world's greatest rain forest. We even captured the ever-serious Dave Lawrence on film swinging like Tarzan across a ravine.

The election of Alberto Fujimori in 1990 brought macro-economic stability to Peru and eventually the capture in 1992 of Abimael Guzmán, ending the horrors perpetrated by the Shining Path. Also that year, because he was unable to move his program through Congress for want of a majority, Fujimori ordered tanks into the streets, dissolved the Congress, suspended the constitution, and dismissed dozens of judges including 13 of 23 Supreme Court justices. He justified the so-called auto-coup saying he needed a free hand to combat terrorism, corruption and drug trafficking and to implement economic reforms. With the capture of Guzmán, Fujimori's popularity soared, and he won control of the Congress in the subsequent elections.

In my mind, Alberto Fujimori falls into a category with Venezuela's Hugo Chavez and Russia's Vladimir Putin as leaders who believe in what some call "illiberal democracy." These are regimes that respect free, although not always fair, elections, but do not respect constitutional guarantees. Their methods range from legal harassment of the media to the illegal tactics of the Fujimori regime of bribery, fraud, kidnapping or worse.

After Fujimori's self-coup, space for criticism in the news media narrowed dramatically until only a few courageous journalists dared confront the regime. Still, Fujimori himself would have gone down as a savior of his country had he limited himself to a single term. Instead, he became ever more authoritarian and ran and won in 1995 against Javier Perez de Cuellar, the former U.N. secretary general, and again in 2000 against Alejandro Toledo.

The independent media, led by *El Comercio, La Republica* and Channel 2 Television, uncovered numerous of the regime's crimes. My friend Alejo Miró Quesada led the way by hiring Peru's most renowned investigative journalist and fearless reporter to found and head the Investigative Unit at *El Comercio*. Ricardo Uceda had made his reputation as editor of the news magazine *Sí* by implicating military officers in the 1991 massacre of 15 people in a barrio of Lima, and revealing the existence of a clandestine grave containing the bodies of nine college students and their professor who had been abducted by the military. Uceda much later would become executive director on the Institute of Press and Society (IPYS), the prestigious local organization fighting for press issues in Peru and elsewhere, including Venezuela.

In 1998, *El Comerico* exposed the misuse of state funds intended for victims of the El Niño floods and mudslides that led to the arrest of the regime's civil defense chief. After numerous smaller battles, the key confrontations between the *El Comercio* organization, including its cable television station, *Canal Ñ*, and the regime occurred in 2000. In March of that year *El Comercio* revealed that Fujimori's re-election campaign had forged more than one million signatures on a petition it filed for his re-election. Fujimori won the election in a second round when Alejandro Toledo withdrew in protest.

Then, on Sept. 14, *Canal Ñ* broadcast the first of the "Vladi-videos" showing Vladimiro Montesinos, Fujimori's Svengali-like national security advisor, bribing an opposition Congressman with $15,000 to change parties. Eight days later Montesinos fled the country and Fujimori would follow before the year ended.

The videotapes of Montesinos also brought to light numerous instances of various media owners receiving large payments in exchange for support—selling themselves to the government. Television channels implicated plunged toward bankruptcy as their audiences and then advertisers boycotted them. The circulation of the second largest newspaper plummeted to less than 10,000 copies, and ultimately most of the press funded by Montesinos closed.

In early 1999, in the midst of these years of tension between *El Comerico* and the Fujimori regime, Alejo's young daughter Isabel was kidnapped on Montesinos' orders as a warning. She was held only briefly, but the episode profoundly disturbed Alejo and his wife Elizabeth, who thereafter became justifiably cautious as they faced additional life-threatening challenges. The kidnapping did not became public knowledge, and upon her release Isabel was hurried off to California to live with an aunt.

Early in 2000 Montesinos brought to a head a long-simmering *El Comercio* stockholders' dispute with the intention of seizing control of the newspaper through the court system. The ploy had many of the earmarks of a similar attempt years earlier in Panama, when the Omar Torrijos regime successfully took control of *El Panama America*. In both cases minority stockholders who were relatives cooperated with the government with the intent of taking over from the majority owners. Fortunately, the threat to *El Comercio* died with the end of Fujimori's presidency.

Just two weeks before *Canal Ñ* broadcast the first "Vladi-video" that would lead to the government's fall, I joined four other members and two staffers on an IAPA investigative mission to Lima headed by then IAPA President Tony Pederson of the *Houston Chronicle*. Our principal purpose was to support *El Comercio*, although we looked into other serious press-freedom issues, especially the case of Baruch Ivcher, who had lost his opposition television station, *Canal 2*, as a result of a trumped-up dispute about his citizenship. We met with President Fujimori August 29 to express our concern about press freedom in Peru, and we were temporarily elated later that day when he told a press conference that he believed the issues we presented would have a "happy resolution (resolución feliz)."

At the meeting with Fujimori our delegation was disturbed to realize we were quietly being taped by a videographer. At first we hadn't noticed, but as the session progressed it became more apparent. The experience reminded me of the six-hour interview I led with Fidel Castro in 1998, which also was videotaped. In that case the tape was played later on Cuban television. In the case of Fujimori, the tape, so far as I know, has not been made public, but as a result of the experience, when we learned later Montesinos had taped his bribery sessions, we were less surprised than others.

Should the tape come to light, it will show that as the meeting was breaking up I presented Fujimori with a small glass box engraved with the seal of Kansas State University, located in my hometown of Manhattan, Kansas. I had learned sometime earlier that the president's youngest son, Kenji, was attending KSU, where a former colleague of his father from the president's earlier studies in the United States, Robert Hudgens, was an assistant dean. Fujimori was obviously very pleased to receive the gift and told me he came to Manhattan quietly from time to time. He said he dressed incognito with sunglasses and went unrecognized. I invited him to call me the next time he came so we could get together for dinner. I assured him my newspaper would respect both his privacy and that of his son.

President Fujimori's revelation that he came to Kansas did not come as a complete surprise to me. A year earlier he had created a flap in Kansas City at the end of one of his incognito visits when American Airlines downgraded his first-class ticket to economy. He tried to tell the airline agents he was president of Peru. They were incredulous. A Japanese man could be president of Peru? They searched his luggage, and he was outraged. "It seems impertinent, unacceptable to me that a common employee of American Airlines searched my baggage," he later told reporters. "What they should be doing is looking into whether American Airlines employees are smuggling drugs." Upon his return to Peru, American Airlines published ads in all Lima's dailies expressing "deepest apology for any inconvenience we may have caused the president."

Even after the Fujimori regime fell, Alejo and Elizabeth Miró Quesada did not see their lives return to normal. They lived with threats from alleged drug trafficker Fernando Zevallos. In 2005, when Alejo was IAPA president, U.S. authorities prepared a case against Zevallos, a Peruvian whose meteoric rise in little more than a decade saw his jungle-based charter airplane service become Peru's largest airline, AeroContinente. *El Comerico* managed to secure and publish U.S. documents tying Zevallos to a major role in cocaine trafficking. One document even said he was believed to be one of several men behind the killing in 1989 of Todd Smith, a 28-year-old *Tampa Tribune* reporter who had uncovered a planned drug shipment. I had worked on the Todd Smith case that year as in-coming president of IAPA.

Alejo and Elizabeth were attending IAPA's mid-year meeting in Panama City with their family when his newspaper's revelations were published, and colleagues at *El Comercio* advised them not to return to Peru. Threats had been made against Elizabeth. Alejo sent her and two of their daughters to California, but returned to Lima himself. Eventually, Elizabeth returned as well, but in late 2006 she lived with high-level security including constant body guards.

Like virtually all daily newspaper owners around the world, the Miró Quesadas have had to endure their share of criticism, some of it deserved such as support for the 1968 military coup. But since 1839 they have demonstrated outstanding leadership and courage, often under dangerous and trying circumstances. The public at large sees their affluence and influence and undoubtedly envies them. Seldom does it learn that these benefits often come at a high cost.

9. Ecuador
Off the Rails

With the possible exception of stable Costa Rica, I had thought the country in Latin America most unlikely to legislate the mother of restrictive press laws would be Ecuador. Venezuela with Hugo Chavez, yes. Nicaragua of Daniel Ortega, yes. But the normally accommodating citizens of Ecuador, no way.

Karen and I had lived there in the mid-1960s and had returned nearly annually since. We have many friends there, several in the media with their own intriguing stories, but none ever suggested the country was about to go off the rails on press freedom. Some abuses of press freedom, yes; but not outright wreck.

In 2013 that's what happened. The Ecuadorian Congress passed a communications law meant to silence voices critical of the government. It gave authorities the power to impose arbitrary sanctions and censor the media. It created a special agency to audit, issue sanctions and enforce its provisions. Simply put, it is a gag law. I had led several press freedom missions there, but the issues were always relatively straightforward: distribution of government advertising or confrontational style of a president. Ecuador has a long history of weak political parties and strong populist rhetoric that often led to volatile and unstable politics. But its press had lived relatively untouched for decades.

From the beginning President Rafael Correa was no friend of the press. After coming to power in 2007 he fought relentlessly against press freedom. He followed the lead of his Venezuelan mentor but went well beyond Hugo Chavez with regard to the printed press. Both confiscated TV channels and co-opted media outlets through business-owner friends. They both managed to gain control of not only the legislative branch but also the judiciary, resulting in a complete lack of judicial independence. They both prosecuted newspapers and journalists.

But Correa surpassed his mentor with the 2013 communications law regulating not only electronic media but the printed press. Fines and arbitrary sanctions by a new government press tsar became commonplace—a first in the Americas for newspapers and magazines in a nominally democratic country.

The World Association of News Publishers characterized the law as "a sophisticated strategy to marginalize every voice independent of official authority." The law provides for surveillance by the Superintendency of Information and Communication (Supercom), which controls, censors and intrudes on journalistic content under loosely defined regulations. It orders crippling fines and jail terms that have forced some media to cease operation. To avoid heavy fines the press is forced to self-censor.

Furthermore, newspapers and other media have been prosecuted for devoting insufficient coverage to the president. The Quito daily *Hoy*, founded 32 year earlier by my good friend Jaime Mantilla, was fined for not covering as required President Correa's trip to Chile where he received an honorary doctorate from the University of Chile. *Hoy* ceased its print publications shortly thereafter. Other newspapers were threatened with prosecution for insufficient coverage of a government supported lawsuit involving Chevron Corporation. Many have been fined for not fully complying with orders to rectify headlines.

Cartoonist Xavier Bonilla was the first journalist fined under the law after he published an illustration that the government deemed defamatory. In 2014 journalist Fernando Villavicencio was sentenced to prison under the law for defaming President Correa. The law also introduced the novel concept of "media lynching," defined in Article 26 as "dissemination of information in a coordinated and reiterative manner . . . with the purpose of discrediting or harming the reputation of a natural or legal person or to reduce their public credibility."

More than 500 cases were brought in the law's first two years with 313 resulting in punishment. A total of 185 fines were levied. The Guayaquil daily *El Universo* was fined $350,000 for not publishing in the same position, dimensions and type as the original story a complete reply (replica) to an investigation of the national health system.

In 2017 Correa's vice president Lenin Moreno was elected by a razor-thin margin to succeed him. Subsequently, fines were imposed on seven media outlets for having declined to reproduce a story published in a leftist Argentine daily, *Pagina 12*. Fines of US $3,750 on each were imposed for not having used the story during the campaign alleging defeated opposition candidate Guillermo Lasso evaded taxes. The government regulator said the failure constituted prior censorship.

Breaking from Correa, President Moreno subsequently undertook to modify the communications law to be less onerous, although he did not have it repealed. In 2019 at a Quito ceremony he pledged unbridled support for press freedom and formally signed the Declaration of Chapúltepec, IAPA's 10 principle Magna Carta.

The repressive law grew out of events in 2010 when President Correa was held captive at a police hospital in a pay dispute. He was freed, but a few months later Emilio Palacio, a columnist for *El Universo*, wrote that Correa was a dictator and should be criminally charged for ordering soldiers to fire on the hospital, which was full of civilians.

Correa sued Palacio and the owners of the newspaper for libel. He demanded $80 million in damages and three-year prison terms for the defendants. Ultimately, after much stress for the columnist and owners as well as many international protests including from the IAPA, the president withdrew the lawsuit. He then called for passage of the communications law "to strengthen freedom of expression and promote a good press" in Ecuador.

Late in 2015 a constitutional amendment was approved granting the government power to regulate information as a public service like water, electricity, health or public safety. The amendment gives constitutional legitimacy to the 2013 Communications Law that itself did not support the degree of censorship being applied. Under Article 314 of the Constitution "the State is responsible for the provision of public services," now including the media.

I participated in two IAPA missions to Ecuador in hopes of heading off the Communications Law and to support journalists facing various threats and lawsuits. The first was in October 2009 when we met with key congressional leaders as well as a group of top officials at the seat of the government, Carondelet Palace. Among the latter were five cabinet ministers including Fernando Alvarado, the communications minister, and Minister of Defense Javier Ponce. President Correa's personal secretary, Galo Mora, was also present.

I had known Javier Ponce for many years and enjoyed seeing him at numerous social occasions. He was a gifted editor and political writer for years at Quito's *Hoy* and had frequently faced severe pressure from his country's presidents, especially President León Febres Cordero in the mid-1980s. Recalling his history, I told the ministers that to understand just how dangerous the proposed communications law would be "the government should think again about what a government such as that of Febres Cordero would have been able to do had it had similar legislation at hand."

At the conclusion of the formal meeting I spoke with Javier. He assured me that the proposal was nothing more than a sword the administration was bandying over the press and would not become law. His comments were encouraging and I was pleased with the meeting's outcome. Our delegation concluded that "this bill is restrictive and would create government censorship, encourage self-censorship and limit investigative reporting along with its exposing of corruption. It would gut the role of the press in a democracy."

Unfortunately, despite our optimism in 2009 and after the events of 2010, we again saw a need in 2011 to be on site in Quito concerned that the law would be passed by the Congress. At the time we were also extremely worried about the fate of Guayaquil's *El Universo*, the country's largest and arguably most important daily, facing the $80 million lawsuit. Although we had been assured of a meeting with President Correa, shortly after our arrival we were told he refused to meet with us. For two days we met with congressional, media, judicial and religious leaders and then held a press conference. Just hours after we departed came a shock. A Quito judge issued a ruling in the *El Universo* case sentencing columnist Emilio Palacio and his newspaper's two owners to three years in prison. The newspaper was fined $40 million.

A substitute judge had taken control of the case only 30 hours earlier, yet managed to issue—with President Correa in the courtroom—a 156 page ruling. In that short time he had "studied" the more than 5,000-page file. We knew then we had lost the battles in Ecuador itself and our only hope was an appeal to international human rights institutions.

The morning after the ruling *El Universo* published a blank front page except for an Ayn Rand quote saying when corruption is honored and honor is converted to self-sacrifice, "your society is condemned." The strategy of President Correa since taking office in 2007 had been to discredit the media and journalists with insults on his radio and television programs not unlike President Donald Trump would do in the United States. Broadcasting Correa's programs was mandatory under existing law. He called the media "corrupt," "mediocre," "mafiosos," "miserable human beings," "savage beasts," "brutes," "racists," "discriminators" and "liars."

Later came a stage of harassment, new taxes, lawsuits and closings as well as inciting the public to take action. Then his government, with intent of telling its own story, dramatically expanded the number of government-owned media outlets through direct or indirect purchases and confiscations including direct ownership of five TV stations, five radio stations, four magazines, three daily newspapers and a news agency. The expansion came thanks to a massive increase in investment in official publicity, from two million dollars by the previous government to 129 million dollars in 2012.

By 2015 the government had appropriated 55 radio and TV station under the law. According to media watchdog Fundamedios, a network of more than 300 radio stations were editorially aligned with the government. In 2015 even the owners of the stalwart *El Comercio* succumbed to the pressure and sold the daily to Latin American media mogul Remigio Angel González, a Mexican who launched his TV empire in Guatemala and is known for avoiding editorial conflict with governments.

The worrisome developments were condemned as early as 2009 by the Organization of American States (OAS). It was in this context that the IAPA appealed to the OAS's Inter American Commission on Human Rights on behalf of Emilio Palacio and the owners of *El Universo*. We also sought intervention by the commission against the proposed communications law. The United Nations Human Rights Commission also weighed in.

The president eventually withdrew the lawsuit. But he subsequently launched an offensive against the OAS Human Rights System and in particular its Office of the Special Rapporteur of Freedom of Expression. A month before the *El Universo* decision was announced, the OAS had created a Special Working Group of member states assigned to strengthen its human rights system. President Correa mounted a campaign within the members contravening that purpose. The Rapporteur had fought censorship throughout Latin America. It worked to end impunity in crimes against journalists, campaigned to eliminate insult and criminal defamation laws and fought for access to information laws. The office had promoted the advancement of freedom of expression in the hemisphere since 1997.

By December 2011 President Correa had accomplished what he set out to do. The working group issued a report with three proposals that contradicted the intended purpose and undermined the work of the Rapporteur. Specifically, the Ecuadorian government proposals would require the rapporteur to abandon its annual report, which criticized Ecuador and other governments, instead producing only a summary in the commission's general report. They would weaken the office by starving it of funding by prohibiting the raising of independent money. The proposals also would create a code of conduct to increase state control.

Facing a vote on the Working Group's proposal at the OAS March 2013 General Assembly, IAPA's president Milton Coleman of the *Washington Post* launched a hemisphere-wide campaign to defeat it. He had worked closely with the current Special Rapporteur, Catalina Botero, a Colombian attorney, and fully understood the importance of the issue. The Office of the Special Rapporteur had been established at the urging of IAPA. By using IAPA's press freedom leaders in each country to lobby their OAS ambassadors, he managed narrowly to head off the proposal and defeat Correa and his allies. But winning that battle did not stop President Correa from pushing through the new communications law, which was implemented in June, 2013.

In 2015 President Correa moved to close down Ecuador's leading press-freedom monitoring organization, Fundamedios, and relented only in the face of international condemnation. Also in 2015 Freedom House rated Ecuador's press as "not free." The communications law has been criticized continually by press organizations and human rights institutions around the world. In July 2016, for example, the United Nations Human Rights Commission again called for its revision to conform with Article 19 of the Universal Declaration of Human Rights guaranteeing full freedom of expression. Late in 2016 the United Nations Special Rapporteur for Freedom of Expression and the Inter American Human Rights Commission Rapporteur issued a joint warning of its "serious effects . . . to freedom of expression in Ecuador, urging authorities to bring (the act) in line with international standards on the issue."

"It has been used as an instrument to unduly interfere in the content of media outlets and punish them," they said, "especially when their coverage is unfavorable or questions the government's actions and decisions." They also called "concerning" that "certain obligations established in the Act are not defined by law, and their application together with the severe punishments for failure to comply gravely inhibit freedom of expression and opinion in Ecuador."

They said Supercom is "insufficiently independent from the executive branch." Of particular concern was "the application of the Act's provisions that seek to protect the honor and reputation of public officials, as well as the section on the right to correction and response." They requested open dialogue with the government on these and other issues.

These developments stemmed at least in part from reaction to the government's censorship of independent media coverage of the devastating April 2016 earthquake near the northern coast of the country. The quake, 7.8 on the Richter scale, resulted in nearly 300 deaths and 16,000 injured. It was the worst such disaster since a 1949 quake near Ambato.

The censorship prohibited independent coverage for three days. Government social media were the only source for Ecuadorians to learn what happened or how to help. Widespread resentment to the censorship played a role that year and later leading up to the 2017 election and its aftermath.

In the spring of 2006 the country's dailies served as hosts for a splendid mid-year meeting for the IAPA highlighted by the celebration of the 100th birthday of the Quito's most important daily, *El Comercio*. The occasion was highlighted by, among many memorable touches, thousands and thousands of roses, as would be expected in a country known for exporting gorgeous flowers. The Ecuadorian President Alfedo Palicio delivered a somewhat unexpected but eloquent speech supporting press freedom. Later that year elections were held to choose his successor.

From 1997 to 2005 three elected presidents—Abdalá Bucaram, Jamil Mahuad and Lucio Gutiérrez—were forced by popular protests and congressional opposition to leave office before completing their terms. Protestors called for a constituent assembly and a new constitution—a clean sweep of the country's institutions. Karen and I were in Quito at the time Bucaram left the country and three top officials, including Bucaram, claimed to be president at the same time—perhaps a first in Latin America.

At the outset of his presidency Palacio appointed Rafael Correa, a U.S. trained leftist economist, as minister of economy. Correa was a fierce critic of neoliberal economic policies and his tenure was brief because market-oriented Ecuadorians, foreign governments and the World Bank opposed him.

Thirteen candidates, including Correa, entered the 2006 presidential contest and two emerged from a first round. Alvaro Noboa won 27 percent and Correa, who billed himself as unequivocally on the left and an architect of change who would deliver a "Citizens' Revolution," had 23 percent.

Correa was victorious in the second round 56 percent to 43 percent, not incidentally with the help of a longtime friend of mine, Freddy Ehlers, the popular host of a highly rated Sunday evening television show. Freddy was named Minister of Tourism by the new president and later "State Secretary for the Presidential Initiative for the Construction of a Society of Good Life." His role then was to launch a television series promoting dialogue on government programs.

Correa adopted a populist approach to governing and grew widely popular as a result social programs that reduced poverty and built infrastructure. Strong oil prices and a mandated raise from 13 to 87 percent in the government share of oil profits, as well as default on $3 billion in bonds, underwrote his success. As pointed out, he became a key ally of Venezuela's Hugo Chávez and successfully rewrote Ecuador's constitution through a constituent assembly. Among its many changes were the worrying provisions on the press. Correa was re-elected in 2009 under the new constitution and again in 2013.

The wreckage of press freedoms by Rafael Correa was unprecedented. Because of my affinity for Ecuador, I led or participated in a number of IAPA investigative missions there earlier and have followed the activities of many friends in the media for nearly half a century. In addition to the missions confronting the Rafael Correa government, I especially recall investigations of press abuse by President León Febres Cordero and later treatment of the press under President Lucio Gutiérrez.

Back in 1985 my friend and colleague Wilber "Bill" Landrey of the *St. Petersburg Times*, who was then chairman of IAPA's Freedom of Press Committee, and I spent three days in Quito at the request of Ecuadorian editors. Our mission was to look into the state of press freedom in the country. At the time I was the chairman of IAPA's Executive Committee.

The visit grew out of allegations by the Quito daily *Hoy* that it was victim of discrimination by the government of President Febres Cordero. His government complained the alleged violations of press freedom reported by *Hoy* and others were untrue.

We interviewed 36 people including two past presidents of Ecuador as well as sitting government officials, newspaper and broadcast executives, politicians and reporters. Among them were Osvaldo Hurtado, Febres Cordero predecessor as president, and the renowned Galo Plaza Lasso, who had served a highly successful presidency from 1948 to 1952. Galo Plaza later was Secretary General of the Organization of American States from 1968 to 1975.

I had interviewed Galo Plaza about Ecuador's military government in 1966 when I was a Fulbright student in Ecuador. On the 1985 occasion he invited Bill Landrey and me to a memorable luncheon at Zuleta, his 4,000-acre working hacienda near Quito. Zuleta today is a destination for tourists with luxury accommodations and a still-working farm. Embroidered textiles produced there by hand are among the best in the country.

He and Hurtado both confirmed the heavy-handed style of Febres Cordero, but he put a much more positive spin on it, saying the challenge would help the county's democracy mature. Hurtado told us he routinely encountered pressure, even from the president himself, seeking to prevent television stations and newspapers from airing his views. Several media owners suffered significant financial sacrifices to bring his opinions to the public, he said.

Carlos Pérez Perasso, the editor-in-chief of *El Universo* whose sons later would do battle with President Rafael Correa, flew from Guayaquil in support to have breakfast with us. He was the president of the then newly formed AEDPA, the newspaper editors' association. He spoke of "alarming signs" of the government's attempts to manipulate the news by rewarding friends and punishing those regarded as enemies, including *Hoy*.

National Press Secretary Patricio Quevedo replied point by point to IAPA's report from its previous March meeting in Panamá that had been based largely on a report from *Hoy*. His government, he said, upholds the same ideals of press freedom, democracy and private enterprise as does the IAPA. Proof of its dedication to press freedom, he said, is the tolerance of *Hoy*. To its credit the government had annulled a decree passed under the military dictatorship authorizing the requisition of news media under the National Security Law. Virtually everyone we contacted, except Quevedo, confirmed *Hoy* was not getting a fair share of government controlled advertising and that the government also tried to influence advertising decisions of commercial advertisers.

A disturbing allegation we also encountered was that *Hoy*'s director, Benjamín Ortíz, was a leader of the leftwing terrorist organization Alfaro Vive and that *Hoy* provided a refuge for the group. Benjamín had been a friend of mine since my student days in Quito. Journalists had said Febres Cordero himself had made the allegation in August shortly before a kidnapped banker, Nahim Isaías, had died in a shootout between government forces and his captors. Quevedo told us he did not know whether the president said it but "if he did, then he had proof."

Benjamín Ortiz later served as foreign minister in the government of President Jamil Mahuad in the late 1990s. In that capacity he put on an elaborate dinner at the foreign ministry in my honor when I was president of the American Society of Newspaper Editors.

In the report on the mission to the 1985 IAPA general assembly in Colombia we said given the increasing importance of government-controlled advertising in Latin America, objective standards based on audited circulation figures should be adopted for the distribution of government-controlled advertising.

We concluded Ecuador is a democracy whose government is using its power to favor its friends and punish enemies. Most newspapers go along, we said, but *Hoy* has "insisted on a path of independence and criticism and has, in some measure, suffered for it. The IAPA shares many ideals with the government but must defend *Hoy*. IAPA should continue monitoring the situation."

Under the presidency of Lucio Gutiérrez, a former Army colonel who was elected to serve as president in 2003, press freedom deteriorated. He flirted with a proposal to regulate the press, but soon backed off. Journalists and the media were targeted with physical and verbal abuse which an IAPA report characterized as the greatest difficulties for them in 25 years.

Gutiérrez did, after first declining to do so, sign IAPA's Declaration of Chapúlepec, and supported the passage of a new Freedom of information law. However, he delayed issuing regulations for its implementation as confrontations between his government and the press mounted. There was constant hostility against what he called "mediocracy"—the political power wielded by media. He accused various media of lying and reporting "half-truths." A serious concern existed that the final FOI regulations would be drafted in a way, rather than to facilitate access by media, to make it more difficult.

In this environment IAPA President Jack Fuller and I went to Quito in the summer of 2004 with hopes of calming the situation. Jack, President of the *Chicago Tribune* company and a good friend, and I were assured in a cordial meeting with President Gutiérrez that he would implement the regulation proposal supported by the country's media. He would also try to improve relations with them, he told us. We were complimented in media coverage of our meeting and felt we'd achieved our objectives. The ultimate outcome, however, was the opposite. Gutiérrez ignored the proposed regulations. What he implemented would become an obstacle to accessing information.

The government escalated its verbal attacks. Gutiérrez characterized several journalists as "nasty, rotten, shameless, childish stooges." Jaime Mantilla, owner of *Hoy*, was targeted with an investigation of his assets. An investigative reporter at *Hoy* was threatened with death at gunpoint if he continued writing about government entities.

Early in 2004 President Gutiérrez described himself as a "dictocrat," which he defined as a dictator for the oligarchy and a democrat for the people. Government advisors announced a "blacklist" consisting of enemies including, among others, my friend Jaime Mantilla.

The president orchestrated approval by Congress in 2005 of changes in the makeup of the Supreme Court, which he alleged was biased in favor of his political opposition. Massive demonstrations took place in Quito and on April 15 he dissolved the remade court trying to placate the protesters. This move was widely viewed as unconstitutional and on April 20 the Congress removed him and appointed his vice president, Alfredo Palacio, to replace him. It acted without the participation of Gutiérrez' party. Lucio Gutiérrez and his political party continued to figure in Ecuadorian politics. It finished third with his brother Gilmar Gutiérrez as its candidate in the 2006 election won by Rafael Correa. Lucio ran again in the 2009 election, finishing behind Correa with 27 percent of the vote.

As the situation worsened in 2005, we made plans for another mission to Ecuador in which the president of IAPA, its freedom of press chairman and I were scheduled to participate. We would arrive April 24 for three days. President Gutiérrez had agreed to receive us, as had former president Hurtado, the mayors of Quito and Guayaquil and several leading politicians. But the mission was cancelled after Gutiérrez's removal from office.

New and much improved regulations implementing the FOI law were issued by the new President Alfredo Palacio within months.

A formally stated objective of the Inter American Press association is "to work collectively for the solution of common problems and for the preservation of the peace and tranquility of the New World." Two of my good friends, now both former presidents of the society, took that goal to heart by working together to end the 1995 border war between their two countries, Ecuador and Peru. Jaime Mantilla of Quito's *Hoy* and Alejo Miró Quesada, editor in chief of Lima's *El Comercio*, had known each other well for years at our semi-annual meetings.

Called the "Cenepa War," hostilities broke out between their counties in January that year at the border near the headwaters of the Cenepa River. It was the third armed confrontation in a long-standing territorial dispute dating to the first decades of the 19th Century. A full-scale war in 1941 and a brief clash in 1981 had both seen Peru's military prevail. Facing World War II, a settlement in favor of Peru to the 1941 war was brokered by the United States with help from Argentina, Brazil and Chile—the Guarantors. Known as the 1942 Rio Protocol, the agreement gave the entire border region to Peru and eliminated Ecuador's access to any tributary of the Amazon River. Thereby precluded was access for trade to the east as well as possible natural resources in the region.

Ecuador had always claimed the right for a sovereign access to the Amazon and disputed the treaty as it applied to the Cenepa and adjacent area. In 1960 it declared the Rio Protocol null and void. When my wife and I lived in Quito in 1965–66, virtually everyone we knew could recite the national refrain: "Ecuador is an Amazonian country and always will be."

At IAPA's late-March 1995 mid-year meeting in St. Petersburg, Florida, Jaime and Alejo developed a joint report reviewing the situation and calling for a resolution. It was the beginning of a newspaper cooperative effort toward a definitive settlement.

Mutual causalities for both sides stood at about 500.

Mediation by the Rio Protocol Guarantors led to the opening of diplomatic conversations, and with support from the newspapers, a formal peace agreement (the Brasilia Presidential Act) was signed in late October, 1998. By that time Ecuador was led by a new president, Jamil Mahuad. His foreign minister in the negotiations was Benjamín Ortiz, the longtime editor in chief of Jaime Mantilla's daily.

Detractors in both countries were upset, but the newspapers' role helped calm the situation. This was especially important in Ecuador because the Guarantors ruled that the border was in fact what Peru had claimed since the 1940s. Ecuador was compelled to cede its decades-old territorial claims. Peru, in exchange, ceded as a "private property," but without sovereignty, one square kilometer of its Peruvian territory where the Ecuadorian military base Tiwintza on the Cenepa River and focal point of the war had been located. A road no more than five meters wide was provided connecting Tiwinza to Ecuador.

The agreement requires the two countries grant reciprocal most-favored-nation status, obligating any privileges enjoyed by any other trade partner. It provides Ecuador its long-standing demand for access to the Amazon River. Its non-military ships have the right to "free, untaxed and perpetual" navigation to the Amazon.

Permanent peace might have come without them, but Jaime, Alejo and especially Benjamín clearly helped bring a peaceful outcome.

Two additional and unfortunate Ecuadorian memories involve Jaime Mantilla of *Hoy*. Jaime was the victim of a baseless slander, what he called "extortion," by a television station previously seized by the government.

The episode began when a female reporter for the Saõ Paulo daily *O Estado* came to Quito in 2000 to report on the country's economy, which had recently adopted the U.S. dollar as its currency. Jaime was a friend of the Brazilian newspaper's editor, Julio de Mesquita, who put the reporter in touch with Jaime as a source. Jaime, in his typical friendly manner, gave her a warm welcome and provided guidance during her five days in Ecuador. He followed up with a couple of emails which exuded his normal enthusiasm.

The reporter had been hired previously from another paper by her lover, *O Estado*'s managing editor (*jefe de redacción*). The managing editor was in his 60s, she in her early 30s.

He became insanely jealous of anyone with whom she came in contact, and when she decided to end the relationship, he killed her. He even told Julio de Mesquita's cousin the day before the murder that he planned to kill someone. The cousin thought he was kidding.

Murder investigators identified at least 20 names of men who got her editor's jealous attention. The emails Jaime had sent surfaced. The Ecuadorian government's television launched a crusade against Jaime claiming he and the reporter were lovers and that's why she was murdered.

Jaime's family suffered from the scandal. His wife had to go into a convent for a period. As he told me after I gave him this account as related to me by Julio de Mesquita, "My family's trust and love has helped me overcome the problem."

Another unfortunate episode involving Jaime Mantilla took place in 2009. Driving home about 7 p.m. on a Saturday from a family visit to a sick friend, his car clipped an 11-year-old girl as she tried to cross a busy traffic way with a group disembarking a bus. The girl was caught by his new Mazda's side mirror and somehow also injured by a windshield wiper. She suffered traumatic head injuries and her mother, who had earlier been holding her hand, at first thought she was dead. The mother and a police lieutenant both said they smelled liquor on Jaime's breath as he left his car. He had been driving at less than 35 mph in heavy traffic.

Jaime was asked to take a sobriety test ("Alco check"), but declined knowing he had not been drinking and was to be taken to a hospital for various tests. These did not show traces of alcohol. He told authorities the smell of alcohol may have been the Listerine he "habitually" used. This would make sense in Ecuador where restaurants traditionally have Listerine in bathrooms for washing away breath odors. Clearly, Jaime would have been wise to submit to the original sobriety test. Upon leaving the hospital he was contacted by a broadcast friend saying police were being pressured to turn the case over to the Correa government. A government friend confirmed he had himself received a note "that Mantilla, being drunk, ran over a minor."

Within minutes of this confirmation a television station controlled by the government reported Mantilla had run over a minor in an alcohol (*etilico*) state and had threatened to abandon her. Jaime was jailed overnight before being released on condition he not leave the country for 30 days. The girl's mother told the judge she appreciated the attention she had received from Jaime and his family. Jaime paid all the child's medical expenses. The girl was released from the hospital after two weeks.

A judge ruled Jaime's offense was a misdemeanor.

When Jaime Mantilla became the president of the Inter American Press Association three years later at our general assembly in São Paulo, the Correa government news agency, ANDES, put out a scathing attack. It assailed his business practices and recounted in detail the allegation, quoting its affiliated government-owned daily newspaper, of his "romance" with the murdered Brazilian reporter.

It also reported on the traffic accident. It said Mantilla "bought" the silence of the mother of the girl he "ran over."

10. Brazil
Even Song Lyrics

I have attended five of IAPA's general assemblies or mid-year meetings held in various Brazilian cities. I've made visits to other cities as well, but because I don't speak Portuguese, my participation in press freedom issues for Brazilians has been limited. I speak Spanish or English to Brazilians and those from Southern Brazil can usually understand my Spanish. The Southerners live close to Argentina and many there are bilingual.

Numerous Brazilians have over the years become friends, including Julio de Mesquita Filho and Julio C. F. de Mesquita, father and son. Both served as publishers of *O Estado de São Paulo.* One of my favorite anecdotes from earlier IAPA history is about Julio the father during the Castelo Branco military regime in the mid-1960s when the government imposed a draconian censorship on all media, even on song lyrics.

At first Julio the father would leave blank spaces where a censored article should have been. When the military ruled this was a violation, he replaced the censored story with irrelevances—whole columns on the front page with recipes or poems. A copy of the real story would be pinned on the notice board. The public caught on quickly.

A memory from the 1981 IAPA general assembly in Rio de Janeiro, where I organized the program, involves then U.S. Vice President George H. W. Bush, who was making a highly-secured, three-nation tour to Latin America. We were very fortunate that his short Brazil visit corresponded with our assembly.

What still gets my attention is his departure from our Rio hotel after his speech to us. I happened to be watching a side entrance as a black limousine pulled up and the heavily-guarded vice president came out of the building, stepped into the vehicle and it pulled away. About a minute or so later another limo drove up, a heavily-guarded vice president came out of the hotel and left in it.

I never knew which "vice president" was the "double."

Raúl Kraiselburd

Violeta Chamorro

Pedro Chamorro

José Napoleón Duarte

Juan Manuel Santos

Joaquin Balaguer

Aldo Zuccolillo

Alejandro Miró Quesada Garland

Oliver Clarke

José Rubén Zamora

Roberto Eisenmann

Óscar Arias

Bob Cox

Alejandro Junco

Argentina Interior Minister General Harguindeguy | Fidel Castro | Venezuela President Chávez

Ecuador President Correa | Uruguay Dictator Bordaberry | Panama Ruler Noriega

Chile Dictator Pinochet | Paraguay Dictator Stroessner | Nicaragua President Ortega

Raúl Kraiselburd of Argentina, a press freedom champion, speaks at an IAPA event.

Nobel Peace Laureate and Colombian President Juan Manuel Santos is greeted by the author at a 2018 IAPA meeting in Medellín, Colombia.

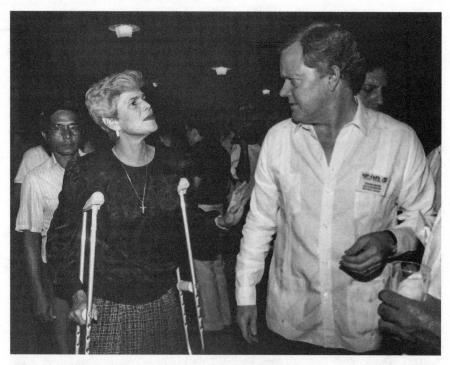

Violeta Chamorro gestures to IAPA President Edward Seaton in Managua a week after she defeated Daniel Ortega in the 1990 presidential election.

José Rubén Zamora above Guatemala City.

NICARAGUA TO END PRESS RESTRAINTS

Announcing Plan for Repeal, Ortega Accuses Contras of 'March of Vengeance'

By LARRY ROHTER
Special to The New York Times

MANAGUA, Nicaragua, March 6 — Acceding to opposition demands, President Daniel Ortega Saavedra announced today that the Nicaraguan Government intends to repeal the country's press law, long condemned by critics of the ruling Sandinista Front as an unconstitutional restraint on freedom of expression here.

"There will be no type of restriction, only the responsibility of the reporter to exercise journalism," Mr. Ortega promised in an address to the Inter-American Press Association, which is meeting here. But he added that he expected the country's press to act "not by the law of the jungle, but by the law of reason, maturity and patriotism."

Mr. Ortega preceded his conciliatory gesture on press freedom with a demand that all armed resistance to the Sandinista Government end immediately. He said that his Government had gone ahead with elections even though the Nicaraguan rebels had failed to honor international accords and that with the Sandinista defeat in the vote there was no excuse for them to continue their military activities.

"Nicaragua has kept its word," he said. "As President, I am proud of having kept my word. Now they have to keep their word. The counterrevolution must disarm."

In a communiqué issued Monday, the army accused the rebel forces of attacking army units and civilian settlements after the elections.

President Daniel Ortega Saavedra of Nicaragua, acceding to opposition demands, said yesterday that the Government would repeal the country's press law. He spoke with Edward Seaton of Seaton Newspapers after an address in Managua to the Inter-American Press Association.

Reuters

"They have broken the truce and are on a march of vengeance, thinking that now is the time to settle accounts with the peasants who have resisted the action of the counterrevolution," Mr. Ortega charged. "They think now is the time to make heads roll."

"The contras must think carefully about the steps they are taking," he continued. "It is best for them and for Nicaragua that they demobilize and disarm immediately."

Mr. Ortega urged the United States to take steps to force the rebels to demobilize. The American Government, he said, "created them, financed them and armed them" and should now support efforts by the United Nations and the Organization of American States to bring about peace.

Gesture Is Applauded

Mr. Ortega's analysis of what he called a "delicate" military and political situation was received quietly by members of the press association. But his audience, consisting of editors and publishers from newspapers throughout Latin America and the United States, applauded enthusiastically applause when he announced he would propose to the National Assembly that the press restrictions be lifted.

Eight years ago, the Sandinistas imposed a state of emergency that required prior censorship on all news material printed or broadcast. Restrictions on newspapers and radio stations have gradually eased since August 1987, when Nicaragua and its neighbors signed the first of several agreements aimed at bringing peace and democracy to Central America.

Mr. Ortega said that rescinding the press law would pave the way for the opening of private television channels, viewed by many in the opposition as one of the most important steps to removing the remaining barriers to free expression. Since the Sandinistas came to power in July 1979, both of Nicaragua's television networks have been operated by the state.

On several occasions in recent years,

The New York Times/March 7, 1990

The contras and the Sandinistas accused each other of breaking a truce in Nueva Segovia province.

private groups have sought to obtain authorization to open a third channel, only to be turned down by the Ministry of the Interior.

Guatemalan Says U.S. Is Unfair on Rights

GUATEMALA, March 6 (Reuters) — President Vinicio Cerezo, responding to the recall of the American Ambassador for consultations on the deteriorating human rights situation in Guatemala, attacked the move today as unfair and inconsistent.

"The attitude of the United States is unjust and unfairly critical," Mr. Cerezo said. "We didn't hear this kind of criticism with dictatorships in the past."

The United States, he added, "has been much more critical with the present Government, that's made an effort toward democracy, than with dictatorial governments, with whom, in some cases, they've been silent accomplices."

Mr. Cerezo, a Christian Democrat, was elected to a five-year term in 1985, ending 17 years of military rule. He has been widely criticized for the Government's failure to identify suspects in the recent assassinations of five university student leaders, a prominent Salvadoran politician, a Nicaraguan diplomat and more than 100 peasants.

The State Department announced on Monday that it was recalling Ambassador Thomas Stroock for a week's consultations on human rights in Guatemala because no one had been prosecuted for the killings.

The human rights dispute erupted after Mr. Stroock delivered a speech at a Rotary Club luncheon last week in which he questioned the Government's ability to deter rights abuses.

Daniel Ortega and the IAPA president at the IAPA 1990 meeting in Managua. In his formal introduction of Ortega, Seaton urged Ortega to accept the election results. In a true democracy he would get another opportunity, Seaton said.

El Salvador President José Napoleón Duarte, right, *when he spoke at Kansas State University in 1984.*

Fidel Castro and then ASNE President Edward Seaton debate about human rights in Havana.

Former Costa Rica President and Nobel Peace Prize winner Óacar Arias listens to the author at an IAPA-sponsored conference.

THE TEN PRINCIPLES OF THE DECLARATION OF CHAPULTEPEC

(Adopted by the Inter American Press Association in Mexico City, Mexico, on March 11, 1994)

1. No people or society can be free without freedom of expression and of the press. The exercise of this freedom is not something authorities grant, it is an inalienable right of the people.

2. Every person has the right to seek and receive information, express opinions and disseminate them freely. No one may restrict or deny these rights.

3. The authorities must be compelled by law to make available in a timely and reasonable manner the information generated by the public sector. No journalist may be forced to reveal his or her sources of information.

4. Freedom of expression and of the press are severely limited by murder, terrorism, kidnapping, pressure, intimidation, the unjust imprisonment of journalists, the destruction of facilities, violence of any kind and impunity for perpetrators. Such acts must be investigated promptly and punished harshly.

5. Prior censorship, restrictions on the circulation of the media or dissemination of their reports, forced publication of information, the imposition of obstacles to the free flow of news, and restrictions on the activities and movements of journalists directly contradict freedom of the press.

6. The media and journalists should neither be discriminated against nor favored because of what they write or say.

7. Tariff and exchange policies, licenses for the importation of paper or news-gathering equipment, the assigning of radio and television frequencies and the granting or withdrawal of government advertising may not be used to reward or punish the media or individual journalists.

8. The membership of journalists in guilds, their affiliation to professional and trade associations and the affiliation of the media with business groups must be strictly voluntary.

9. The credibility of the press is linked to its commitment to truth, to the pursuit of accuracy, fairness and objectivity and to the clear distinction between news and advertising. The attainment of these goals and the respect for ethical and professional values may not be imposed. These are the exclusive responsibility of journalists and the media. In a free society, it is public opinion that rewards or punishes.

10. No news medium nor journalist may be punished for publishing the truth or criticizing or denouncing the government.

CENTRAL AMERICA/MEXICO

11. Nicaragua
Revolution in a Family

In 1975 Pedro Joaquin Chamorro sent a letter to Nicaragua's President Tachito Somoza. "I am waiting, with a clear conscience, and a soul at peace," the country's most prominent editor wrote, "for the blow you are to deliver." In less than three years Pedro was dead, the victim of Somoza's assassins. Pedro fought a long and courageous battle against the Somoza family. In the end, the victory was his. But Nicaraguan journalism is more than Pedro's story, it involves his entire family.

The subtitle of Shirley Christian's 1985 book is "Revolution in the Family." No better characterization describes Nicaragua, especially in the era of the Sandinista Revolution, and no family illustrates her point better than the Chamorros. The history of modern Nicaraguan journalism is also the history of the Chamorros.

The family had included major players in the country's history since its founding. Fruto Chamorro was the first president (1853–55), and three other Chamorros held the office: Pedro Joaquín (1875–79), Emiliano (1917–21), Diego (1921–23) and Emiliano again in 1926. The latter's nephew, the bookish Dr. Pedro Joaquín Chamorro Zelaya, ran the newspaper he acquired in 1932, *La Prensa*, without controversy until his eldest son and successor editor, Pedro Joaquín Chamorro Cardenal, became active in protests as a 20-year-old university student in 1944. The students tried to prevent Nicaraguan President Anastasio "Tacho" Somoza Garcia from seeking re-election. While the effort succeeded, Pedro as a result spent several weeks in jail and *La Prensa* was shut down for two years.

Ultimately Pedro, a colleague of mine on committees in my early years in the IAPA, spent more than four years in Nicaraguan prisons and one under house arrest. While he never became president of Nicaragua, he made *La Prensa* the most important communications voice in Nicaragua and probably had a greater impact on the country's history than any of his ancestors. Pedro's student protests sought an end to the Somoza family dictatorship, which began in 1937 and was to last more than 40 years under three Somoza presidents—"Tacho," Luis and "Tachito"—with brief intervals served by surrogates. Pedro's professional journalistic and political careers unfolded during these years until he was assassinated on February 10, 1978.

With *La Prensa* closed in 1944, Pedro and his parents went into exile. He studied law in Mexico City and also made a point there of learning what he could about managing a newspaper. He returned to Nicaragua in 1948 to collaborate with his father at *La Prensa*. He married the strikingly handsome Violeta Barrios in 1950 and, upon his father's death in 1952, became editor and publisher of *La Prensa*. Ownership of the newspaper was bequeathed in equal shares to him, his mother, his two brothers and two sisters. Together they formed the board of directors.

Pedro crusaded against the Somozas his entire adult life, much to their displeasure. As a result of being unfairly jailed on arbitrary accusations of taking part in an overthrow plot in 1954, tortured and sentenced to prison, Pedro went into politics full time. He resigned as editor so as not to involve the newspaper in his political battle. His two-year prison term was commuted to house arrest in 1955.

Just three months after completing this punishment, he was arrested again during a bloody crackdown—this time for conspiracy in the assassination of the first President Somoza. The initial charge was based on publication in *La Prensa* of photographs of the shooting. It was amended to rebellion after his torturers extracted a false confession, and he was banished for 40 months to the small town of San Carlos on the San Juan River, which forms Nicaragua's border with Costa Rica. Violeta, leaving their children with her mother-in-law, joined him.

On the eve of Easter 1957, the pair slipped away and down the river in a skiff with the help of an accomplice. Their escape was fraught with danger. Tachito Somoza, then head of the National Guard, had said Pedro had been sent to San Carlos in hopes he would attempt an escape—thereby providing justification for killing him.

Eventually Pedro and Violeta had to row up a tributary and finally walk the last leg of their journey. They would remain in Costa Rica two years. He found work on the San José daily, *Prensa Libre*. Some 32 years later I was a featured speaker at *Prensa Libre*'s centennial, but I didn't know until later that its publisher had provided Pedro refuge.

La Prensa was shut down in the aftermath of Tacho Somoza's assassination, and IAPA sent its freedom of press chairman, Jules Dubois, to Nicaragua. According to a later account by Pedro's youngest brother, Jaime, Jules told their mother, "Doña Magarita, the paper must come out even though it may be banned, because we will back you up any way we can." Though all the executives were in jail, she took his advice, rounded up a few journalists and reopened.

In San José, Pedro wrote columns as well as a book, *Bloody Stock: The Somozas*, an expose of the family's cruelty including the hideous torture he suffered himself. Encouraged by Fidel Castro's successful revolution in Cuba, Pedro and colleagues on the democratic left organized an expedition in 1959 to overthrow the original Somoza's eldest son and successor, Luis Somoza Dabayle. They went to Havana seeking arms, but departed convinced that Castro wanted to control their movement. This revolution, in which his brother Jaime also participated, failed after just two weeks. Pedro for the third time faced a military court. He was sentenced to nine years for treason. Why the Somozas didn't have him executed, Pedro's cousin who edited *La Prensa* in his absence, Pablo Antonio Cuadra, would later explain: "They didn't kill Pedro Joaquín because he was among the best of Nicaragua, and there would have been a terrible uproar."

In prison Pedro wrote another book, *Diary of a Prisoner*. Visitors would smuggle segments out to Violeta, who managed to piece together the result. In it he elaborates his rationale for struggle against the dictatorship. He was released a year after his trial in a general amnesty. Press censorship was lifted and Pedro's life achieved a certain normalcy. He published editorials and essays in *La Prensa*, went daily on the airwaves with them and brought them out in book form. In 1963 he was elected a director of the Inter American Press Association, which had pressured Somoza for his release from prison.

Luis Somoza did not seek re-election in 1963 and named René Schick as the candidate to succeed him. Schick turned out not to be a yes man, and Tachito Somoza announced he would run to succeed him in the 1967 election. Unfortunately, Schick died of a heart attack in 1966 and was succeeded in violation of the constitution by his interior minister, who was guided by Tachito, the third Somoza. Pedro was incensed by this power play and organized a campaign against Tachito's candidacy in the upcoming election. Forty opposition supporters were killed in a demonstration, and Pedro was detained. *La Prensa* was occupied and closed for more than a week. Forty-five days later Pedro was released—after Anastasio "Tachito" Somoza was safely elected president, a position he would retain until deposed in 1979 by the Sandinista Revolution.

During these years until his assassination in 1978, Pedro's secretary was Rosario Murillo, Sandinista leader Daniel Ortega's common-law wife. A poet, she would be the future president's close advisor in his first presidency and his communications tsar and lead spokesperson in the second.

The Somoza dynasty might have lasted much longer had a devastating earthquake not struck Managua two days before Christmas 1972, killing 10,000 people and leaving three-fourths of the buildings in rubble or damaged beyond use. *La Prensa*'s buildings and main rotary press also were damaged. The Somoza government would not permit it to reopen under the pretext that the vibration of the newspaper's presses could bring down the precarious structures, endangering lives. For help in this situation, Pedro summoned to Managua the then president of the IAPA, Rodrigo Madrigal Nieto of Costa Rica.

Government agencies had permitted *Novedades*, the Somoza family daily run by Tachito's cousin, to reopen. Madrigal cleverly met with Tachito's cousin, whom he knew through IAPA, and suggested it would not look good for the newspaper or the country if he were to tell the international news agencies that *La Prensa*'s closure was a maneuver by the government and *Novedades* to get rid of the opposition newspaper permanently. The president's cousin immediately arranged a meeting with Tachito, and *La Prensa* was given permission to resume publication that same day.

As international aid for earthquake victims poured in, the Somozas capitalized on it, skimming off vast amounts, which then found their way to the black market. Financial aid passed through Tachito's banks. Construction materials were manufactured in his shops. Downtown was not rebuilt and the building that took place did so on Somoza's land. More than $24 million in U.S. financial aid in the first six months was never accounted for, and $16 million in private assistance from the United States mostly vanished.

Pedro immediately decried the corruption, first circulating mimeographs and then in *La Prensa*. In 1976 he would publish *Richter 7*, a novel about the earthquake and its aftermath. In it he recalls circling Managua on his motorcycle observing how aid was being squandered. He concludes the book with a plea against censorship.

Strikes and organized resistance took place. In 1974 the long-moribund Sandinista rebels received new life after a spectacular hostage taking and exchange. Blaming *La Prensa*, Somoza seized the moment to impose two years of press censorship. As it had in 1954 and 1956 when Pedro was implicated in plots to assassinate the elder Somoza, and in 1967 when it requested he be granted asylum in Costa Rica, the IAPA came to his aid. As his brother Jaime later expressed it, "In response to each of these aberrant actions against the press, we always had the support of the IAPA, which ceaselessly put pressure on the dictator." In less than five years the Sandinistas would be in power. Their support grew, but the event that catalyzed the moderate opposition to join them—and thereby brought their success—was the assassination of Pedro Chamorro.

In 1974 Pedro united the democratic opposition under the banner of the Democratic Union of Liberation, where he was elected president. There were numerous threats, but Tachito could not throw him into prison again because, as one scholar later put it, "he had become too influential an adversary, too well known among the press corps and, in particular, among the members of the Inter American Press Association."

It was during these years that I came to know him. He used IAPA assemblies as a forum to attack the Somozas. In 1975 he spoke at our meeting in São Paulo drawing from a newspaper series about human rights abuses in Nicaragua that he had been unable to publish because of the censorship. We worked together to craft resolutions at the IAPA's 1977 spring meeting in Cartagena, Colombia. Initially, he was denied permission to leave the country to attend our October meeting that year in the Dominican Republic, as he had been on other occasions, but the Nicaraguan Supreme Court upheld his right to travel and ultimately he was permitted to come. There, he had a vitriolic exchange about unwarranted press censorship and human rights abuses with a representative from Tachito's newspaper, *Novedades*, who denied everything.

Somoza's man gave an interview at the meeting saying Pedro was going to end up like a man who was said to have committed suicide—this less than 90 days before his assassination. Pedro responded in an interview himself, "It was like telling me, 'we're going to kill you, and there will be no assassin's sign.'" With travel restrictions lifted he also was able to go to New York to receive the Maria Moors Cabot Prize from Columbia University—just two months before his death. In presenting the award Columbia officials said: "Chamorro, in his battle against corruption in his county, has known how to replace the power of the sword with the power of the written word." No one in the hemisphere was more deserving of the most important prize awarded in the United States for Latin American journalism, they commented.

At age 53, Pedro was cut down by shotgun in broad daylight while driving his car to work. His Saab had been forced off the street into a lamppost. To hold down the size of the crowd, his funeral was required to be advanced two and one-half hours and bus service curtailed. Nonetheless, 30,000 mourners managed to attend. Looting and burning went on for 48 hours and an estimated $7 million in damage occurred in response to the assassination. Violeta joined the mourners shouting "Viva Pedro Joaquín Chamorro," "Viva la libertad" and singing the Nicaraguan national anthem.

In a commentary published on the front page of *The Manhattan Mercury*, I wrote: "Pedro's death forces those of us who knew him to stop what we are doing and reflect. It does not come as a surprise. We almost expected it. . . . What makes life meaningful to a principled and thoughtful man like Pedro Joaquín Chamorro is doing what you think must be done under the circumstances, and his circumstances dictated that he be an editor and a freedom fighter. Even Violeta knew this and therefore could join the chanting crowd."

Pablo Cuadro, Pedro's cousin who eventually became editor of *La Prensa*, spoke for the nation when he said: "I went to the hospital and saw Pedro Joaquín with some thirty shotgun wounds. If he's not a hero, I don't know who is. Pedro's valor was spent for ideals. He was one man alone with a pen in front of a dictator who had the National Guard, prisons and torturers. He stood alone before all of that—one man with a newspaper, a bullfighter without a sword."

Just 18 months after Pedro's death, the Sandinistas were in power. *La Prensa* had been turned into an opposition headquarters. The Sandinistas inside *La Prensa* formed secret cells, and the Chamorro family loaned the revolution $50,000 (which was never paid back) for an unspecified "revolutionary operation" which they believe culminated in the famous takeover of the National Palace by Edén Pastora and his commando team in August 1978.

In that year seven machine gun attacks and an attempted bombing of *La Prensa* occurred.

As Somoza's impending defeat became apparent, he unleashed one final blow against his old nemesis. The National Guard destroyed *La Prensa's* building on June 11, 1979, with rockets, an armored vehicle and gasoline. Just a month later, Somoza fled to Miami and the Sandinistas took over the country.

With international assistance, *La Prensa* was able to re-appear 27 days after the Sandinista triumph. Printing was at the newspaper in León, 50 miles northwest of Managua. Within a year the Managua plant was again fully operational with the help of equipment sent by IAPA members and a generous loan from a German foundation. Meanwhile, the new government took over Somoza's daily, *Novedades,* and renamed it *Barricada.* Pedro and Violeta's youngest son and most radical offspring, Carlos Fernando, became its editor-in-chief. During this period the Sandinistas also began issuing repressive legislation and regulations that made freedom of press contingent on ambiguous criteria and permitted prior censorship on economic and national security matters they considered threatening.

With Carlos Fernando heading the Sandinista daily, the Pedro Chamorro family became a microcosm of the nation. Violeta for a brief period joined the Junta set up by the Sandisistas to run the country. Young Pedro Joaquín, the oldest, returned to *La Prensa* and eventually became a strong anti-Sandinista. Claudia, the elder daughter, stuck with the Sandinistas and eventually served as Sandinista ambassador to Costa Rica. She was also her mother's personal assistant and advisor the nine months Violeta served on the Junta. Cristiana, the younger daughter, wrote sympathetically for *La Prensa* until her sentiments shifted to those of her husband, Antonio Lacayo, who as a businessman was wary of the Sandinistas from the beginning.

Early in 1980 the IAPA sent a delegation to Managua to meet with Violeta and the other members of the Junta about growing concerns regarding restrictions on the press and to suggest to her that time may have arrived for her to resign, which she had attempted to do previously on five occasions. From the beginning Carlos Fernando, who knew the true direction of the revolution would not suit his mother, had urged her to leave. Finally, after serving nine months, the Sandinista leadership agreed. It was a graceful exit blamed on her health.

Meanwhile, tensions at *La Prensa* developed between those who supported the Sandinistas and those opposed. The paper criticized the Sandinistas as intolerant. The Sandinistas tried to buy out the family through the auspices of Pedro's brother, Xavier, who was the co-editor-in-chief. The family declined and problems arose between Xavier, who sympathized with the revolution, and the board of directors. The board called for his resignation, which resulted in a work stoppage, apparently orchestrated by the Sandinista leaders. They said Xavier was the only editor-in-chief acceptable to them, and threatened to confiscate not only *La Prensa,* but the personal property of the directors, if the decision were not reversed. The directors stood firm.

The IAPA attempted to mediate in May of 1980. I participated in those efforts conducted by telephone from Miami with the Chamorros in Managua. In the end a deal was cut in which Xavier received 25 percent of *La Prensa*'s capital and newsprint to start a new pro-Sandinista daily, *El Nuevo Diario.* Seventy percent of *La Prensa*'s employees, mostly from the technical and mechanical side but including Xavier's co-editor-in chief, Danilo Aguirre, joined him at the new daily. After the month-long crisis, *La Prensa* reopened. Chamorros would now run all three dailies in Managua: the official Sandinista *Barricada* (Carlos Fernando), the pro-revolution *El Nuevo Diario* (his uncle Xavier), and the anti-Sandinista *La Prensa* (his uncle Jaime and brother Pedro Joaquin).

I made nearly a dozen trips to Nicaragua in the next decade on behalf of *La Prensa* and its owners. Key Sandinistas had earlier been affiliated with Pedro Joaquín and *La Prensa,* but as an opposition newspaper it suffered repeatedly under these very former colleagues. Among them, as noted earlier, was Pedro's personal secretary, Daniel Ortega's common-law wife Rosario Murillo. Tomás Borge, the interior minister who would oversee persecution and censorship of the newspaper, was a distribution agent before Somoza Garcia's assassination. And Sergio Ramirez, the Sandinista vice president, had contributed poems and prose.

Initially, the Sandinistas did not dare confront the newspaper—symbol of opposition to the Somozas. But the true colors of the Sandinistas emerged within months. The government decreed a Provisional Law Governing Communications Media that contained a list of prohibitions deemed by the government to be undesirable, including material the government believed offensive or disrespectful of "established institutions." As its opposition grew, Daniel Ortega accused *La Prensa* of harboring counterrevolutionary sentiments, and in due course cut its access to foreign exchange for purchasing newsprint. U.S. President Jimmy Carter intervened and arranged for regular shipments of paper. By 1981 the prohibitions were extended to any material the government believed threatening to internal security or compromising of the economy. In the next six months, *La Prensa* was shut down five times. Then, in March 1982, a state of emergency brought with it prior censorship. All pages had to be submitted in advance for review by the Office of Communications Media. On 46 occasions the editors decided not to publish due to excessive censorship. The newspaper was suspended ten times, normally for 48-hour periods, before it finally was closed permanently in June 1986.

Violeta had always served to anchor Pedro in his struggles, but after his assassination she, too, went to battle. Less than two months after his murder, she brought her own problems with Somoza to the IAPA's 1978 spring meeting in Cancún, Mexico. She spoke there of censorship and Somoza's failure to investigate the assassination, then distributed copies of editions censored by Somoza. Using the approach Pedro had used earlier, whenever a story didn't pass the approval of Somoza's censors, the new editors substituted a really ludicrous account of UFOs or a photo of a movie star. Readers knew a story had been banned. After the Sandinistas first censored the newspaper in October 1980, Violeta or her colleagues again appeared at IAPA meetings distributing censored newspapers. At our October 1981 meeting in Rio de Janeiro, the general assembly voted to send a mission to Nicaragua the next month led by IAPA President Charles Scripps, chairman of Scripps-Howard Newspapers, to investigate the situation and support *La Prensa*.

I participated in the mission and visited Sandinista Nicaragua for the first time in November, 1981. I had not been in Managua since 1966 when Karen and I passed through on our way north after our Fulbright year in Ecuador. In addition to me, the delegation included my good friends Raúl Kraiselburd of Argentina and Bill Landrey of St. Petersburg, Fla., along with other representatives from Mexico, Costa Rica, Argentina and IAPA staff. Young Pedro Joaquín, Cristiana and Violeta received us at *La Prensa* and supplied copies of the laws and decrees the Sandinistas were using to restrict freedom of the press. Violeta later welcomed us at her spacious home for a buffet and a chance to see the horrifying artifacts she now displayed in Pedro's library surrounded by photographs and highlights of his remarkable career. In a glass case she had displayed, and even today displays, the clothing he was wearing with traces of blood, sweat and dust from the assassination. His broken glasses and other personal effects there stopped all conversation. In front of her home, covered by a tarp, sat his wrecked Saab.

We also met with then Archbishop Miguel Obando y Bravo, whom Pope John Paul in 1985 made the only Cardinal in Central America in order to enhance his standing as an important opponent and mediator with the Sandinists. He detailed for us the Sandinista attacks on church officials. We also heard of mass graves and attacks on opposition parties from the Nicaraguan permanent Commission on Human Rights.

One vivid memory that has stayed with me was our interview with the 25-year-old Carlos Fernando Chamorro in his impressive office at *Barricada*. Accompanying us was his uncle and *La Prensa* editor, Jaime Chamorro. Carlos Fernando was so ill-at-ease that he appeared totally out of place as the editor of the official Sandinista daily. He seemed to us to have been taken advantage of in every respect by the revolutionaries. He did his best to explain that Nicaragua was going through a very difficult time and that criticism from the press could damage the country. The laws were not intended to limit press freedom, but rather ensure it was exercised responsibly, he said.

Then his uncle Jaime, who never minces words, likened the Sandinistas to Nazis in their approach to governing. Carlos Fernando simply came unglued and so agitated he scolded Jaime and said it was impossible to carry on such a dialogue. The interview was over. We also held a formal session with members of the Junta as well as meetings with other officials of the government and were promised respect for a "responsible" press, but our visit had no visible or lasting impact of which I am aware.

In 1983 I became vice chair of the IAPA's Executive Committee and began playing a larger role in the society's approach to *La Prensa*'s problems. Two years later I was elected to chair the committee and was serving in that capacity when the Sandinistas—reacting to Congressional approval of President Reagan's additional $100 million in military assistance to their Contra opposition—closed the newspaper in June, 1986.

As tensions mounted over the closure, Xavier Chamorro again made overtures about buying *La Prensa*. He approached the board in April with an offer he said was not prompted by the government but rather of his own volition. Again, the buyout was turned down. The closure resulted in a desperate financial situation for *La Prensa*, which had to lay off a majority of its staff even in the face of a possible government or worker takeover on behalf of "neglected workers"—the excuse Juan Peron used in 1951 to justify confiscating Argentina's *La Prensa* after he closed it that year.

After several meetings including a special one in October in Miami with several members of the Chamorro family, we concluded not to involve the IAPA in any official way in the raising of funds for the maintenance of *La Prensa*—despite my initial impulse to create a "Save the Newspapers Fund."

Jaime Chamorro had told us he could retain the 90 remaining staff with $5,000 to $8,000 a month in hard currency. Our reservations were founded on concerns that *La Prensa* might have received money clandestinely from the CIA, and the damage disclosure of that, if true, would do to the IAPA. A recent article in *Common Cause Magazine* had strongly suggested the possibility. Oddly, covert funding is viewed as reprehensible in Latin America, while above-board support, even from government sources, is generally acceptable.

We decided we had to know the facts, and the Miami meeting was called for October 3. We invited not only Jaime Chamorro and several IAPA leaders, but also Roberto Eisenmann and Aldo Zuccolillo. Roberto had taken self-imposed exile in Miami just two months earlier as a result of death threats against him in the on-going struggle between his daily in Panamá, *La Prensa*, and Gen. Manuel Noriega. Aldo's *ABC Color* in Asunción, Paraguay, had been closed by the Stroessner government two years earlier. Both these men had first-hand experience in dealing with authoritarian repression. Aldo, who is independently wealthy, told how he was managing to pay his staff through the ordeal, which was to last another three years until Stroessner fell.

Jaime was direct with us. He told us since the troubles began with the Sandinistas *La Prensa* had received more than $250,000 from the National Endowment for Democracy—a quasi-private U.S. group that receives funds overtly from the U.S. Congress to support democracy abroad—money from a foundation supported by the German government, and $400,000 from a Venezuelan business man whose name he said he didn't remember. The latter was in the form of a "loan" but did not have to be repaid. He said that Interior Minister Tomás Borge, who had once worked as a distribution agent for the paper, had privately given his permission for the receipt of aid from all three sources. An additional $100,000 had come from Venezuelan President Luis Herrera Campins, but it had not been "registered" with the government, although the Nicaraguan ambassador went with Jaime to receive it.

Jaime characterized the $400,000 "loan" as "presumably from the CIA," although he had no way of knowing for sure. He said a U.S. Embassy official told him about the money. As a result, we feared if true the exposure of a CIA subsidy would taint our effort and therefore opted for bringing international pressure rather than IAPA-sponsored financial assistance.

Private financial assistance was undertaken by several of our Latin American colleagues, but it remained completely independent of the IAPA. In the name of the IAPA we launched a campaign to raise international pressure on Managua to re-open the newspaper as well as to solicit donations for the legal expenses of our effort. With the hope of insulating the IAPA, at least to some extent, from the heated debate about leftist Nicaragua, we determined to mount the campaign on behalf of both *La Prensa* and Paraguay's *ABC Color*. Cases previously had been brought on behalf of *ABC Color* at both the United Nations and the Organization of American States. We joined those and brought cases on behalf of *La Prensa*. IAPA President Alejandro Miró Quesada Garland testified both at the OAS's Inter-American Commission on Human Rights in Washington and at the United Nations Human Rights Commission in Geneva. I assisted him in preparing these presentations.

Before our meeting in Miami, the U.S. Congress had again considered an earmark of $450,000 for *La Prensa*. Jaime said he had become nervous about such assistance since the Contra aid approval, and he didn't know how the Sandinistas would react. They could use it as a pretext to confiscate his newspaper, he told us. Ultimately, the money was not approved because Republicans said the amendment would force a conference committee on Contra aid, which they did not want to risk.

Earlier that same year, with hopes of helping *La Prensa*, I had become deeply involved in promoting the peace process then under way in Central America. On April 14 Secretary of State George Shultz had delivered a Landon Lecture at Kansas State University. As chairman of the patrons of the series, I had the privilege of being on stage with him and exchanging views in private. In a follow-up letter three days later, I suggested the United States make a highly visible offer to the effect that, if Nicaragua signed the Contadora peace agreement, the United States would cut off aid to the Contras. I made the point that the Contadora proposal had well-defined security and verification provisions that would restrict Nicaragua's ability to export revolution and at the same time require the Sandinistas to pursue internal reconciliation and democratization. I said I believed the treaty, if complied with, would protect U.S. interests in the area. At the very least, I told him, such an offer would call President Ortega's bluff on the Contadora issue. "If he signs," I said, "we will have won the struggle."

I was aware this approach was on the table because my local congressman, Jim Slattery, was on the fence about Contra aid votes and using his indecision to push the Reagan administration toward this solution. He had had conversations with Philip Habib, the president's special envoy to Central America, and received assurance in writing from Habib that if the Sandinistas signed the Contadora agreement, which would ban foreign support for insurgencies in the region, the United States would halt support for the Contras.

On May 6 Secretary Shultz responded to my letter through Richard Melton, his director of the Office of Central American and Panamanian Affairs. In the letter Melton repeated what Habib had told Slattery: "The United States will abide by the terms of a "comprehensive, verifiable, and simultaneous implementation of the Contadora Document of Objectives of September 1983. . . . The criteria for our own compliance as set forth in the letter (to Slattery), make clear that all twenty-one points of the Document of Objectives must be agreed upon and formulated in a way that is verifiable before any provision takes effect. . . ." He attached a copy of the Habib letter.

With this encouragement that the moment was at hand to resolve the problems in Central America if the Sandinistas could be persuaded to accept and sign the agreement June 6, the negotiating group's self-imposed deadline before the Contra Aid vote in Congress, I launched an effort to bring as much pressure as I could. I wrote letters to key editorial page editors, including *The Washington Post, The New York Times, The Los Angeles Times, The Miami Herald* and several Latin American newspapers. I explained that a narrow window of opportunity existed to achieve peace in Nicaragua and to save *La Prensa*. "If the Sandinistas can be persuaded to sign the Contadora agreement June 6, the crisis will end," I said, and I urged them to push the Sandinistas with editorials. In conclusion I wrote: "My judgment is that this window may be among the last for a negotiated solution. In its present form Contadora would restrict the Sandinistas' ability to export revolution and require them to pursue internal reconciliation and democratization. I see it as the best way out of a bad situation."

I was further encouraged in May when Vice President George H. W. Bush, attending the inauguration of Oscar Arias, the youthful new Costa Rican president, told Latin American leaders at a breakfast the United States would halt support for the Contras if the Contadora treaty were signed.

Unfortunately, as the June 6 deadline grew near, the hawks in the Reagan administration, who were determined on victory, managed to sabotage Habib and the opportunity. Two weeks before the deadline a high administration official briefed reporters without attribution saying the Habib letter was "imprecise" and "in error' in promising action "on signature." If he could rewrite the letter, "I'd just change the word 'signing' to 'implementation.'"

On June 5 the administration officially backtracked on its position with an on-the-record spokesman saying the United States had revised its negotiating position and would abide by the Contadora treaty only upon "implementation." The upshot was that on June 25 the U.S. Congress approved $100 million in Contra aid and the next day Daniel Ortega reversed himself on Contadora, blaming *La Prensa* for the aid vote and characterizing Violeta Chamorro as an enemy of the revolution who deserved a 30-year prison sentence. The next day he shut down *La Prensa*, the only independent media voice in the country. Its press would remain idle for sixteen months—until Ortega signed the Arias Peace Plan under which he had to begin steps toward democratization.

Under the lead: "Color the Sandinistas hammer-and-sickle red," my newspaper, *The Manhattan Mercury*, said "The closure was announced for an 'indefinite period,' but informed observers see it as all but irreversible." We quoted an assessment I had written in 1981: "La Prensa has become much more than simply an independent newspaper. It is the symbol of pluralism just as the assassination in 1978 of its late editor, Pedro Joaquin Chamorro, became a symbol and catalyst of the revolution against Somoza. If it is closed permanently, the world will know that the commanders have decided to follow their (Marxist totalitarian) bent."

"For four years," we said, "the newspaper has operated under a draconian censorship that has forced it to miss publication at least 41 times and involved the loss of nearly $6.5 million. Yet out of patriotism and devotion to democracy, the Chamorro family and the editors, reporters and employees have doggedly refused to quit. The pretext for its closure Thursday was a vote in a U.S. Congress with which *La Prensa* had nothing to do."

At the end of that year, at the request of Congressman Slattery, who was still deeply involved in diplomatic efforts to resolve the situation, I helped organize a trip for a Kansas group to Honduras and Nicaragua. We spent three days in Honduras investigating the U.S. Contra side including a visit to the U.S. Palmerola Air Force Base in Camayagua and a session with President José Azcona. Jim flew to the Contra camp with another friend I had invited to join the group, U.S. Army Maj. Gen. (retired) Neal Creighton. None of the others in our delegation had security clearance. They returned with a changed view of the Contras, who at the time were portrayed as feckless. The two were highly impressed with the Contra potential, especially their communications capabilities. We then spent a week in Nicaragua.

Christiana Chamorro had sent word to me before our trip that the Sandinistas probably would declare an end to the state of emergency shortly before our arrival and a new "democratic" constitution including so-called guarantees for freedom of expression was to be signed into effect the day we were to leave from Miami. Taking advantage of this development as well as the ninth anniversary of her father's assassination January 10, she and the family might "request" permission to publish again, she said.

Violeta and Cristiana received our entire 18-member delegation January 13 in a visit to their closed newspaper. Such visits are always depressing experiences for me. I had had the unhappy occasion to endure similar ones previously in Paraguay and Panama.

Our hosts briefed us on their current hopes of publishing under the new constitution and provided us a proof copy of the edition they planned to issue two days later, January 16. They hoped Congressman Slattery's presence at the time, as well as that of three other members of the U.S. Congress, would help their cause. They had asked permission to renew publication on January 10, but were still waiting an answer. Permission was officially denied early on the 16th. Within days they filed a protest with the Inter American Human Rights Commission. Violeta sent me copies of all her exchanges with the government as well as the protest. "Here each time is worse—nothing positive—just tricks for the (foreign) visitors," she wrote in a personal letter accompanying the documents.

The evening of our visit to the newspaper plant, Violeta invited Congressman Slattery and me to join her and Cristiana at her home, where the congressman was much taken with both Violeta and her "museum."

We also had a session with poet and Vice President Sergio Ramirez, who had visited Kansas the previous November, and interviewed advocates for both the pro- and anti-Sandinista viewpoints. President Daniel Ortega cancelled a scheduled meeting with the group in order to appear on a local talk show. We also journeyed to Matagalpa, on the edge of the war zone two hours north of Managua, to visit a Sandinista military installation, where we were briefed by the regional commander.

Congressman Slattery and I then departed with his staff of two for San José, Costa Rica, for an evening meeting with President Oscar Arias at his private home. Arias and his foreign minister, my old colleague from IAPA

Rodrigo Madrigal Nieto, gave us an off-the-record briefing on Arias's peace plan, in skeletal form, which would eventually prove successful and win him the Nobel Peace Prize. The plan had many similarities to a plan Slattery had been pushing and its key was asking that democratization be achieved within a fixed time period. The underlying thrust of the plan was to substitute democracy for arms in solving Central America's conflicts. Required were free and fair elections in which opposition groups had a chance. Both plans emphasized reconciliation, ceasefire, amnesty, dialogue, full freedom of the press, an end to foreign military aid and advisors (U.S. and Soviet) as well as a return to democratic solutions to problems. As the Arias plan evolved, the key would be challenging Daniel Ortega to live up to his professed democratic bona fides, which he ultimately did in acknowledging electoral defeat to Violeta Chamorro in 1990.

Arias formally announced his plan the next month on February 15 and, to the surprise of most observers including Washington, the five Central American countries signed it Aug. 7 at Esquipulas, Guatemala. It set a 90-day deadline for compliance. On October 1 *La Prensa* resumed publication. After a two-year hiatus, peace talks resumed October 4 between the Salvadoran FMLN guerrillas and President José Napoleón Duarte. For the first time in 27 years, peace talks began October 7 in Madrid between Guatemalan officials and the URNG guerrilla leaders. October 13 Oscar Arias learned he would be awarded the 1987 Nobel Peace Prize.

In an emotional editorial October 8 Violeta Chamorro wrote: "If to achieve reconciliation and peace among Nicaraguans I'd have to pay the price of seeing the hired killers of my beloved husband go free, then I am ready to pay it."

Just three weeks before the Nobel Peace Prize was announced, President Arias came to Manhattan, Kansas, at my invitation to deliver on September 21 a Landon Lecture at Kansas State University. Congressman Slattery, who had become Arias' principal contact in the U.S. Congress, was key in his decision to visit Kansas on a trip that included an address to an informal joint session of Congress in Washington and then to New York to speak at the General Assembly of the United Nations. The fact that José Napoleón Duarte had given a Landon in 1984 on the topic of the search for peace in El Salvador may also have had a bearing on Arias' coming, as well as the possibility of influencing Kansas' two senators, Nancy Landon Kassebaum and Bob Dole, the Senate minority leader. Both were players on the Contra aid issue.

In his Landon Lecture Arias outlined the details of his peace plan and at a press conference called on the United States not to extend Contra military aid, which he said would jeopardize the plan. Give peace a chance, he urged. The day he spoke in Manhattan, the Sandinistas announced they would permit *La Prensa* to resume publication without censorship. The paper came out swinging—without prior censorship after years of censorship—by publishing a list of opposition members who had died in prison, coverage of an opposition march and criticism of the Sandinista *comandantes.*

Again playing a role in an agreement to permit *La Prensa* to reopen was Rodrigo Madrigal Nieto, the former IAPA president and now President Arias' foreign minister. President Ortega had called Violeta saying he wanted to meet and discuss conditions under which he might agree to let the paper reopen in compliance with the Arias peace plan, and brought Rodrigo to the meeting at Violeta's house. "His administration wanted to assure me in the presence of our mutual friend Madrigal Nieto," she later wrote, "that *La Prensa* could reopen with minimal censorship." Violeta told him she could not agree unless she was guaranteed complete freedom of expression.

The discussions lasted for hours with both sides wanting success under the circumstances, and in the end Ortega accepted complete freedom. A joint communiqué was drafted and "entrusted to Madrigal Nieto," she wrote, "so that he, an eyewitness and trusted friend of both parties, could be the one to let the world know that the worst inquisition ever to have hit Nicaragua was at last over."

The communiqué acknowledged the role Rodrigo Madrigal played in negotiating the deal: "The government authorities of Nicaragua and the management of the daily *La Prensa* thank the foreign minister of Costa Rica for his valued efforts that made this understanding possible." *La Prensa* wrote: "Under terms of the Accords of Esquipulas and through the mediation of the foreign minister of Costa Rica, Mr. Rodrigo Madrigal Nieto, we achieved a negotiation with the Sandisista government in which the sacred right of the people to freedom of the press and information was once again defended by the daily *La Prensa,* this time emerging victorious."

Decades later in 2016 the President of Costa Rica, Luis Guillermo Solis, told me at a dinner party that as a young diplomatic advisor to Rodrigo Madrigal he participated in these negotiations. He in fact had the job of typing up the agreement at Violeta's house—on Pedro Joaquin Chamorro's personal typewriter, which Violeta kept in her study. He was in Manhattan, Kansas, to deliver a Landon Lecture.

Guido Fernandez, President Arias' ambassador to the United States, invited my wife Karen and me to attend a dinner in Washington at his home in early November shortly after the November 7 deadline for implementing the Arias peace plan had to be delayed and reset for January 4. Subsequently it was extended to January 15, when it successfully brought a ceasefire in Nicaragua and eventual peace. Guido was a former editor of Costa Rica's *La Nación* in San Jose and an old friend through IAPA. The dinner was to bring together the five Central America ambassadors to the United States for the first time in years, perhaps ever. The Guatemalan ambassador had attempted a similar dinner without success. Neither the Nicaraguan nor El Salvadoran ambassadors showed on that occasion.

This time they all appeared—with spouses. Guido had stayed at our home at the time of Arias' visit in Manhattan, Kansas, and was reciprocating our hospitality. He thought my participation would aid in a trip I was organizing to Central America for the American Society of Newspaper Editors (ASNE). He may also have thought the presence of an American at the dinner would keep the conversation on the peace effort. Karen and I were the only outsiders, and the conversation for us was riveting.

At issue was how to overcome the issues holding up implementation of the August 7 agreement signed by all five countries. Talks had bogged down on the question of who sits at the negotiating table, but the real issue was timing. The Sandinistas insisted aid to the Contras end before they restored civil liberties and lived up the other provisions of the agreement. The Contras insisted on an end to the state of emergency, complete press freedom and a general amnesty as conditions for halting the fighting. Meanwhile, the United States was proposing direct talks with the Sandinistas on U.S. security issues, especially the Soviet and Cuban presence in Nicaragua.

At dinner the fear was that President Ronald Reagan would declare the peace plan a failure when he spoke the next week to the Organization of American States and call for the OAS to reopen the issue. After considerable discussion the ambassadors concluded he would not do so. My friend Guido said he hoped Reagan would propose bilateral talks between the United States and the Sandinistas in concert with the Contra-Sandinista talks. I suggested there had been indications he would do this, and the ambassadors were very interested.

Toward the end of the evening the Honduras ambassador Roberto Marti-nez gave a carefully worded toast on the Arias plan alluding the fact that all of them were "in this together" and they would ultimately find a solution even if the Arias plan failed.

Given that the Arias plan succeeded within two months, the dinner bring-ing together all the ambassadors for the first time undoubtedly was a positive step in the peace process. All five ambassadors agreed that direct U.S.-Sandi-nista talks would put the war in a diplomatic stalemate with an end to Contra aid, but it was not clear the Nicaraguan ambassador, Carlos Tunnerman, was speaking for his government or just himself. Earlier, without the presence of Tunnerman, who was the last to arrive, the other four were very supportive of the Arias plan. Once Tunnerman entered, the conversation became more cautious.

Tunnerman's wife, Rosa Carlota, told me she thought Nicaraguans were like Violeta Chamorro's family, where even after the political split, they all still attended Claudia Chamorro's wedding. "We will get back together and will be a family again," she said. She was right, and the peace agreement ultimately brought not only Nicaraguans back together but ultimately also the Salvador-ans and Guatemalans.

In the critical January days of 1988 with the Arias agreement taking hold, I led a 14-member delegation of U.S. editors to Mexico and Central America at the request of Katherine Fanning, editor of *The Christian Science Monitor* and ASNE president. The two-week trip concluded with an interview with Presi-dent Arias at his home just four days before a scheduled Congressional vote on more aid, including additional weapons, for the Contras. Arias urged us to push limiting any aid to humanitarian assistance. Many of the participants, who included top editors from Washington, Baltimore, Chicago, Hartford, Boston and the Scripps-Howard chain, reported his views and several, includ-ing me, endorsed them editorially. At least one of their stories was cited by the White House and another on the floor of the Congress during the aid debate. The aid bill, the last attempt to pass lethal arms support, was defeated in the House.

The trip included personal interviews with the presidents or top leaders of the five countries bound by the peace agreement. The presidents of Guate-mala, El Salvador, Nicaragua and Costa Rica met with us personally in their own countries, and all expressed the view that the peace effort would not be destroyed by approval of the aid package. We also held scores of interviews with other highly placed figures of all political persuasions including Contra leaders. The trip began in Mexico with interviews with President Miguel de la Madrid and presidential candidate and eventual successor Carlos Salinas. Leaders of the Guatemalan and Salvadoran guerrilla movements were also interviewed in Mexico.

In Nicaragua Violeta Chamorro invited the group to her home for a reception, which turned out to be one of the highlights of the trip. We also visited her newspaper, where her daughter Cristiana had been managing editor since the reopening the previous October. She had an inexperienced, skeletal staff and significant production issues. Upon my return to Kansas, I helped arrange for a seminar on reporting for her staff. I forwarded a request to Apple Computer for assistance. In March at the IAPA meeting in the Dominican Republic, I hand delivered surge protectors to Violeta to address one of their principal concerns—the frequent power outages in Managua. At the time surge protectors were not in common use.

Unfortunately, within weeks of our visit the Sandinistas launched vicious attacks on Violeta and *La Prensa,* implicating her personally with television spots every half hour showing the deaths of children followed by a scene of her meeting at *La Prensa* with Jeanne Kirkpatrick, U.S. ambassador to the United Nations. She was accused of "crimes of war" and being a CIA agent. She also was subject to indecent telephone harassments and anonymous letters. The IAPA, of course, condemned these attacks at its March meeting and, fortunately, they stopped after the ceasefire was reached with the Contras at Sapoa on March 26, 1988.

In Costa Rica our group of visiting journalists interviewed Oscar Arias at his home and presented him an invitation to speak at ASNE's April convention in Washington, which he eventually accepted. I introduced him at the convention. I had read a book about his presidential campaign by Guido Fernandez, my old friend who was now Costa Rica's ambassador to Washington and who had been Arias' campaign manager, which provided me interesting details for the introduction to the American editors. In his address President Arias reported that the peace plan was "in good health." He called on the editors to support the peace effort and to give as much attention to the agreements among Central Americans as to their conflicts.

Young Pedro Joaquín Chamorro, now a Contra leader, organized at my request a session for us while we were in Costa Rica with several of the Contra commanders including himself.

In compliance with the peace plan, the Sandinistas scheduled presidential elections for February 25, 1990, and after some hesitation Violeta Chamorro agreed to stand as the candidate for a united opposition to Daniel Ortega. Virtually everyone believed he would win. With a view to the democratic opening that was required, I saw an opportunity: As president-elect of IAPA I managed to persuade the membership, despite considerable opposition, that a meeting in Managua a week after the election might push the Sandinistas toward maintaining the opening, however limited, enjoyed by the press in the campaign.

I went to Managua in July to investigate that possibility and was delighted a few weeks after my return to receive a letter from the secretary general of the ministry of foreign affairs, Alejandro Bendaña, confirming that Nicaragua would welcome the IAPA meeting in March and outlining procedures for obtaining visas. I had met with him seeking approval. I also met with the editors of *La Prensa* and Xavier Chamorro's pro-Sandinista *El Nuevo Diario*, which ran a front-page story on my visit. In his letter Bendaña also commented on an op-ed I had written for *The Wall Street Journal* after my trip pointing out the restrictions in a new media law.

I did not know at the time that Bendaña was married to the daughter from an earlier marriage of Daniel Ortega's common-law wife, the radical poet and former Pedro Chamorro secretary Rosario Murillo. The Ortegas had seven children of their own. In 1998 Bendaña's wife publicly accused Ortega of sexually molesting her as an adolescent—something that had long been suspected by Sandinista Party loyalists. Bendaña, a one-time Harvard lecturer and widely published left-wing author, issued an open letter to the press begging his wife's forgiveness "for not doing enough to stop Daniel Ortega in his aggression against you" and for "having participated in the creation of an idol" powerful enough to get away with it. "I realize now," he told *Time* magazine, "that I subordinated my conscience to the Sandinista cause."

Bendaña and his wife soon separated. She later filed a lawsuit against Ortega and has pursued the case for a decade all the way to the Inter American Human Rights Court. The issue has been a constant headache in Ortega's subsequent political career. Curiously and despite being a saga of sex, political fealty and conflicting family ties, the issue has not undermined his ambitions in Nicaragua, with its legacy of machismo.

In mid-January 1990 as IAPA president I led a delegation to Managua to examine treatment of the independent press in the electoral campaign. Cristiana Chamorro and her husband, Antonio Lacayo, served as our hosts, as they had for my July visit. By January Antonio had become Violeta's campaign manager and subsequently would be Minister of the Presidency in her government. The environment in January was heavily biased in Ortega's favor. His banners were everywhere and he had a monopoly on television access. Nearly all the polls said he would win easily. However, when we attended a mass on the 12th anniversary of Pedro Joaquin's assassination, we saw the quiet resolve of the opposition.

The situation became even dicier toward the end. Ten days before the election President Ortega declared that if the Sandinistas were to win, the government would confiscate opposition property including *La Prensa*. "I anticipate if we win we are going to bring them to account and they can be without the newspaper, and we will convert Mrs. Chamorro's house to a child development center," he told a Sandinista gathering.

After Violeta's victory, it became obvious that voters, fearing retribution, had not been honest with pollsters. The IAPA meeting a week later in Managua was a resounding success and celebration. Violeta, now 60 years old, attended several of the events and was as warm as ever with her long-time friends. As IAPA president, I had the privilege of introducing both her and President Ortega for their formal remarks. Violeta also invited the entire meeting to her home for a reception.

In introducing President Ortega for his keynote address just a week after he had lost the election, I decided to speak directly to the question of his government's willingness to turn over power. There was much speculation that the Sandinistas would not do so despite the fact Ortega had accepted the defeat as a result of marathon negotiations led by former President Jimmy Carter. I saluted him as a democrat for accepting the results and noted that by respecting democracy he and his party might return to power in the future, which they eventually did 16 years later. To the delight of the IAPA audience, he pledged to repeal the repressive press law.[1]

The meeting was held at Managua's best hotel, the Inter-Continental.

1. The IAPA meeting received significant coverage in the U.S. press. *The New York Times* used a Reuters photo of me talking the President Ortega before his keynote. Other photos of me with Violeta, the newly elected president, appeared around the hemisphere.

Karen and I enjoyed the excitement of staying in the presidential suite which just a week earlier had been occupied by President and Mrs. Carter while he monitored the election. Three weeks later I returned to Managua again to represent the IAPA at Violeta's inauguration. She invited me to a buffet at her home the night before, and upon arriving I learned that heavy negotiations were underway in a separate room regarding the role of the Sandinistas in the new government. Violeta, Antonio Lacayo and their advisors accepted a compromise that let Violeta and her team control the government but left Daniel Ortega's brother Humberto as defense minister.

In April 1992 Violeta came to Manhattan, Kan., at my request to deliver a Landon Lecture at Kansas State University. Her visit was part of a trip that included a speech to the American Society of Newspaper Editors, also at my invitation, and a visit to Baltimore, where her gravely ill grandchild, daughter Claudia's son, was being treated. In her lecture, "Changing the State of History in Nicaragua," she spoke of her policies of dialogue, conversation and reconciliation. She said the two "plagues" affecting the Nicaraguan people—war and hyperinflation—were now history as a result of her election and policies. Her address at ASNE in Washington was similar. I gave her a lengthy introduction, as is customary for major addresses there, by putting her election in the context of the long-held conventional wisdom that Marxist regimes, once entrenched, wouldn't give up power, even at the polls. I then reviewed her record of accomplishment along with her personal history.

Later during Violeta's six-year presidential term I participated in an IAPA mission to Central America to secure signatures by heads of state on the Declaration of Chapultepec, the IAPA's Magna Carta of press freedom. As always, she was extremely warm and in the formal ceremony recognized my past role in helping her and her newspaper. She also spoke at an IAPA March meeting in Costa Rica in the last year of her presidency.

At the time of Violeta's election, a Nicaraguan graduate student at Kansas State University, a pro-Sandinista, wrote an op-ed piece for *The Manhattan Mercury* in which he expressed a view with which I agreed: "I do not doubt Doña Violeta's sincere love for Nicaragua. In fact, I believe that it was this love, the love of a mother who wants to stop the fighting of her children, that led to the run for president in the first place." The Chamorro family was a microcosm of Nicaragua's national agony, and she brought harmony to the family and her country—at least for a while.

Later, in her autobiography co-written in 1996 with my friend Guido Fernandez, she explained that she declared all political discussion among her children off-limits at her home, which enabled the family to remain reasonably close despite ideological differences. "When I was elected president," she wrote, "after the country had been polarized by years of political extremism, I remembered the lessons I had learned in those days of family strife. Tolerance, reconciliation, and the right tactical approach are the three premises on which to build peace."

I would see Violeta several times later and on many occasions spend time at various journalism events with her children, especially Cristiana and Carlos Fernando. After Violeta's defeat of Daniel Ortega, Carlos Fernando worked to convert *Barricada*, the Sandinista daily, into a more traditional opposition newspaper, even on occasion criticizing Ortega and his supporters. Undoubtedly as a result, in 1994 he was forced out by former Sandinista Interior Minister Tomás Borge.

Subsequently, Carlos Fernando emerged as one of the country's most respected independent journalists on both television and in print. As Daniel Ortega consolidated his power two years after his 2006 election to a second presidency, a U.S. human rights leader writing in *The New York Review of Books* summed up Carlos Fernando's role in terms reminiscent of descriptions of his father three decades earlier: "Chamorro's supporters in Nicaragua and throughout Latin America believe that he is the only figure left in the country with the moral authority, the credibility and the journalism skills to hold Ortega to account."

The story of Nicaraguan journalism and the Chamorros—and Nicaragua's agony—continues.

12. Mexico
Young and Bold

A little-remembered but important event in the gestation of a functioning democracy in Mexico occurred at a 1971 fair in Houston, Texas. A tragic fall high from a carnival ride there claimed the life of Elba Valeria González, the mother of Alejandro Junco de la Vega, the renowned Mexican publisher. She was on the ride with her husband, Rodolfo Junco de la Vega Gómez, who could do nothing to save her. Rumors swirled, perhaps fanned by rivals among company stockholders, suggesting maybe it wasn't an accident and perhaps even premeditated. Alejandro's father was paid $900,000 by an insurance company, which determined, at least legally, it had been an accident.

Within a short time Rodolfo brought to a stockholders' meeting a woman suspected of being his lover and announced his plans to marry her. At the time he was sole administrator of *El Norte*, one of the company's two dailies in Monterrey. This angered Rodolfo's parents, who had built the dailies and controlled the family stock, and they *ipso facto* fired him from *El Norte*. Alejandro's father immediately moved to Texas with his intended wife and was joined by his youngest son. Alejandro and his older brother Rodolfo, who both worked for the newspapers, stayed in Monterrey along with two sisters.

Risking their fortune, Alejandro's grandparents had founded first the afternoon daily *El Sol* in 1922. In 1938 they added the morning *El Norte*. In both ventures another family, the Sadas, contributed capital and eventually sought influence that led to tensions and litigation not resolved until 1973—after the events precipitating the dismissal of Alejandro's father from the company. Alejandro's grandmother would not forgive her son for what she considered the shameless act of immediately marrying "the other woman," and when the family finally had full control in 1973, the grandparents decided to turn over to Alejandro and Rodolfo both the management and inheritance of the newspapers, bypassing their father. Alejandro was then 24 years old, Rodolfo 25. Later Rodolfo sold a part to Alejandro giving his younger brother 75 percent of the stock and the positions of president and general manager.

At the time Mexican journalism generally was both corrupt and subordinate to the government, a lap-dog press. It was part of what Nobel winner Mario Vargas Llosa called "the perfect dictatorship." It was dull, wholly pro-government and pliable. The government party, the PRI (Partido Revolucionario Institucional) stayed in power through a blend of patronage and iron-fisted rule. Its routine included repression, corruption, lying, impunity and fraud. Journalists did not make waves but made out. Had Alejandro's mother not died in that tragic accident, Mexican print journalism might still be that way. Alejandro might not have led the way to today's thriving, if somewhat flawed, democracy.

"Not all of Mexico's newspapers were complicit partners with the government," according to former Associated Press (and PBS) Mexico correspondent and now American University professor Rick Rockwell (2002): "For decades, a small but influential group of publications has bucked the trend and ushered in a different ethical standard for journalism. Many observers point to Alejandro Junco de la Vega and his newspaper group as leading the 'Mavericks,' as they were called."

In the democratic opening, the role of the media is hard to overstate. "Much of what might be called the political liberalization in the broader sense was actually the product of changes in Mexico's mass media," writes Chappell Lawson, an MIT professor in his 2002 book on the subject. "The rebirth of civil society, the erosion of regime legitimacy, and opposition victory at the polls were all deeply influenced by changes in media coverage during the 1980s and 1990s." Lawson calls the news media the "locomotive of change."

Just a year after graduating in 1969 from the University of Texas with a bachelor of journalism degree, Alejandro Junco began to play his role in those changes. In 1970, with his grandsons back at the newspapers, their grandfather, Rodolfo Junco de la Vega Voigt, created a training program with Alejandro and Rodolfo as instructors. The idea was to bring young "untainted" talent into journalism. The six-week program had a heavy emphasis on news values but also offered training in writing leads, story organization, interviewing techniques and editing skills. There was a stringent code of standards.

When Alejandro took over as publisher of *El Norte* in 1973, he hired one of his former University of Texas journalism professors, Mary Gardner, to do the training. "She was a demanding teacher," Alejandro said recently. "She would question our writing and our journalistic practices, and she would challenge us vigorously. If she saw us falling short, she would let us know in no uncertain terms."

Mary Gardiner was also active in the Inter American Press Association, where I came to know and admire her. In 1967 the University of Texas Press published her history of IAPA: *The Inter American Press Association: Its Fight for Freedom of the Press, 1926–1960.* Her affection for IAPA undoubtedly influenced Alejandro in his early years to take an active role in IAPA, where I worked closely with him. He served as IAPA president in 1992–93.

With Mary Gardner guiding the way, Alejandro prohibited his reporters from accepting kickbacks or favors from sources or, as was a common practice, selling advertising to officials they were covering. He also initiated other changes including better pay for reporters and editors to reduce the temptations of graft. In the early years he brought university graduates from fields other than journalism into the program and trained them to be journalists. Later, as university training in Mexico improved, he included journalism graduates. The program was overseen by a director of training with a master's degree from Harvard in business administration.

Alejandro said of the school, "The significance of the experiment is that it formed a number of Mexican journalists. Over the years, we brought people to our model of journalism."

The results have been remarkable. His initiative changed the face of Mexican journalism. Alejandro's top editor once explained, "We sell credibility. In this country, that is something that is very scarce." Other important newspapers followed Alejandro's lead and Mexican journalism grew in credibility, but not before Alejandro had seen his original staff of 17 reporters grow into a fleet of more than 1,000 working at his seven dailies including important newspapers in Mexico's three largest cities. Of particular importance was his founding in 1993 of *Reforma* in Mexico City. "The newspaper immediately became a change leader, and analysts cite its opening as a watershed event in Mexico City journalism," Sallie Hughes, a journalism professor at the University of Miami, wrote in her 2006 book, *Newsroom in Conflict: Journalism and the Democratization of Mexico.* "It changed the rules of Mexican journalism," concludes Chappell Lawson in his 2002 book.

Alejandro may have explained the new rules best when he said to Lawson in an interview, "In this business we have only one god, the reader, and he demands regular worship." Earlier, in speaking with Hughes for her book, he commented about starting the training program, "At the time, *El Norte* had a lot of shortcomings, but it was known for being outspoken. We had more maneuvering room in the provinces. A lot of people came because it was one of the few newspapers that told things as they were. People came and said they wanted to work there to exercise their freedom of expression. We told them that 'Rather than work for a newspaper so you can exercise your freedom of expression, we're going to teach you something more important. You are going to be a depository of the reader's right to know and that is a right superior to your personal freedom of expression.' We started to shift the paradigm of what freedom of expression is and is used for."

Alejandro's success did not come overnight or without risk. A year after his taking over in Monterrey, *El Norte*'s newsprint supply was cut 83 percent when Mexican President Luis Echeverría was angered by its reporting and editorials. This was when I first got to know Alejandro as he turned to IAPA for support. It was a time when the Mexican government's monopoly of newsprint production and importation let it turn on and off supply to punish enemies or reward friends. To friends it even subsidized newsprint through generous terms.

Alejandro told IAPA at the time that there were days he did not have enough newsprint for the next morning's edition unless paper arrived from the government. He was kept on a tight rope. He had to cut *El Norte* to 12 pages. Eventually he was able to supplement his supply with imported newsprint, but *El Norte*'s editorial posture, although retaining its reputation for independent coverage, softened somewhat for nearly a decade after this trial and a similar one in 1979. Other pressures continued. The government at one point even founded a daily in Monterrey to compete with *El Norte*.

In the fall of 1981 Alejandro felt forced to move his family to Texas for a year after police agents of the José López Portillo government visited his children's school, took pictures and determined their routine. He moved them back to Monterrey as Lopez Portillo turned the presidency over to Miguel de la Madrid.

While *El Norte's* aggressive posture softened somewhat in this period, its finances thrived. Alejandro changed the paper's content and format in an effort to appeal to Monterrey's growing middle-class by introducing sections on fashion, food, automobiles, real estate and suburban life. He added a Sunday supplement. The contrast with the established Mexican approach of drab, complex display and coverage focused on politics and sports produced dramatic results. Sales of *El Norte* soared to levels normally seen only in the developed world. By 1983 *El Norte* had a news staff of 400 and was shifting to computerized production.

My wife Karen and I visited Alejandro and his wife Rosa Laura in Monterrey that year and witnessed these dramatic changes. *El Norte*'s format seemed avant-garde even for a modern U.S. daily. It was still produced in the facility built by Alejandro's grandfather, who died that year, but it was a bustling place with state-of-the-art technology. At the time he was even initiating an electronic library, which eventually would be expanded into a nationwide electronic information system and ultimately the largest Internet content provider in Latin America.

Karen and I had grown close to the Juncos over the years as part of the younger crowd at IAPA meetings. Alejandro and I often enjoyed good contests on a tennis court with each of us winning about the same number of games. At the time of our visit to Monterrey the Juncos had recently moved into a beautiful new home next to Rosa Laura's mother's house. We even played a match on his new tennis court and enjoyed a marvelous formal dinner with them, our two boys and the Junco's son, "Ale"—later known also as Alejandro. Another evening we were introduced to a meal of Monterrey-style goat, which Karen and I still seek out when we can find it. Alejandro's brother, Rodolfo, took us to a bullfight, which our boys found fascinating. The matadors were young and had trouble with the kill, but it was a singular spectacle.

Alejandro in those days suffered regularly from migraine headaches. I put him in touch with a program at the Menninger Clinic in Kansas that used bio-feedback to help patients control migraines. He was very appreciative and soon learned that his problem was lactose related. He quit consuming milk products and brought his condition under control.

When I became president of IAPA in 1989, Alejandro and *El Norte* served as hosts for the society's general assembly in Monterrey. Rosa Laura organized elaborate social events as a project for her master's degree. The highlight of the meeting was the participation of the new Mexican president, Carlos Salinas, who was from Alejandro's home state of Nuevo León. The Juncos organized a fabulous dinner with the president for a few of us in their home. And, most importantly, at Alejandro's urging, President Salinas announced plans to privatize PIPSA, the government newsprint monopoly. Mexico would begin unrestricted importation of newsprint in concert with Mexico's economic opening to the world. This was a dramatic event and the culmination of years of struggle between IAPA and the Mexican government.

"I await the response of publishers and journalists on this (PIPSA's) destiny," Salinas told the IAPA general assembly. Interestingly, while IAPA and press organizations around the world hailed his move, the Mexican press was not unanimous in approval. Many publishers depended on the credits and discounts they received for favorable treatment of the government, and they feared losing these financial advantages. In some cases they could not survive without the government support in this and other forms.

At the closing banquet where I gave my inaugural address, I recall a guest of Alejandro was the president's brother, Raúl, whom Alejandro introduced to me. Raúl Salinas would later be a quiet beneficiary of the president's other major gesture toward media reform—the sale of two state-owned television channels. He also would benefit from the privatization by the Salinas government of roughly 60 percent of the 600 firms owned by the state when his brother took office. Raúl's legendary corruption played a role in the appetite the Mexican public developed thereafter for political reform. He later spent ten years in prison accused of the murder of a brother-in-law, but was acquitted in 2005.

When Alejandro became IAPA president three years later, I joined him on missions on behalf of the press including a mission in Mexico. We met in Mexico City, where he was deeply into planning for his new capital-city daily, *Reforma*. I shall never forget riding along the city's major thoroughfare, Paseo de la Reforma, with Alejandro and his top editor. They asked me to suggest possible names for their projected daily. I threw out "Verdad" (Truth), "Integridad" (Integrity) and several other ideas. Even as we drove past the famous Angel of Independence statue—the symbol of the boulevard—they said nothing. Only later did I realize they had already settled on a name (Reforma) and were just having fun with me.

The mission itself was interesting. We flew on Alejandro's jet to Cancún, where we investigated the death of an outspoken journalist who had claimed harassment by local authorities, although we could not corroborate his accusations. We also investigated a labor dispute in Chihuahua and the death of an editor in Juárez. In that border city I could hardly restrain myself with the police investigators we interviewed when I saw their Rolex watches and gold chains. Alejandro and I drafted the mission's report over dinner at one of Mexico City's best restaurants, Hacienda de los Morales. We had planned also to fly to Chiapas, where the local newspaper was threatened and armed rebellion would break out within a year, but Alejandro decided against going there. I have since come to believe he thought it too risky.

The first issue of *Reforma* appeared on November 20, 1993, which marked the anniversary of the start of the Mexican Revolution. Many would agree with Chappell Lawson, "It was destined to be Mexico's finest and most influential newspaper." Originally Alejandro had hoped to partner with the owners of *The Wall Street Journal* but ultimately failed and had to raise the required $50 million through his own company earnings and bank loans. A key to convincing him to undertake such a costly venture was President Salinas' decision to privatize PIPSA, the newsprint monopoly, as well as the president's other reforms opening the economy.

The risk was apparent. At the beginning of the Salinas presidency in 1988, a dynamic young businessman with excellent connections, Javier Moreno Valle, decided to launch *El Independiente*, a new national daily, by assembling a team of honest journalists. With aspirations similar to Alejandro's, he thought he had the blessing of the Salinas team and spent nearly $1 million planning and training. But sometime before the launch, according to journalists involved, he was told his other businesses would suffer if he insisted in upsetting the journalistic waters. He abandoned the effort.

Once Alejandro launched *Reforma* near the end of Salina's six-year term, his most serious challenge came from the pro-government Union of Newspaper Vendors, which enjoyed a monopoly on newspaper distribution in Mexico City. The union refused to distribute *Reforma*. Although perhaps he had no alternative, Alejandro's gutsy decision was to send his reporters and executives into the streets to sell the daily. He joined them himself and garnered international attention as "the publisher newsboy" peddling his daily on the Mexico City streets. In only a month's time they established a distribution system that managed to reach readers several hours before other dailies relying on the union.

Unfortunately, the Inter American Press Association did not come to Alejandro's aid in that crisis. Its president at the time, my good friend Raúl Krailselburd, apparently viewed the situation as a business issue rather than a challenge to press freedom. He perhaps also was reflecting on the situation in his own Argentina, where newspapers were distributed by a similar monopoly union. In any case, at the very time of the crisis Raúl led a mission to Mexico following up Alejandro's previous mission, but he ignored the issue. He didn't even contact Alejandro. The result was that Alejandro quit active participation in IAPA. He continued financial support but never attended another major IAPA semi-annual meeting.

Just a year after *Reforma*'s founding came a wrenching economic crisis in Mexico at the end of Salinas' term that required Alejandro's astute management to navigate. He managed to reschedule his debt, lock in long-term advertising, cut the staff 12 percent, trim the paper's width by 30 percent and double the street price. His new newspaper survived.

Before the distribution crisis, in March of 1994, just after Alejandro launched *Reforma* and before its headquarters was completely finished, he played a central role in organizing the conference that wrote the Declaration of Chapultepec, which I've described elsewhere as the Magna Carta of press freedom for the Americas. Not only did he secure the famous Chapultepec Castle as the site for the conference, he managed to deliver as participants several of Mexico's most prominent intellectuals, including Nobel winner Octavio Paz and acclaimed historian Enrique Krause.

As the years passed, Alejandro's newspapers focused coverage on bringing honesty and transparency to Mexico. From the beginning he put resources into exposing electoral fraud and pushed for opening up government. In the July 2000 election that saw Vicente Fox defeat the PRI, Alejandro's group devoted 100 reporters to election-day coverage, especially to monitor possible fraud. Another 18 reporters tracked radio and television coverage throughout the campaign. Its polling operation was viewed as one of the most reliable.

Immediately after Fox's victory as the first non-PRI president in 71 years, I wrote Alejandro a note saying I believed his efforts over time had been essential to the change in his country. I received a letter of response from him dated July 14, 2000. He wrote:

Dear Edward:

Thank you for remembering your Mexican friends at this very special time.

We are indeed looking forward to a new era and hopefully accomplishing some additional worthwhile things like creating some disclosure and access laws.

I would like to share my plans with you in this respect. Keep me

posted on any travels that might bring you in the vicinity of Texas or
México.
   Regards,
   Alejandro

In 2002 the Mexican Congress passed and President Fox signed a free-dom-of-information law, often described as the best-designed law in the hemi-sphere. This remarkable development was the result of many contributors including the Inter American Press Association. The language itself emerged from a 2001 academic conference in Oaxaca attended by legal experts, NGOs, media owners, foundations and others. The alliance became known as the Grupo Oaxaca. IAPA organized a follow-up conference in Mexico City where I gave a presentation on the U.S. Freedom of Information Act. A memorable contribution to the campaign was Alejandro's fictional character, Juan Ciu-dadano (John Citizen). Through a Web site, *La Reforma* offered $10,000 to anyone who could find the answers to any of 10 sample questions about Pres-ident Fox's first federal budget. Among the questions were: How much does Mexico spend on government offices outside Mexico? How much is spent fighting drug traffickers? Only two questions came close to being answered.

Subsequently, a shield law allowing reporters to protect their sources from disclosure was passed in 2006.

While other media leaders played important roles in the changes in Mex-ico, especially Julio Scherer at *Proceso* magazine, without Alejandro Junco's contributions, I believe Mexico would not be the vibrant democracy it is to-day. He took advantage of the liberalization of the country's economy under presidents De la Madrid, Salinas and Zedillo. In fact, as former U.S. Ambassa-dor to Mexico Jeffrey Davidow has written, "Mexico is a textbook illustration for the argument that economic reform can generate political liberalization." Alejandro earlier on had pushed for economic reform. As it unfolded, he took advantage to produce a more aggressive journalism discrediting the authori-tarian political culture, which in turn produced additional economic and po-litical reforms.

As a result of Alejandro's success, other publishers followed his example. Many of these became active in the Inter American Press Association. In the early years they included José Santiago Healy of Hermosillo, Enrique Gómez of León and most notably Juan Francisco Ealy Ortiz, publisher of Mexico City's market leader, *El Universal.* The latter made a complete conversion in 1999 to civic, investigative journalism from its long-standing lap-dog approach. The change came not so much from democratic ideals as, initially at least, to hold its number one position. *Reforma* was making inroads on its market dominance.

The conversion of *El Universal* was real. By 2002 Ealy Ortiz' support for the access and shield laws illustrated the change. *Reforma* and *El Universal* put aside their commercial rivalry and became key players pushing for these changes. They were joined by more than 100 other publications.

Subsequently, Juan Francisco Ealy Ortiz became very active in IAPA and one of its principal benefactors. His participation grew out of his experience in 1996 as he began to move his paper toward a more independent stand. He had hired columnists known for their criticism of the PRI. The Zedillo administration sent its tax men calling and then a phalanx of riot troops to arrest him on a tax evasion charge. It apparently intended to make Juan Francisco a symbol in its desire to expose past corrupt cronyism of previous governments. Juan Francisco first fled, then turned himself in under protest. The IAPA strongly denounced the excessive use of force. The charges were eventually dropped, but Juan Francisco was struck by the fact that other Mexican publishers did not come to his aid. He determined that IAPA was his best bet for protection—viewing it as others from many countries often had in the past as a sort of insurance policy.

I came to know Juan Francisco fairly well through his participation in IAPA. At the beginning of the presidency of Felipe Calderón in early 2007 I joined him with a half dozen others for a private meeting with the new president at Los Pinos, the Mexican White House. Our purpose was to push Calderón to do something about the flagrant impunity in crimes against Mexican journalists. As a result of the meeting and other efforts, Calderón's government eventually federalized such crimes, taking investigation out of the hands of corrupt local jurisdictions.

In 2007 Juan Francisco was host for a lavish—the most impressive in my then more than 40 years—IAPA general assembly in Mexico City. He reportedly spent $600,000 putting it on.

Another IAPA leader I came to know was Rómulo O'Farrill, an icon of an earlier generation who continued to participate in and support IAPA until his death in 2006. Rómulo, who owned the Novedades newspaper chain but was most visible as a long-time major stockholder of Televisa, the Mexican television monopoly, was IAPA president in 1963. His general assembly was in Miami, and in those years the annual assemblies lasted an entire week. On Monday night November 18, 1963, the speaker was President John F. Kennedy. It was to be his last major speech. He was assassinated 72 hours later.

Rómulo introduced Kennedy, but first greeted the president at the Miami airport and then met with him in his hotel suite. "A curious thing," he wrote later about the occasion, "was that dress for the dinner was business suit, but President Kennedy wore a tuxedo—in contrast to everybody else."

As is still customary when a major speaker addresses IAPA, a small group of leaders met with the president in a reception before the formal address. The speech focused on the Alliance for Progress. Rómulo later reflected that in the two hours he spent with the president they chatted on a wide range of subjects and, apparently as a result, President Kennedy invited Rómulo and his wife Hilda to spend a weekend at Hyannis Port. That visit, of course, did not take place.

The 1963 general assembly was at lunch that Friday when, as Rómulo remembered, "we received the dramatic and dreadful news of President Kennedy's assassination, which cast a pall over the proceedings. The reactions were of surprise, shock and dismay at the magnitude of the tragedy. At the assembly's final session, an emotional posthumous tribute was paid to the memory of this great man. We all wore black in mourning and our Venezuelan colleague Monsignor Bellín led us in prayer for the departed."

Rómulo was already a radio and newspaper entrepreneur in 1949 when, through his connections to then President Miguel Alemán, he received the first commercial television license in Mexico. Also receiving early license concessions were Aleman's son and, in 1951, Emilio Azcárraga. According to a newspaper account, by 1955 neither Rómulo nor Aleman's son was making money and Azcárraga was asked by then President Adolfo Ruiz-Cortines to form a partnership with the other two, who were politically affiliated with him. The merger took place. Nineteen years later they merged with the only other large competing network (in Monterrey) to form Televisa. Until 1993 Televisa held a virtual lock on Mexican television and even today continues to dominate. Throughout these years it enjoyed a cozy relationship with the government. In the 1970s and 1980s, for example, it agreed to provide the government with 12.5 percent of all airtime in lieu of paying taxes.

In 1990 Azcárraga founded *National,* a national sports daily in the United States. The paper folded in 1991 after losing $100 million. When faced with the heavy loses, he declared *National* a Televisa venture. Reportedly, Rómulo in response told Azcárraga to buy him out or be bought out by a group of investors aligned with Rómulo. For Rómulo's third of the company, Azcárraga turned over to Rómulo a French restaurant, three houses in Cancún, four automobile dealerships, a plane, a yacht and a rumored $350 million.

With assistance from my influential Mexican friends and their key executives, I was privileged to meet and spend time with every Mexican president from Miguel de la Madrid forward. With the help of Rómulo and his staff I led a group of U.S. editors who interviewed President De la Madrid in 1988. Alejandro Junco arranged several encounters with President Carlos Salinas, and in 1995 Alejandro was key to my securing President Ernesto Zedillo as a speaker at the annual convention in Dallas of the American Society of Newspaper Editors. Also appearing at that convention were the presidents of the two other partners in launching the North American Free Trade Agreement: Bill Clinton and Jean Chretien, the Canadian prime minister whom I secured for the program through an IAPA Canadian colleague.

Shortly after his presidency Zedillo came to Manhattan, Kansas, at my request in 2001 to deliver a Landon Lecture at Kansas State University. I was also successful with the help of Juan Francisco's staff in successfully inviting Vicente Fox to Kansas for a Landon Lecture in 2008.

Late in 2006 an envelope arrived at my office with the return address: Cria Cuervos (Raise Ravens), San Antonio, Texas. It contained a letter and video from 84-year-old Rodolfo Junco de la Vega Gómez denouncing his two sons, Alejandro and Rodolfo. He claimed they illegally "snatched" his stock in the company and he was going public at his late age so later generations will not "continue living this trickery." He said the stock was still his and he planned to bequeath it to a journalism school. He sent the same letter and video to all members of the executive committee of the Inter American Press Association.

At the same time he went on Telvisión Azteca with these allegations and set up the web site criacuervos.info. Among other allegations, he claimed his sons had committed acts of violence including sacking his residence and even an assassination plot.

At least one commentator in México attributed the attacks to the work of Ricardo Salinas Pliego, the owner of Televisión Azteca. Alejandro's publications had undertaken a campaign promoting the licensing of an additional television network to compete with Televisión Azteca and Televisa. In any case, the attack had the appearance of an act of revenge after many years of silence. It certainly put Alejandro in an uncomfortable position and opened him to attacks by those who might want to curb his aggressive journalism.

Also, despite remarkable economic growth in Mexico spawned by the transparency and openness pushed by Alejandro, the country today is experiencing extremely serious problems. Violence is rampant in many parts including Alejandro's hometown of Monterrey. For the several years he had to move his family to Austin, Texas, and commuted during the week to his various offices in Mexico. Just as I am writing this (July 2012) comes a report of three attacks within the last month against *El Norte*. The newspaper has been targeted by gunfire and grenades six times the past two years. In the most recent attack three masked men entered a suburban office, subdued a guard, and set the building on fire after drenching the reception with gasoline. The men fled in a waiting caravan of vehicles. Seconds later a police car showed up but didn't give chase.

A few days earlier two of the newspaper's other offices in Monterrey were attacked with grenades and automatic-weapons fire. The attacks followed by one day publication of an investigation into massive corruption in the state public transportation department.

What is certain is that Mexican journalism—and Mexico—are not what they were before Alejandro's rise. Back then, to cite one illustrative example mentioned by Sallie Hughes in her book, a reporter asked President Miguel de la Madrid at his first press conference in 1982 the following:

> Today, as you grant us the first press conference of your government, we wish to thank you for granting it to us and offer you testimony of our support for your work. We have been witnesses to your untiring labor and we have tried to inform our readers, listeners, and viewers of your work and of the necessity of supporting it. Do you wish, Mr. President, to direct a message to the people of Mexico . . . and to give us the answer to some question in particular that you would have wished us to ask?

Lapdogs don't bite.

13. Guatemala
Risks and Rewards

Among the most courageous newspaper publishers I know personally in today's complex world is José Rubén Zamora. His daily is *elPeriodico* in Guatemala City, and he sees his role as the agent of change for eliminating the corruption of his country. Or, as he puts it, "Journalism guards the door to the Apocalypse."

As a result, he has spent the last three decades flirting with his own death and the fragmentation of his family.

I had been to Guatemala on 10 separate occasions, many including lending support for José Rubén, who for many years had been the most innovative and aggressive editor in the country. He was almost always under pressure. When he was editor of Siglo XXI (21st century), which he founded, a coup occurred and censorship imposed. His immediate step was to publish the next morning under the name Siglo XIV (14th century).

José Rubén sees Guatemala, a nominal democracy that elects presidents every four years and does not permit re-election, as a "klepto-dictatorship that is born and dies every four years and co-governs with crime."

His education as an engineer took him into business originally, but when his country emerged from military rule in the 1980s he saw the need for a bold newspaper willing to investigate and print views from all sides if democracy was to take root. Perhaps this was in his genes. His grandfather, who had served as vice president of the country, had founded a daily with similar objectives aimed at change and building a nation in 1920.

On our 2014 mission to Guatemala, the threats to José Rubén didn't seem as deadly, although as my colleagues and I were holding a press conference to offer our assessment, an unknown assailant fired gunshots at the home of José Rubén's attorney. In view of the fact that among the issues were lawsuits filed by the country's president and vice president against José Rubén—lawsuits defended by his attorney—it was difficult to see that incident as isolated.

As a five-member delegation of the IAPA, we had held a joint two-hour meeting with President Otto Pérez Molina and Vice President Roxana Baldetti. They said they had brought criminal charges against José Rubén because he authored stories and columns alleging corruption generally and in particular lavish properties owned by the vice president. She had come from a modest background and had limited earnings as a congresswoman and then vice president. They denied the corruption and were especially irked by the exposés and mention of their children. The vice president said she made her money as owner of a beauty salon.

Our concerns were the lawsuits as well as an advertising boycott and tax audit of the newspaper that had been ordered. We had success in that the criminal complaints were dropped after we announced we would be coming. We pointed out the new constitution prohibited criminal charges in such circumstances. But we were told the suits were being re-filed with an Honor Tribunal which dealt with freedom of expression and does not carry criminal sanctions.

President Perez Molina claimed the newspaper was not getting government advertising because it had a circulation of only 2,000 copies—less than a tenth of the true distribution.

In 2015 prosecutors presented evidence of President Perez' involvement in a corruption ring and the Congress voted unanimously to strip his immunity. He resigned the next day. In 2017 he was ordered to stand trial on charges related to bribes channeled to officials helping businesses evade customs duties. At this writing, he has remained in custody since 2015.

Also in 2015 Vice President Balteddi resigned amid the corruption scandal. In 2018 she was sentenced to 15 years in prison and faced drug trafficking charges in the United States.

José Rubén's problems at the time of our 2014 mission seemed almost minor compared to those he'd experienced earlier.

In 1995 his car was forced off the road and he was threatened with death by two people linked to the Guatemalan military after the paper published allegations that the military had links to organized crime.

Two grenades were thrown at his car in 1996 although he was unhurt. Shortly after that latter incident, he was forced to leave the paper by the board of directors.

Within months he persuaded 125 investors who supported his stand on the role of the press to back him in a new daily, *elPeriodico*. Among them was the yet-to-be president, Otto Peréz Molina. José Rubén's reporting in the new daily again was to expose corruption, drug trafficking and human rights violations.

In 2003 during the presidency of Alfonso Portillo, José Rubén and his family were taken hostage in their home for nearly three hours. His children were beaten and he was stripped and forced to kneel in front of them at gunpoint. One gang member told him, "If you value your children stop bothering the people above. I don't know who you've annoyed high up the ladder, but we have orders that someone up high despises you. Whatever you do, do not report this."

He wrote later that the first 40 minutes he believed they were all going to die. The next hour-and-a-half he believed he was the one who would die. The last 40 minutes he was sure his wife and son would be kidnapped.

José Rubén today is confident President Portillo was behind the attack, but Portillo unexpectedly visited him shortly after and blamed the Army. Portillo also gave him access to the government's photographic database. *elPeriodico* published photos of the 12 attackers, including a senior member of Portillo's staff, an employee of the Attorney General and a counter-intelligence specialist. Eventually, one member of the military was sentenced to 16 years imprisonment.

President Portillo eventually fled to Mexico and was extradited to the United States, where he was accused of laundering $70 million of Guatemala's money through U.S. banks. He was convicted and served a year in the federal prison in Colorado, then released to return to Guatemala.

In 2008 Jose Ruben was kidnapped and beaten after enjoying a cocktail with his cousin. He was drugged and left unconscious and nearly naked in a garbage dump some 26 miles outside Guatemala City. He nearly died but was noticed by a woman who walked three miles to get help. His wife and children believed he had been killed.

I first visited Guatemala in 1966 with my wife Karen on our return trip from our Fulbright year in Ecuador. We were enamored at the time by similarities with Ecuador, especially the predominance of indigenous Guatemalans in their traditional dress. As a result Guatemala seemed a favorite venue for a return.

Unfortunately, I didn't return until 1988 when I led a fact-finding trip to war-torn Central America for members of the American Society of Newspaper Editors. At the time our focus was primarily on Nicaragua and El Salvador.

On our two-night stay we encountered a very interesting situation. We interviewed President Vinicio Cerezo, the first democratically elected president in two decades, at the presidential residence. The last democratic election had taken place just after Karen and I had visited Guatemala City after our Ecuador year. That president was overthrown by the military after a short term.

In the interim more than 100,000 Guatemalans were killed and another 36,000 "disappeared." In the 1970s and early 1980s somewhere between 40 and 100 journalists lost their lives, depending on how you define a journalist.

Cerezo, who had survived three assassination attempts before becoming president, told us he now had about 50 percent of the power for a normal democratically-elected president. The balance was held by the army and exercised mostly by Gen. Héctor Alejandro Gramajo, the secretary of defense. Gramajo confirmed this when we met with him.

Others, including Jorge Serrano Elías, an evangelical political leader and member of the National Reconciliation Commission, and Nineth Montenegro, the leading human rights advocate, also agreed. Serrano would become president of Guatemala in 1991.

We also met with civic leaders and media, but on this visit did not weigh in on media struggles. Those would be the focus of my second visit that year. During an attempted coup that May by a small group of army officers, President Cerezo had ordered the closure of a television station whose news program contained apparent backing for the insurgents. The closure was reversed by a court, but the offending program was dropped by the station.

The newscaster, Mario David García, who had earlier been an unsuccessful candidate for president and had displayed the insurgents' red bandana on the broadcast, brought his case that October to the IAPA General Assembly in Salt Lake City. He denounced the government for the loss of his program as well as harassment of the press in other instances.

A government spokesman contested these charges at the Salt Lake assembly and shortly afterwards President Cerezo invited IAPA to send a mission to Guatemala City for an independent report.

As vice president of IAPA I joined this six-member mission headed by Costa Rican Manuel Jiménez Borbón, our president. We met with President Cerezo, who said it was the first time in Guatemalan history a court had ruled against a sitting president and the president followed the ruling. "Earlier presidents would have just killed him (the broadcaster)," he said, "or at least blown up the station."

We also investigated other issues, including a fire-bomb attack in June that had eliminated *La Epoca*, a new weekly.

Our mission condemned the television closure but issued a statement saying journalists should not hide behind their local equivalent of the First Amendment to foment a coup. "It is trite but true," we concluded, "that democracy cannot exist without a free press and that a free press cannot exist without democracy."

Early in 1990 I travelled as IAPA president to Guatemala City with Francisco ("Pacho") Santos, later vice president of Colombia and subsequently that country's ambassador to the U.S. We had also included a visit to Panama to assess press issues in the taking down there of strong-man Manuel Noriega. Pacho was then managing editor of Bogota's *El Tiempo*, and we wanted to confront Guatemala's Defense Minister Gramajo.

Gramajo had recently been making threatening comments about the media. We asserted that given his country's history of violence, his comments would likely result in dead journalists. I still remember Pacho telling me after our session that I was too confrontational, that a cabinet officer, especially a general, should be shown more respect. I did get the point across and can hope lives were saved.

In January 1991 José Serrano Elías succeeded Venicio Cerezo as President of Guatemala. It was the first time in decades that a sitting president had surrendered power to an opposition victor. Serano's election was controversial because in the early 1980s he had been an advisor to the government of General Efraín Ríos Montt. The general had taken power as a result of a coup and later was convicted of genocide and crimes against humanity.

That same month Kansas' junior Senator Nancy Landon Kassebaum, a member of the U.S. Senate Foreign Relations Committee, met with my newspaper's editorial board and expressed strong concerns about Guatemala and especially Serrano. After the meeting I drafted a letter to her suggesting she consider getting behind Serrano "at least until he proves ineffective."

I explained I had met Serrano and recently spent two hours talking to him in the airport after Violeta Chamorro's inauguration in Managua, which we both attended, and had developed a high regard for him.

I told her he held an education doctorate from Stanford and later lived in exile in the United States. for several years after receiving threats. As a member of the National Reconciliation Commission he had been instrumental in initiating dialogue with the URNG, the Guatemalan guerrillas. Because of his conservative credentials, I said, Serrano might to able to accomplish things Cerezo could not in the same way Nixon was able to open up China.

In the end I was mistaken. President Serrano initially had some success in consolidating civilian control over the army, persuading the military to participate in peace talks with the UNRG and reversing the economic slide. But by late 1992 tensions including with the media had grown to the extent that the IAPA executive committee decided to send a four-member mission which I headed.

The government in December that year went so far as to declare publicly that the press was dedicated to "destabilizing the democracy" and "discrediting the State." We met in late February with the president and vice president and brought to their attention eight serious cases of harassment of the press. Both men said they lamented what had occurred in December and that they intended to improve relations with the press. Official protections would be provided for any journalist under pressure. Both men said they would participate in a June seminar about the role of the press in democracy.

I followed up with a letter to President Serrano in March asking what measures had been taken to resolve each of the eight cases, but things got worse.

On May 25th Serrano precipitated a constitutional crisis, a self-coup (*auto-golpe*) that became known as the "Serranozo." He took a page right out of the playbook of Peruvian President Alberto Fujimori, who orchestrated a similar and successful self-coup in April the previous year. Serrano suspended the constitution, dissolved Congress and the Supreme Court, imposed censorship and tried to restrict civil liberties—all in the name of fighting corruption.

Widespread protest resulted. At the forefront was José Rubén Zamoro's *Siglo Veintiuno*. International pressure also grew. The Constitutional Court ruled against the takeover and the Army enforced that decision. President Serrano resigned and fled the country for Panamá. He has never returned to Guatemala.

At the urging of our mission the IAPA held its next Mid-year in Guatemala City. A newly elected president, Human Rights Ombudsman Ramiro de León Carpio, showed renewed support for the press.

In 1997 we held a special conference in Guatemala City focusing on impunity in the assassinations of journalists. Guatemala was chosen as the venue because of so many unsolved cases there.

Historic Antigua, Guatemala, was the site of the 2004 IAPA General Assembly. Memorable speakers included Rigoberta Manchu, the indigenous Guatemalan human rights activist and 1992 Nobel Peace Prize winner, and Oscar Arias, the 1987 Nobel winner and twice president of Costa Rica. The presidents of Guatemala, Oscar Burger, and of El Salvador, Tony Saca, also spoke.

Karen and I were at all of these events. I attended alone the 2017 mid-year, also in Antigua, where I was honored by José Rubén Zamora. He was asked to give an account of the threats and encounters he and his colleagues had experienced in their country. Before he began, he paused. "I want to make a personal comment," he said. Without the support of "my dear friend Edward Seaton" and a couple of his colleagues, "I wouldn't be here to make this presentation."

His tribute to me in Antigua was among my proudest moments.

14. Panama
Upending Dictators

The tortured history of newspapers in Panamá, a country to which I have a family connection from its founding, has afforded numerous opportunities for editors and publishers to take on heroic roles. It has been my privilege to know quite well two who did so.

If fiction, these stories wouldn't be credible. The bizarre truth includes trashed newspaper plants, nearly $1 million in found cash, an unpaid electric bill covering 21 years, voodoo at Manuel Noriega's home and a decapitated corpse.

Rosario Arias de Galindo is the scion of one of the leading families on the isthmus, a family that played a key role in the 1903 revolt creating the country and later provided two of its elected presidents. "Mommy," as she is affectionately known, Rosario Arias is the daughter of the first one, Harmodio Arias Madrid.

A gifted corporate attorney educated in England and regarded as the most astute man of his time in Panama politics, Harmodio Arias was elected president in 1932 as the "candidate of the poor." His election came on the heels of a successful revolt a year earlier in which his brother Arnulfo was a leader. Harmodio Arias built a cattle and journalistic empire, acquiring ranches while he was president and *The Panama American* shortly after he completed his four-year term. He later became a founding member of the Inter American Press Association. He maintained his lucrative law practice while overseeing his media properties and died in 1962, leaving his daughter and her lawyer brother in charge.

Meanwhile, Arnulfo Arias, a medical doctor who attended Harvard as an undergraduate, served as a diplomat in Europe in the era right wing dictatorships ruled in Italy, German and Spain. Like Juan Peron of Argentina, he caught the fever of National Socialism and returned home to stand for Panama's presidency in 1940. With the aid of a news blackout of the opposition by his brother's newspapers, *El Panamá América* and *The Panama American*, Arnulfo was elected. He established a policy of neutrality in deference to the Nazis.

That policy, along with a decision to slip out of Panama without the necessary congressional consent in order to keep a secret date with his girl friend in Cuba, led to his ouster only a year into his term, which he read about in a Havana newspaper. It came with the blessings of the U.S. State Department. During his year in office, he tried to remake the government through constitutional reforms and racist laws. He also established a social security system, enhanced labor laws and instituted women's suffrage. But as was often the case throughout his political life, he put his expedient political interest ahead of the national interest. He waged an undeclared war on the press, including brother Harmodio's newspapers, despite their help in his election, and he steered the country toward censorship. He also managed to frustrate the United States in its desire to build defense bases and landing fields for the defense of the Panama Canal.

Arnulfo returned home at the end of World War II and again stood for the presidency in 1948, but lost in an election marked by allegations of fraud. The winner died of a heart attack less than a year afterward. Arnulfo then led a campaign of agitation and subversion, and in the resulting turmoil, the chief of police refused an order to crack down, which led to the new commander in chief's resignation. His constitutional successor was them sworn in, but lasted only three days after he, too, tried to push the police chief. The police chief then summoned Arnulfo Arias, who was sworn in as president. His supporters said he was the legitimate successor to the office because fraud had prevented his election a year earlier.

He might have completed the full term this time had he not made a grasp for dictatorial powers. In May 1951, he decided to declare himself dictator. He decreed censorship of all newspapers and radio, which led to his undoing. The owners of the major radio network defied his censorship decree. Arnulfo ordered the master station closed. A majority of the National Assembly then gathered secretly and voted to impeach him. Arnulfo was ordered, again by the police chief, to abdicate. He refused and a gun battle ensued resulting in casualties to both the police and the palace guard. In his white suit stained with blood, he was taken away by police and shouted: "*Volveremos!*" We shall return.

He was then impeached, tried, convicted and deprived for life of his civil rights and the right to hold public office. Panamanian politics being Panamanian politics, he was not to lose his rights forever. Ultimately, he was a major candidate in five presidential elections. Two of them he lost amidst allegations of fraud. His last successful run was a landslide victory in October, 1968, but again was short-lived and ended in a crucial event that underlies the polarization in modern Panamanian politics. Just eleven days after his election, he was overthrown by General Omar Torrijos and the Panamanian National Guard. They were supported not only by Arnulfo Arias' traditional enemies but significant factions of Panama's elite.

Wrenching change followed. The government seized control of the Arias family's newspapers, which now included not only *El Panamá América* and *The Panama American*, run by Rosario Arias, but also a new paper, *Expreso* and the tabloid *Crítica*, the most popular daily in the country, that had been started by her brother Gilberto. Much of the family, including Arnulfo and Gilberto, was forced into exile. Censorship was established throughout the country and two non-Arias newspapers also were closed. The government selected editors for all private media under decree power.

The fight for return of the Arias media properties to the family would require more than two decades. The two younger Ariases were not joined in the long fight by three other brothers, one of whom died earlier and two who had sold their stock to Rosario and Gilberto. One of those, Roberto (Tito) Arias, was undoubtedly the most famous of the siblings. Tito was married to Dame Margot Fonteyn, the world-renowned British prima ballerina. In 1959 Tito was among those who persuaded Fidel Castro to assist in an invasion of Panama from Cuba to capture the government. The unsuccessful invasion was mounted ultimately by fewer than 100 men. Dame Margot apparently purchased a yacht for the invasion from a seller in Miami, and she accompanied Tito on the yacht, flush with arms for the rebels, at the height of the invasion. She was later arrested, and Tito took asylum in the Brazilian embassy. Four years later, while running for deputy to the National Assembly on the ticket of his uncle Arnulfo's party, he was shot in an election dispute. He survived as a paraplegic.

I saw Rosario and Gilberto throughout the 1970s and 1980s as they brought their case for the return of their dailies to the meetings of the Inter American Press Association. Gilberto lived in exile until 1978. From 1984 on, as I participated in special IAPA missions to Panamá, I grew close to them, especially the effervescent Rosario. Their case was compelling but complicated. Just 11 days after the Torrijos coup, their newspapers were closed. A month later they again were publishing, but with censors and government-appointed editors. The following July, a judge opened hearings that resulted in the company, Editora Panamá América, being liquidated. Its assets were to go to a new company, Editora Renovacion S.A. (ERSA). The machinations leading to these events are not unique. A ploy later in Panama was similar, and another was nearly successful against the owners of Lima's *El Comercio* 25 years later. Others probably had occurred elsewhere earlier.

An unhappy minority stockholder had brought suit seeking a stockholders meeting and examination of the books. The judge—a supporter of the government—used the litigation to declare the company bankrupt and liquidated it, paid its debts and turned the assets over to a new company whose directors and officers included Torrijo's vice president, his brother-in-law and Manuel Antonio Noriega, then head of the intelligence service and acting commander-in-chief of the Armed Forces. At least that's what happened—officially.

In fact, the dissident stockholders had inherited their 13 percent of the stock from their father, Antonio Arias, the brother who died. They were minors and their shares were controlled by Antonio's widow, now remarried, who had apparently been kept in the dark about the financial condition of the company. Before he died in 1962, Hermodio Arias had initiated plans for a new newspaper plant with offset printing—just the third offset in Latin America—and the plans had gone forward. The company owed nearly half a million dollars to Chase Manhattan Bank, but it was satisfying the bank's terms and had no other unsatisfied creditors.

The company by-laws required a petition from a minimum of 20 percent of stock to mandate a stockholders meeting (*"asemblea general"*), but the judge let the case go forward and eventually ruled for liquidation, which had been requested at one point by the dissident stockholders' lawyer and proxy. Several months later the dissidents, apparently having realized what was happening, attempted to withdraw their petition requesting a liquidation, but the judge ruled that the liquidation had been decreed and a reversal would be "in conflict with the principle of public order."

The new company soon converted *Expreso* from tabloid to standard format and re-named it *Matutino*. The popular *Crítica* with its lead in circulation was maintained, as was *El Panamá América* until 1977, when its name was changed to *La República*. These papers became the propaganda outlets for the military dictatorship for 21 years. In 1980 Editora Renovación S.A. (ERSA) applied for membership in the Inter American Press Association. An investigation was ordered and the application denied.

Rosario and Gilberto brought their case regularly to the IAPA from the outset of the problem, and IAPA protests were routinely made to the Panamanian government, but to no avail. When Gen. Torrijos regime and President Jimmy Carter initiated negotiations that led to the new Panama Canal Treaty, hopes increased that the properties might be restored to their rightful owners. Torrijos was permitting a political opening and making a number of concessions to give the appearance of respect for democracy and human rights, including permitting the founding of a new daily, *La Prensa*. The ERSA papers were also having financial difficulties. But nothing was to come of the hopes, and Torrijos was killed in a strange helicopter crash in 1981.

In 1985 the IAPA held its mid-year meeting in Panama City. The Editora Renovación personnel pushed its case for ownership with a slick-cover booklet called "Así Se Liquido La Editora Panama America, S.A." (Thus Was Liquidated Editora Panamá America). After the meeting concluded, they held a mock funeral for IAPA in the patio of the newspaper plant, complete with a floral wreath, a casket with the society's initials and a cross as well as an engraved marker which read: "*Aquí pacen los restos de la S.I.P. Murió el 12 de Marzo de 1985 (q.e.p.d.)*" (Here lie the remains of the I.A.P.A. Died March 12, 1985 [R.I.P.]).

My first mission on behalf of Rosario and Gilberto came in January, 1984. I was then vice chairman of the society's Executive Committee and joined a delegation named by IAPA President Horacio Aguirre, the publisher of Miami's *Diario Las Americas*. When he first went into exile from his native Nicaragua years earlier, Horacio had been given work by Hermodio Arias on *El Panamá América*. We made a point of hearing both sides but were never in question about who the legitimate owners were. The opposition paper, *La Prensa*, was permitted to campaign for the return of the Arias newspapers while we were in the country, and as a result of what seemed an opening, the Panamanians decided to invite the 1985 March meeting of IAPA. We felt our mission had made progress. Before we departed, Gilberto put on an elegant buffet for us at his beautiful hillside home, where we met many of the country's leading citizens.

In keeping up the appearance of a political opening, Manuel Noriega, the dictator who succeeded Omar Torrijos, also staged elections. At the mid-year meeting I joined several IAPA leaders in a private session with President Nicolás Ardito Barletta, a respected former World Bank official who had been hand-picked by Noriega, but who barely won in a controversial recount over former President Arnulfo Arias, then an octogenarian. We came away encouraged that the Arias family might get its newspapers back. I recall in the meeting fumbling once in a nervous Spanish. My friend Raúl Kraiselburd, also on the mission, said Barletta spoke English and suggested I switch. As I recall, I continued to stumble along in Spanish.

We were still hopeful as we left Panamá despite the appearance of our opponent's victory suggested by the mock funeral. What we didn't realize is that the political situation was soon to come apart. That September Noriega forced Barletta to resign in an effort to divert a growing murder scandal that implicated the Army. The president had hinted he might appoint a commission to investigate the killing of Dr. Hugo Spadafora, a medical doctor and leading exiled Noriega critic who in recent months had spoken of his hopes of overthrowing Noriega. Spadafora's decapitated body had been found near the Costa Rica border two weeks earlier. Barletta was summarily ordered back from a United Nations General Assembly in New York and initially refused to resign, but gave in after 14 hours of intimidation.

Two weeks after Barletta resigned, Wilbur Landrey and I made a brief visit on behalf of *La Prensa*, the opposition daily founded during the opening Torrijos initiated. Bill went as vice chairman of IAPA's Freedom of Press Committee and I as vice chairman of its Executive Committee. *La Prensa* was at the center of revelations about the Spadafora murder, and we were extremely concerned about its future.

We issued a press statement expressing our concern and called for reassurance. The release also referred to our recent March meeting in Panamá and the promising future then seen for free institutions. We requested a meeting with Barletta's vice president and successor, President Eric Arturo Delvalle, but were told such a meeting was "inconvenient." During our mission, however, Noriega's number two, Defense Forces Chief of Staff Roberto Díaz Herrera, issued a statement vowing what we hoped would be hands off. "The Armed Forces has plans against no entity of the press or individual journalist that are not within the legal system or the express order of authorities in their role within the legal norms of the state," he said

The statement was directed to two U.S. organizations, the American Society of Newspaper Editors, which had released an expression of concern that I had written, and the Committee to Protect Journalists. We believed it was not addressed to IAPA, despite our being present in Panamá, because of our campaign on behalf of *El Panamá América*.

The individual journalist Díaz Herrera had in mind was Guillermo Sanchéz Borbón, an investigative reporter and columnist for *La Prensa*, who was the most widely read journalist in Panamá. In his column, "Pocas Palabras" (A Few Words), he had tied the authorities to the murder and decapitation of Dr. Spadafora through witnesses who provided names and descriptions of some of those involved. A 61-year-old who had had to seek asylum in another political crisis in the 1960s, Guillermo was again in hiding.

Bill Landrey and I held a clandestine interview with him in an office building where he explained that the morning after his story appeared he was paid a visit by someone close to Noriega who said they were going to overthrow Barletta, and that they were desperate and would come after him. The day Barletta resigned, he went into hiding. He said he was against hiding but his family and the newspaper insisted. However risky, he said he had to reappear and planned to do so in a few days as the IAPA opened its annual general assembly in Cartagena, Colombia, which he did. "I won't let up in "Pocas Palabras," he said, although he had promised management he would go lightly to begin. He was good on his word, but soon realized for his own safety he had to go into exile, where he remained until Noriega fell.

The next four years were tense and filled with repeated demonstrations against the dictatorship. All opposition newspapers and electronic media were closed. The end came only with the U.S. invasion, overthrow and arrest of Noriega. After the invasion Rosario Arias was back in her office at *El Panamá América*. She had been a 49-year-old publisher in the prime of her career when Omar Torrijos and his supporters took her newspapers. Now she was 70-year-old and faced the challenge of establishing her legal right to ownership.

A week after the December 20, 1989, invasion, Rosario and brother Gilberto simply walked in and took back their three newspapers after a 21-year absence. People clapped, Gilberto told me a month later when I went to Panamá heading an IAPA mission to investigate reports that the United States had closed radio stations by blowing up their towers, which turned out to be true.

Most of the journalists and editors departed the Arias newspapers after the invasion, including the woman in charge, the mother of Noriega's long-time mistress, Vicky Amado, who took refuge in the Cuban embassy. The three newspapers had been subsidized by the government and loaded with political cronies. The Ariases had to cut the staff from 375 to 125. Many had walked away at the time of the invasion. Others demanded legal severance, which could be up to three years pay, but Rosario and Gilberto took the position that their company had never employed them.

As de facto owners, they found not only $875,000 in cash with no record of its origin, but also two arsenals and a room filled with passports, primarily Cuban and Chinese. The installation had seriously deteriorated. The offset press that before could print 30,000 newspaper in an hour could now generate only 7,000 hourly. Rosario also found a measure of the usurpers' clout when she discovered a direct fax to Noriega's bunker as well as the large subsidies and many unpaid bills. She called the electric company to have the bill returned to her name and was told it had never been changed. It also had not been paid in 21 years. "You owe us $300,000," she was told.

Another three years would pass before Rosario finally obtained legal authority over her property. She and Gilberto wisely had never appealed their case to the dictatorship's Supreme Court. "We would have burned out the candle," Gilberto said of the due process case they would have lost. Now, they appealed and won on constitutional grounds. But the government-owned Banco Nacional de Panamá, which had been ERSA's steady source of ready cash for 21 years, refused to lift liens it had until the Arias family repaid the full debt incurred by the usurpers.

The Panamanian congress ultimately took a dim view of the situation and, more than two years after the Arias's de facto possession of their property, passed a special law restoring to them all rights and turning away hundreds of suits filed by Noriega era employees. However, the new president installed by the United States, Guillermo Endara, vetoed the law. He was unhappy with the Arias' editorial policy. Finally, nearly a year later on April 22, 1993, the Supreme Court overturned the veto. Thus the battle that had gone on just short of a quarter of a century finally ended.

I've always treasured a fax Rosario sent me the day she and Gilberto walked back into El Panamá América. I had been president of IAPA for two months. On her personal stationary with Rosario Arias de Galindo printed at the top and the typed date, December 27th, 1989, she typed: "At this time, when we begin to see the proverbial light in the tunnel of our vindications, I wish to reiterate my sincere appreciation for the support and encouragement you have given me throughout the ordeal we have experienced in the past two decades. Thanks [*sic*] you, and may God bless you, very cordially yours (signed) Rosario A. de Galindo."

In 1993 I received another fax from Rosario informing me that the Supreme Court of Panama had ruled constitutional a new law exempting them from all obligations taken on by the newspapers while under control of the dictatorships. She concluded: "The constant support you gave us throughout our ordeal is still fresh in my mind and I find it difficult to express the sincere appreciation I feel. Justice prevailed at least in our case for the benefit of Democracy and Freedom of the Press. Please give my regards to Karen, and thank you once again. Sincerely, Rosario Arias de Galindo."

Ironically, Arnulfo Arias' widow, Mireya Moscoso, was elected president in 1999 and oversaw implementation of the Panama Canal Treaty negotiated by Omar Torrijos, the dictator who overthrew her husband. In the election she defeated his son, Martín Torrijos, Then in 2004 she was succeeded in the presidency by Martín Torrijos. To add to the irony, she promised, as had her predecessors, to eliminate the oppressive media laws implemented by the dictatorship, but she was unable to move repeal through the Legislative Assembly. At the 2005 midyear meeting of the IAPA in Panama City, President Martín Torrijos also promised to eliminate what had long been known as the "gag laws." Rosario Arias, age 85, was at the meeting to encourage him. On July 6, 2005, Torrijos signed the repeal. Among the laws were one making insulting a public official a crime, another (No. 67) regulating the practice of journalism and the onerous Law No. 11 regulating the media as well as a 1969 cabinet decree permitting censorship. None of these laws had been used since the return of democracy, but removing them from the books was an important symbolic accomplishment for Panama's press—especially under the leadership of Omar Torrijos' son.

I participated in numerous meetings and debates about the laws, including a dinner party in late 1990 in my Kansas home for two Panamanian legislators. One, the sponsor of a repeal law, would later become president of the Legislative Assembly. The other was chairman of the committee considering the bill. I wrote Bobby Eisenmann of *La Prensa* the next day saying I thought I had made headway with the committee chairman, who was not entirely on board. He returned my letter with a handwritten notation: "Thank you again! Your lobby was very effective. Bobby." Unfortunately, another 15 years passed before repeal. Fifteen years that included gag laws discussions I participated in with Presidents Endara, Perez Balladares, Moscoso and Torrijos.[1]

Another friend and IAPA colleague, Bobby Eisenmann, fought his own battle for Panama's freedom that lasted only a decade, but it was no less important than the long Arias struggle.

In 1979 I. Roberto Eisenmann Jr. and four friends decided to take advantage of a political opening by establishing an independent daily. Torrijos was in negotiations on the Panama Canal Treaty. Bobby was a successful entrepreneur with a graduate business degree from the Wharton School at the University of Pennsylvania. Neither he nor his friends had experience in newspapers, but they set out to learn, first by attending the 1979 IAPA general assembly in Toronto, which is where I first met him.

The assembly's first session included a memorial to Pedro Joaquín Chamorro, the Nicaraguan editor who had recently been assassinated by his country's dictatorial regime, as well as two assassinated South American journalists. Bobby later reminisced: "We knew there were some risks, but. . . . What trouble are we asking for? That day we braced ourselves for the sacrifices that would be required . . ."

They also received substantial pledges of help from several IAPA members, including representatives of *The Miami Herald* and *La Nación* of Costa Rica. Bobby remembers Manual Jiménez Borbón, my predecessor a decade later as

---

1. Thinking back to that first 1984 mission to Panama and my fumbling Spanish, I took a certain pride in the aftermath of a question I asked 21 years later at IAPA's 2005 mid-year meeting there. I decided to ask a question at the joint appearance of Colombian President Alvaro Uribe and Panama's Martín Torrijos. They both spoke of the excellent relationship between their countries. I knew the subject of the absence of a highway connecting their two countries was delicate, so, contrary to my normal practice, I put my question in Spanish despite the presence of simultaneous interpretation: "*Yo quisiera tocar el tema de las buenas relaciones entre los dos países, Colombia y Panamá,*" I said. "*Cuándo vamos a ver una callecita pavimentada entre los dos?*" ("I want to address the good relations between your two countries, Colombia and Panama. When are we going to see a little paved street between them?")

Their answers made the front pages of all the local dailies the next morning, and *La Prensa* devoted its entire op-ed page the following day to a pro and con on the issue. My Panamanian IAPA colleague, Juan Luis Correa, who was our host, told me that after my question his country's vice president asked him: "Who is that gringo who speaks Spanish so well?"

IAPA president, introducing him to top executives of the Abitibi newsprint company with the comment: "I want to present to you Eisenmann and his friend. They are founding a daily that freedom of expression in Panamá has to have. If you want to keep selling newsprint to *La Nación*, open an account for them under the same terms of price and credit that *La Nación* gets." Said and done. *La Prensa* got its newsprint.

La Prensa shone light upon the dictatorship. It became the key voice of opposition for the next eight years, when it was finally closed by Noriega. Initially, Torrijos needed Bobby and his investors in order to create the illusion that a free press could function in Panamá. He did not close or even censor the paper because he believed it would fail after its first year. After all, the government was the nation's largest advertiser. His ERSA newspapers were losing about $1.2 million a year. How was Eisenmann going to make it?

The answer is complicated. *La Prensa* was not an orphan. It had widespread international support through IAPA, including many IAPA members who attended its inauguration. Perhaps more important, Bobby came up with the brilliant idea of spreading ownership of the paper as widely as possible among the Panamanian business and journalism elite. This would make closing it more costly for the regime. No stockholder, including Bobby, was permitted to own more than one percent of the stock. There were 700 stockholders at the outset. In addition, he and his colleagues managed to raise more than the $1 million to start *La Prensa* and set aside $250,000 to cover cash needs the first year, which carried it into the second year, when it began showing a profit.

As the opposition grew, the dictatorship unleashed paramilitary groups and politically motivated mobs, known in Central America as *turbas*, on *La Prensa*'s facilities and employees. The National Guard installed censors on several occasions and shut the paper down for extended periods.

I first visited the *La Prensa* facilities in January, 1984, on the mission to press for the return of the Arias family newspapers. Relations between the opposition newspaper and the Noriega regime were tense but not threatening. Noriega was continuing the Torrijos ploy of presenting the world a facade of openness and elected civilian leadership. After helping organize the midyear meeting of IAPA in Panama City, Bobby Eisenmann even decided to accept a Nieman Fellowship for a year at Harvard. But with the murder of Dr. Hugo Spadafora that September the situation for *La Prensa* deteriorated quickly. Because of threats on his life, Bobby would not be able to return to Panamá for five years. His star columnist and investigative reporter, Guillermo Sanchéz Borbón, had to flee the country a few months after Bill Landry and I met with him clandestinely.

On a trip to Boston for a meeting of the Harvard-affiliated Latin American Scholarship Program of American Universities (LASPAU), where I was about to become chairman, I had an opportunity to brief Bobby and his wife Maruja on Guillermo Sanchéz Borbón and what I had seen in Panamá. We enjoyed a sumptuous dinner at Rialto, the fine restaurant in Cambridge's new Charles Hotel, but we knew then Bobby might not be able to return. After the Neiman, he and Maruja went into exile in Miami, and Bobby became a regular on U.S. network television commenting for the Noriega opposition. When *La Prensa* was closed permanently in 1988, he managed from exile to put out a clandestine version of *La Prensa* distributed via fax and computer modem.

I saw Bobby at least four times a year at IAPA's meetings, often at executive committee meetings in Miami. At the height of demonstrations against Noriega in the summer of 1987, police closed and occupied *La Prensa* and two other dailies. The excuse was "inciting rebellion and public disobedience." Bobby paid his employees for two months, but ultimately was unable to continue doing so and his executives started looking for jobs for them.

That fall *La Prensa* missed a scheduled payment to the Rockwell-Goss press company on its outstanding $120,000 debt. Its political risk insurance would make the payment, but Bobby feared the insurance company would in turn make a claim on the military government. If the government chose to pay the claim it would own a credit against *La Prensa* and could legally take over the newspaper. Although this was somewhat different from the case of *El Panamá América*, Bobby could envision the same result. Fortunately, Noriega's figurehead president, Eric Arturo Delvalle, issued a Christmas season pardon and all the closed media were permitted to re-open January 1, although he warned them to be "responsible."

At Bobby's request, I had helped raise the pressure on Delvalle by organizing an editorial campaign among U.S. newspapers. As vice chairman of the International Communication Committee of the American Society of Newspaper Editors, I drafted an alert in late October to ASNE's 800 members, directing editors of the nation's daily newspapers, outlining the problems faced by the independent Panamanian press and the general political situation. I noted that I. Roberto Eisenmann asked that ASNE members to editorialize on the closed publications and a proposed new draconian press law. I noted that Bobby believed U.S. military authorities had in the past conveyed word privately to Gen. Noriega not to worry. Although this might no longer be occurring, he added, Noriega continued to insist to his officers that it was.

He also expressed his concern the Panamanian military might not respond to additional economic pressures, which the United States was applying, because of the view that, whatever happened, the military would survive. Any meddling with the Canal treaty by the United States would be extremely counterproductive, he added, because it would confirm Noriega's contentions that the U.S. policy was intended to destabilize Panama, which would be a pretext to abandon its commitment to the treaty.

I concluded the ASNE alert by pointing out that *La Prensa*, with the largest circulation in the country, had suffered under prior censorship, had its machinery destroyed by government troops, had its editors threatened, sued, exiled and condemned to jail terms, and had its journalists beaten and shot at. If the paper did not reopen, I quoted Bobby, it would soon be bankrupt.

The chairman of the ASNE committee I worked with to produce the editorial campaign was Norm Pearlstine, managing editor at *The Wall Street Journal*. In 1994 Norm was named Editor in Chief of *Time Magazine*.

After our protest, the new press law, which included numerous additions to the five types of publications already prohibited and subject to administrative sanctions without appeal, was dropped. But the improved relations between the press and Duvalle's government were short-lived. *La Prensa* was shut down again after only a month and its three top editors fled to the United States into exile. It did not publish again until two weeks after the U.S. invasion.

That Bobby and his staff managed to get back on the streets so quickly after the invasion was remarkable. When he walked back into his facility he found chaos. The computers were gone, telephones had been ripped out, acid had been poured onto the electrical controls of the press, and the platemaking equipment had been stolen. When I arrived two weeks later heading a four-member delegation investigating the situation, I was stunned to read a box at the top of the front page of the re-born *La Prensa* offering $100 for each Atex computer returned to its plant. It pointed out correctly that they were useless except for use in *La Prensa*'s proprietary system.

Traditionally, newspapers in Panama seldom sold more than 15,000 copies daily. But on the first day of its comeback *La Prensa* sold 90,000 copies. It had to scale back its circulation to 50,000 copies because of a lack of newsprint. Bobby told me privately at the time the paper was seriously in jeopardy of bankruptcy, and he didn't know how he was going to be able to satisfy his creditors. None of the repairs or new equipment or restored services had been paid for. I jokingly told him I'd be happy to pick up his bills—so long as I could get stock in the company in return. I could see a very bright future of *La Prensa*. Bobby didn't laugh.

Panama City's airport is normally a vast bustling array of duty-free stores and vendors, but what greeted our IAPA delegation was a vacant cavern patrolled by bored U.S. troops, several asleep atop armored vehicles. Our delegation found that several journalists had been arrested, but only one, the general manager of ERSA, remained in custody. We learned that nine radio stations, two television stations and two weekly newspapers had been closed or taken over by the U.S. invaders. Ownership of most of them was complicated at best, and in most cases in question. But as I pointed out at a press conference I conducted as IAPA president, our commission "found that the closed media and arrested journalists are being handled fairly by due process."

In a meeting with President Guillermo Endara, who had been denied his victory in elections leading up the invasion but placed into power by the United States, he indicated he wanted to privatize those media that were in question. We saw him in an important and happy circumstance. While we were with him, he took a telephone call from U.S. President George H. W. Bush, who told him he was recommending $1 billion in aid to Panama.

The delegation I headed as IAPA President included my good friend Eduardo Ulibari, the Costa Rican editor who was vice chair of IAPA's Freedom of Press Committee and later co-authored with me the Declaration of Chapúltepec, a deputy managing editor of *The Globe and Mail* of Toronto, and Francisco Santos, managing editor of *El Tiempo*, Bogotá, Colombia. Francisco, better known as "Pacho," had already accompanied me to Guatemala on the earlier phase of the mission. Later that year Pacho was kidnapped by Medillín drug boss Pablo Escobar.

On most IAPA missions I have participated in, we almost always meet with top government officials, often the president of the country. But I had never met Manuel Antonio Noriega. Along with my three colleagues I did get to visit his home immediately after the December 20 U.S. invasion. A lawyer and member of *La Prensa*'s board of directors had been put in charge of it and other Noriega property, and he arranged for a tour. The large home was decorated for Christmas with presents wrapped and piled under a tree. The home also was brimming with tasteless purchases acquired in Noriega's travels around the world, but his library contained an impressive collection, primarily military history. We also saw there the voodoo shrines that received so much press attention.

Noriega ultimately was proved to have obtained his fortune through corruption and narcotics dealing. It was determined to be $24 million and was confiscated by the Panamanian government in 2005. His career military pay, from 1962 through 1989, had been $648,583.

After elected civilian government was well established, Bobby moved on to other endeavors to keep Panama's democracy healthy—first in the training of journalists and later as founder and president of a foundation promoting civic freedom (Fundación para la Liberatad Ciudadana). When IAPA held its 2005 mid-year meeting in Panamá, he penned an op-ed piece thanking us for the help he received. "The IAPA and all the old friends meeting here now are the midwives of the rebirth of freedom of expression in Panamá," he wrote. "To a large extent they are responsible for the stable electoral democracy we enjoy today. . . . The Panamanian nation is grateful to you."

My personal interest in Panama pre-dates my involvement in IAPA. My wife Karen and I first visited the isthmus in 1965. The ten Fulbright scholarship grantees headed for Ecuador that year gathered first in Panamá for a short visit. It was the first Latin American country I had visited other than Mexico. A much earlier family connection came through my grandfather, Fay N. Seaton. While I am not clear on the extent of his involvement in overseeing the construction of the canal, he undoubtedly played a role as the top assistant in Washington from 1908 to 1914 to Kansas Senator Joseph L. Bristow. He also served as the senior staffer for the Senate Committee on Cuban Relations and became known as an expert of sugar tariff matters. He also was to the top staff member of the joint Senate-House committee which investigated the parcel post service in 1909, one of the scandals of the times.

A Progressive, Bristow was involved from the outset in the Panama Canal project. Vice President William Howard Taft, who was put in charge of the project by Teddy Roosevelt, chose Bristow in 1904 to determine whether the Panama Railroad, which was in severe disrepair, could be used for the massive construction project. Bristow had earned a reputation as a savvy investigator for Roosevelt when he resolved a corruption scandal in Cuba involving the Post Office Department.

Bristow traveled both the Atlantic and Pacific coasts studying freight rates, evaluated the condition of the railroad itself and recommended it be revamped as the key to the project. Historian David McCullough in his seminal book on the construction, *Path between the Seas*, points out that the project was at least as much a railroad project as a canal dig. That is to say, unless what was dug could be hauled away efficiently, the torrential rains of Panama would eventually put it back in the dig. In fact, this is one of the reasons the French failed to complete their canal project twenty years earlier. Bristow also recommended subsidizing the railroads' rates for shipping from the U.S. west coast as a means of breaking the U.S. rail monopolies, which were using predatory pricing to undercut the Panama route.

As senator, Bristow served his entire tenure on the Senate committee overseeing construction of the canal. He drafted the original governing documents for the Canal Zone, the U.S.-controlled zone that contained the canal. Ironically, Bristow was defeated for re-election in the August primary election of 1914. That same month the canal opened to shipping. Neither of these events held the public's attention, though, because World War I broke out in Europe the first week of August. But Grandfather's interest in Panama didn't wane.

15. El Salvador
Ending a War

At the height of the 12-year Salvadoran Civil War in 1984, the newly elected Salvadoran president José Napoleon Duarte initiated face-to-face talks with the FLMN guerrillas at the northern town of La Palma. The talks marked the beginning of the end of the war. Two years later he participated in the historic Esquipulas II agreement with other regional leaders to lay the groundwork for a firm and lasting peace in Central America.

Twenty years later Nicaraguan President Daniel Ortega told the Central American Parliament that Duarte, not Costa Rica President Oscar Arias, should have been the recipient of the 1987 Nobel Peace Prize for the accomplishment.

I managed with help from friends to have President Duarte deliver a Landon Lecture at Kansas State University in Manhattan two weeks after the La Palma talks. He spoke there on November 2, 1984. National and international press coverage was extensive, in part because the spokesman for the leftist rebels, Arnoldo Ramos, came to Manhattan at the same time. After tense discussions, Ramos' local sponsors agreed there would be no debate and he spoke the night before and after the speech.

IAPA executive committee chairman Ignacio Lozano, who had been U.S. ambassador to El Salvador for President Gerald Ford, knew President Duarte and had asked him to speak at IAPA's Los Angeles General Assembly that year. I called on Kansas Sen. Nancy Landon Kassebaum to see if he would speak in Manhattan after the Los Angeles speech. He agreed.

The university arranged a jet to bring him from Los Angeles. When Karen and I rode with him on the plane, he asked us to review the English in his prepared text. It was giving him trouble. We did so, although at K-State he began reading the text, stopped and declared, "I didn't write this. Get me a blackboard." After some scrambling, somebody found a blackboard on wheels and he began by saying he would explain what happened at La Palma and give us a lesson on Salvadoran politics and history.

He drew three overlapping circles representing the right wing, the leftist guerrillas and his government in the middle wanting liberal democracy. His goal was to bring the other two groups to the center, he said, which is ultimately what occurred after several years of turmoil and further negotiations. Both the right wing and the left since the civil war have won elections controlling the government.

What I didn't learn until after the president's speech was that the night before, four Salvadoran men had been arrested at the Miami airport on their way to Manhattan. The U.S. Secret Service feared they were coming to assassinate President Duarte. That brought home to me just how dangerous a situation can be in the midst of a civil war.

A year later at the request of IAPA's president, I was joined by IAPA's press freedom chair, Bill Landrey of the *St. Petersburg Times,* to look into complaints of one of our most vocal Salvadoran members. Enrique Altamirano. I then was vice chair of IAPA's executive committee.

Enrique was allied with right wing forces and claimed the Duarte government was routinely discriminating against his newspaper, including with government advertising, access to government news and foreign exchange for newsprint. After meeting with more than 30 relevant people we concluded there was no doubt Enrique's newspaper, *Diario de Hoy,* received fewer ads controlled by the government than competitors. We found no evidence of foreign exchange discrimination, or of unequal access to news.

President Duarte joined our talks with government officials and reaffirmed his previous statements in Los Angeles of his strong support for press freedom. We urged him to review the amount of advertising being allocated to Enrique's paper and to adopt more measurable and objective standards. What made his presence with us so memorable was that at that moment his 34-year-old daughter Inés was being held by the FMLN guerrillas. She had been kidnapped a month earlier. He said they knew where she was being held but were hoping to secure her release unharmed. In fact, he said he was holding periodic conversations by radio with the kidnappers. "They told me they were not trying to bring down the oligarchy or destroy the army," he said. "Rather, they want to destroy José Napoleon Duarte. That's what they told me."

In this context he alluded to the rationale he had for peace when he delivered his Landon Lecture in Kansas—to bring the guerrillas to the middle ground. Now with the kidnapping he believed they were backing away from this possibility. They no longer cared about winning public opinion that could help them in elections, he said.

Two weeks later Inés and a friend were released in exchange for 22 political prisoners. Also in the deal 25 mayors and local officials abducted by the FLMN were released and 101 wounded guerrillas were turned over to the International Red Cross.

After our meeting with the president, Bill Landrey and I left the Presidential Palace. A week later the gate to the complex we had exited was bombed, presumably by the FMLN—or perhaps the army. Alarming for us, to say the least.

My next encounter with President Duarte was in early 1988 when I organized a tour of worn-torn Central America for members of the American Society of Newspaper Editors. We had a half-hour visit with him at the Presidential Palace where he briefed us on the peace process. In June of 1988 President Duarte was diagnosed with advanced stomach cancer. He finished the one year remaining in his presidency and died at age 64 in early 1990.

A footnote to these experiences is the role of Enrique Altamirano with the Salvadoran death squads. The death squads achieved infamy when they assassinated Archbishop Óscar Romero and raped and murdered three American nuns in 1980. Most squad participants had been members of the Salvador security forces. They were funded by businessmen and landowners. Hundreds if not thousands of left-wing activists and their sympathizers were killed. The height of the killings came between 1980 and 1983 with many under the leadership of Roberto D'Aubuisson, a member of military intelligence. He founded the right-wing ARENA party and later pursued a political career. He finished second in the 1984 presidential election won by Duarte.

In a 1981 classified communication to Washington, U.S. Ambassador Robert White singled out Enrique as one of six wealthy Miami residents who were funding and directing the death squads. Even then rumors circulated among IAPA members that Enrique was involved and had moved his family to Miami. Confirmation became public only in 1984 when White testified at the House Foreign Affairs subcommittee on Latin America. White's classified communication was later obtained and made public by the National Security Archive.

Enrique said at the time he was studying legal options but did not pursue them. He was forced out by the United States in early 1986 and moved his family to Madrid where he continued to run his newspaper by computer link. He was nearly fanatic in opposition to President Duarte and the FMLN, including with his continued participation in IAPA.

After an IAPA Mid-year meeting In San Salvador in 2003, which we attended, Enrique withdrew from IAPA participation, leaving his newspaper's representation to his son Fabricio, who is virtually the polar opposite of his father.

Another Salvadoran of the "Miami Six" was Orando de Sola, a cousin of my good friend from college Francisco R. R. de Sola. "Chico," as we knew him then, was a member with me in the Fly Club, a fraternity-like Harvard social club. Karen and I had visited Chico in San Salvador on our return from Ecuador in 1966. We saw him several times when we were in his country.

The de Sola family are very important coffee growers and business leaders. Orlando de Sola was kicked out of the family enterprises when he began his death squad activities.

16. Honduras
Contras Are Real

In the civil wars in Central America, Honduras was a passive facilitator. I made several visits there both before or after visiting one or more of the war-torn countries. Its role was in assisting the U.S. in supporting the fight against leftist forces. Honduras' history is closely tied to the United States, primarily with the U.S. government support of corporations there in the fruit industry. Its welcoming of a U.S. military presence again in the 1980s was, at the very least, controversial. The U.S. military had invaded Honduras seven times between 1903 and 1925.

On a 1997 fact-finding tour with members of the American Society of Newspaper Editors I had helped organized, we arrived there after two days in Mexico City. In Mexico we held interviews including with Mexican President Miguel de la Madrid in the last months of his presidency. We were in Honduras two days before departing for Guatemala. Most instructive was a tour by helicopter to the U.S. installations at Pomerola Air Base at Camayagua, once the capital city of Honduras. We were briefed by the U.S. commander. A member of our delegation with top security clearance was flown from the base into Nicaragua to visit the Contra camps.

Maj. Gen. (ret.) Neal Creighton, a friend of mine who helped ASNE and IAPA in his role at the McCormick Tribune Foundation, briefed us upon his return. The U.S.-supported Contras, he said, were well-equipped and real. They were going to make a difference in the fight against the Sandinista regime. Needless to say, we had learned something at an important moment. We also interviewed several politicians and human rights leaders in Tegucigalpa as well as Honduran President José Azcona. In 1989 Azcona would oversee the dismantling of the Contra support at Pamerola as part of the Arias Peace Plan that led to the 1990 electoral loss of the Sandinistas in Nicaragua.

My next visit to Tegucigalpa was heading an IAPA mission in 1993 that also went to Guatemala. We were in Honduras to investigate threats to and by journalists, especially aimed at *El Tiempo* of San Pedro Sula, one the nation's four largest newspapers. It was owned by Jaime Rosenthal, a Liberal Party politician and banker who was a perennial candidate for president. A 2006 study by Germany's Friedrich Ebert Foundation listed him as "one of the most powerful men in Honduras." He died in 2019 at age 82.

Our focus was on bomb threats at his newspaper after it had printed internal documents of the National Electoral Tribunal. These indicated the commission had authorized payments to 13 local reporters in November and December 1992. The editor received a death threat from one of the named reporters and a warning to quit pursuing the story.

We interviewed President Rafael Callejas and the armed forces commander as well as Rosenthal. The latter would be labeled 22 years later in 2015 by the U.S. Treasury Department a "specially designated narcotics trafficker" under the Foreign Narcotics Kingpin Designation Act.

We had no clue at the time.

17. Costa Rica
Obligatory Licensing

My most memorable experiences in and about Costa Rica are covered in my Nicaragua chapter, especially experiences with Nobel Peace Prize winner Oscar Arias. In general, freedom of expression and ethics are better supported there than in other countries of the region. Not included elsewhere is the 1985 Stephen Schmidt advisory ruling by the Inter American Human Rights Court against mandatory licensing of journalists.

Schmidt, a U.S. citizen, who was not a member of the obligatory *Colegio* (Guild) *de Periodistas*, worked at the respected English language *Tico Times* and stringed for the nation's leading daily, *La Nación*. He had been warned several times by the *Colegio* for illegally practicing journalism and decided to challenge the law.

At IAPA's 1980 mid-year in San José while Karen and I watched, he declared: "I am covering this meeting illegally. Let me work or sue me." The *Colegio* did the latter.

In court Schmidt was at first acquitted, then that ruling was reversed by the Supreme Court and he was convicted and given a suspended sentence. With IAPA's backing, he and his legal team appealed to the Inter American Commission on Human Rights. The Commission upheld the Supreme Court's ruling, and IAPA's leaders persuaded the government of Costa Rica to join it in seeking an advisory opinion on the issue from the seven-member Inter American Court of Human Rights, the ultimate authority. Costa Rica, as a signatory of the American Convention on Human Rights, is required to follow its rulings.

In 1985 when I was chairman of the IAPA Executive Committee, the Court ruled that obligatory licensing of journalists under national statutes violates the right of free expression. It was a solid victory and one of the most important accomplishments in IAPA's 67-year history. Such statutes began to fall in countries that are signatories of the Convention.

Later, as I moved up the ladder to become IAPA President in 1989, I shepherded a challenge at the Inter American Court to the legal right of reply, which is a statutory or even constitutional right in many Latin American countries. It obligates the media to accept responses to criticism, often in the same venue, even giving the same space, regardless of editorial policy. We hoped the court would follow the licensing precedent in another advisory opinion. It did not.

In the late 1970s a controversy soiled the reputation of Costa Rica's media as objective sources of news. At the time the Costa Rican media played a role in the Sandinista revolution overthrowing the Nicaraguan dictatorship of Anastasio Somoza. No media outlet, even *La Nación*, revealed the presence in their country of the Sandinista use of landing strips, etc. These were being used by the guerrillas, Cubans and Panamanian forces supporting the Sandinistas. In the summer of 1980 the *New York Times* broke the story about the Sandinista presence in Guanacaste Province near the Nicaragua border. A young reporter from *Tico Times* accompanied the New York reporter and wrote about it as well.

The editor of *La Nación* and my friend, Guido Fernandez, resigned from the newspaper that year in a dispute over editorial policy regarding the Nicaragua revolution. He had been chairman of IAPA's Freedom of Press Committee.

CARIBBEAN

CUBA

JAMAICA

HAITI

DOMINICAN
REPUBLIC

18. Cuba
Spring Turns to Winter

Whether I share blame for the death of what once was seen as the "Cuba Spring" will undoubtedly never be clear to me. The term refers to the flourishing of independent journalism and easing of state controls in Cuba that began in early 2001 and reached its height in the months leading up to its tragic crushing that began March 18, 2003.

Dozens of self-described independent journalists had worked outside Cuba's state-run media for several years, facing periodic harassment, including confiscation of their rudimentary equipment. They used borrowed phone lines to transmit their stories abroad, primarily to Miami. Many were political activists writing polemics and seeking asylum abroad. At least 50 had gone into exile since 1995, most in the United States. After 1997, a particularly difficult year, the harassment lessened and by the "Cuba Spring" at least 100 independent journalists were working on the island, many producing fairly balanced reporting.

I had donated $1,000 to the movement annually in its early years at the request of Roberto Suarez, an IAPA colleague and Cuban refugee who was president of *The Miami Herald* and publisher of *El Nuevo Herald*. I came face to face with these courageous journalists in 1998 when I was president of the American Society of Newspaper Editors and took the ASNE board of directors on a fact-finding trip to the island. While there I arranged to have a private dinner with several of them, including Raúl Rivero, a poet and Cuba's best known independent journalist.

The 1998 visit, four years before the end of the "Cuba Spring," was in part a way of offering the ASNE board and past presidents an attractive setting for the semi-annual board meeting. The actual work of the board had to be done in Miami because of the U.S. embargo on spending money in Cuba, but as journalists the participants could visit Cuba for journalistic pursuits. A collateral purpose was to push Cuba to allow news bureaus of American newspapers, which at the time were not permitted.

Getting into Cuba with that agenda was one thing. But never in my dreams had I thought I'd be sitting in Havana beside one of the 20th century's legendary figures moderating a six-hour "dialogue" between him and the leadership of America's daily newspaper editors.

My first surprise was being asked to take a seat at the head table between Fidel Castro and Carlos Lage—the man who people on Havana streets then said might be his successor. Cuba's foreign minister and the president of the Congress sat on either side.

As president of ASNE, I knew I would get to ask the first question. I said in Spanish that I had a question about the future. How did the Cuban leader envision his country evolving when he was no longer president? After some introductory musing, he answered directly: "The day I die nothing is going to happen and perhaps things will be even better." Then came my second surprise. "What is your vision of Cuba's future?" asked the Communist leader.

Uh oh. He wanted to debate. It was to be wonderful theater—and I would be the straw man. What choice did I have? In Cuba, he is the *comandante.* For the next 15 minutes we batted back and forth our contrasting philosophies—I said my vision for Cuba was of democracy with free expression and competitive elections; he said that his government already expresses the will of the people and guarantees health care and good education. I said a focus exclusively on such economic rights undermines political and civil rights essential to democracy. Ultimately, we agreed we hold differing views of democracy.

Now he was having fun. I was sweating. "We're going to have a dialogue," he said, "and you can be the moderator." So began our six-hour "dialogue." It was mostly one-sided. The editors raised 15 topics. Fidel, in starched fatigues—his "working clothes"—used their questions as launching pads for dissertations on topics of importance to him. One rambling but fascinating response lasted 55 minutes.

Castro had agreed to meet with ASNE's board and leadership in part because his first trip to the U.S. after the revolution was for the purpose of an address to our society. As things turned out, that 1959 trip was his only unrestricted visit to the United States. He stated very clearly in that two-hour and 15-minute speech in Washington that he and his fellow revolutionaries were not communists.

Perhaps three hours into our 1998 session, Castro rhetorically asked an editor what Cuba could do to make the United States lift its 36-year-old trade embargo. The editor let the moment pass and raised another issue. I seized the prerogative of a "moderator" to interrupt to say that U.S. officials had told us earlier in our trip that even minor loosening of controls would be matched by comparable loosening of the embargo.

That lit his fuse. He pointed his lanky fingers, he raised his voice, he almost shouted. The United States, he scolded in a 15-minute harangue, "has assumed the role of Goliath and we of David, and the world will always be in favor of David." The U.S. has said the same for years, he explained: the embargo will be lifted "if Cuba cuts its ties with the Soviet Union, if it gets out of Angola. The line has always been Cuba's conduct."

Over the six hours—actually six hours and 15 minutes with a bathroom break after four hours—the Cuban leader was both jocular and defiant, endearing and insensitive. At 72, he seemed to have unlimited energy and gave no indication of reported health problems. Clearly, his bladder and vocal chords were fine.

He sat erect on the edge of his chair throughout. He used a four-inch stack of papers, many heavily marked in his own handwriting, mostly as props for dramatic effect. His hands mostly rested gently on the edge of the table before him. Occasionally, he tapped the stack of papers or, when becoming agitated, pounded lightly on them. Facial dramatics and head nods were his stock in trade.

I surprised the *comandante* at one point. Mysteriously, out of my left pocket came a shrill "pop" like a distant gun shot. It was heavily amplified by the powerful speaker system he employed so he could speak softly yet come across forcefully. It jolted Castro—long a target for assassins. He was alarmed. I pulled from the pocket a miniature tape recorder. Later I realized the noise came when I shut my metal glasses case. Castro scolded me for having a recorder in my pocket and reminded me he was at that very moment talking about an assassination plot against him earlier in the year in the Dominican Republic. Then he made light of the situation. He liked the recorder's small size. "I'd like to have one so small," he mused. Ironically, he had kept the purpose of his recording our session to himself. Only much later did I learn that the video tape being made of our "dialogue" was broadcast in its entirety the next week on Cuban television.

My own discomfort in the session grew as the hours passed. The legendary marathon speaker had warned us at the outset: "I have no time limits. You can stay here as long as you want and until you get bored." I kept thinking, "This is

Fidel Castro, he's the *comandante*. He shuts this off." Finally, after five hours, he had outlasted me. I suggested we continue over the lunch he had promised us. It was now 4 p.m. He responded that we could continue until the lunch was prepared. An hour and 15 minutes later I finally asked, "You hungry yet?"

We got up from the table. But goodbyes took another 45 minutes, including a photo op with each of the 32 editors. Privately, he apologized for putting me on the spot. He also inscribed the famous Alfredo Korda book of photographs of the revolution for me. Lunch, of scarce and expensive lobster, was served promptly at 6 p.m.

The wide-ranging "dialogue"—with Fidel doing 95 percent of the talking—addressed subjects ranging from his belief there should be more cooperation between the United States and Cuba on fighting terrorism (three years before 9/11), to the U.S. embargo, the possibility of U.S. newspaper bureaus, his large daily news digest, his discomfort with permitting the use of dollars (rescinded in 2004), his need to stay in power as long as he was useful, Cuban baseball and the dissidents in jail.

He was vague on whether the newspaper bureaus would be allowed. An ease in the embargo might bring permission, he suggested, but he also said our reporters aren't always objective. He reminded us *The New York Times* knew in advance about the 1961 Bay of Pigs invasion and didn't publish a story.

On baseball he joked that he could have put together a team of Cubans that would have won the two previous World Series. Knowing he had been drafted by the Washington Senators as a young pitcher, I had presented him a gift as a gesture of good will an official national league baseball signed by Chicago Cubs star Sammy Sosa, a Dominican. I was subsequently criticized fiercely for doing so by Cuban American leaders, including in front page stories.

The dissidents, Castro said, were in jail because Cuba's constitution did not permit citizens to criticize the revolution, oppose the socialist state or help the United States. His explanation was later to weigh heavily in my mind after events that occurred when I led another ASNE board trip to Cuba four years later.

Only weeks after our 1998 trip, Castro did give permission for the Associated Press to open a bureau, which we told him would serve all American dailies and would be a good way to start. Subsequently, he permitted the Chicago Tribune and its affiliates, including Fort Lauderdale's *Sun Sentinel,* and the *Dallas Morning News* to open bureaus. Noticeable in their absence even today in Havana are Knight-Ridder and its strongly critical *Miami Herald* and

El Nuevo Herald and *The New York Times*. Castro has a long and unforgiving memory. Presumably permission for the Fort Lauderdale paper was intended as a snub of *The Miami Herald*.

Another ASNE fact-finding trip in 2002, again under my leadership and at the height of the "Cuba Spring," brought us into contact with the webs of intrigue that characterize a totalitarian society like Cuba. We again hoped to encourage greater access for U.S. newspapers, but despite virtually ironclad assurances, we didn't meet with Castro. Our timing may be the explanation, but I suspect our behavior and events in which we participated in 2002 better explain why.

On the 1998 trip we were never assured we would meet with Castro. Cuban officials in Washington had told me only that we might get to see him if we "behaved." When I asked what that meant, the short answer was that we not make a big public issue out of the dissidents on the island. As a result we met with the dissidents privately at our hotel and in private restaurants. In advance of the 2002 trip we were told we would definitely have an interview and we weren't warned we must "behave."

Because of continued economic woes in 2002, the Cuban government at the time was on a charm offensive to attract tourists, foreign investment and subsidized trade. Cuba had recently allowed a visit by former President Jimmy Carter, a trade fair for U.S. companies and a Castro interview with Barbara Walters. The interview on ABC's *20/20* aired the day before our arrival. These developments clearly encouraged dissenters, who four years before had been docile and obviously intimidated. At that time four dissidents had only recently received lengthy prison sentences for "insulting" President Castro by saying Cuba wasn't living up to its international agreements.

Although not so apparent to us in 2002, our success in getting the AP bureau approved in 1998 had made the situation for dissidents riskier. Just weeks before approval of the AP bureau, a new felony went on the books with punishment up to 30 years in prison for supplying information to or collaborating with foreign news media or aiding a foreign nation against the interests of socialist Cuba. The law had clearly been promulgated to keep the dissidents away from the U.S. press as its access increased, but it had not been used before our visit except as a threat.

Despite this threat, four dissident opposition leaders willingly met with our delegation. A total surprise, they joined us midway through an on-the-record meeting at the official residence of James Cason, essentially the U.S. ambassador. Their appearance clearly carried the risk of tainting the participants with U.S. collaboration. Cason told us it was the first time anything of this sort had occurred.

Only after Castro stood us up for the interview we had been assured of, did I come to feel that we had been used by Cason and the U.S. government to push—perhaps even test–Castro by making a public show with the dissidents. The more I observed Cason on later occasions try to provoke the regime, the more sure I became. The Bush administration had abandoned the Clinton approach in effect on our earlier visit of responding to incremental improvements in human rights and the rule of law with incremental improvements in relations. The new policy was "all or nothing." And we were being used. As it turned out, Castro pushed back.

I had arranged for the meeting with Cason and his staff in the belief that a U.S. editors' delegation should hear the views of our diplomats. I'd done the same four years earlier. We had plans to meet with some of the dissidents privately at a later time, but we had absolutely no foreknowledge they would be present at Cason's residence. When the Cuba Spring came to an abrupt end the next March, we realized our meeting had been the beginning of events that resulted in not only three of the four dissident leaders landing in prison, but 71 other dissidents, including 29 independent journalists, as well. The prison terms ranged from 6 to 28 years.

Imprisoned were not only journalists but other non-violent dissidents including human rights activists, librarians, economists, doctors and teachers. Their crimes ranged from writing for Web sites based abroad to collecting signatures to petition for a referendum and setting up independent libraries that included books by prominent dissenters like Vaclav Havel and Martin Luther King Jr.

Vladimiro Roca, one of the four who had been convicted of insulting Castro and who had been released from prison only the previous May, told us at Cason's residence they were willing to assume the risk. "We are accused (of cooperating with Washington) even if we don't come here," he said. He and his colleagues said they felt threatened but believed the regime's campaign to present a positive face to the world gave them some protection. The international celebrity of the leaders, who had won human rights prizes throughout the world, also protected them, they said.

Roca was one of the organizers of a citizens' petition to the National Assembly, signed by more than 10,000 Cubans, calling for election reform, access to the state media and private enterprise. The petition, known as Project Varela, also sought guarantees for the rights the petitioners said are in Cuba's constitution but not guaranteed by law or respected by the government. The project, led by a Christian group headed by Oswaldo Payá, had languished for several years until Jimmy Carter gave it life by revealing it to the Cuban people in a live television address. No Cuban leader had mentioned it publicly. Carter made the address a condition of his visit.

Within weeks Varela got its official response with a counter-petition calling on the National Assembly to make socialism "irrevocable." A three-day holiday was declared to gather more than 8 million signatures, and a constitutional amendment passed June 27. To Varela the answer was "Hell No," Cason told us.

That ended the issue until the Barbara Walters interview Friday, October 11. She asked President Castro whether the Varela petitioners would get an official reply, as required by the constitution. He acknowledged the constitution permits the right of petition and said the petitioners would be answered in due time. This was encouraging to the Varela leaders, but as Payá told me at a private breakfast in our hotel, it had little meaning because Castro was talking on U.S. television, which is not seen by Cubans.

Then, in a surprising move, the Walters interview was broadcast in Spanish translation on Cuban television channels and official radio while we were still in Havana. Cuban citizens learned for the first time from their charismatic leader that they had the right to petition their government and to receive a reply. Varela organizers opened an office the next morning.

Also the next day, in our meeting with National Assembly President Ricardo Alarcón, I asked when the reply to the petitioners was likely to come and whether the petition would be published in the official media. My question may have cost us the Castro interview because it tipped off where the questioning of him might go.

Alarcón, a U.S.-trained lawyer and gifted leader with long experience in the United States as Cuba's United Nations ambassador and foreign minister, became clearly agitated and stumbled in his answer—offering legalisms and diversions. He was unwilling to say when the answer would come or answer forthrightly whether the petition would be published so the Cuban people might know what the now famous Varela petition says. Finally, he echoed President Castro: "They will get an answer."

Why was the Walters interview shown? It may be related to our visit. Apparently Castro was told Payá complained to us that the *Comandante* was willing to tell U.S. television viewers about the rights of Cubans but not his own people. The dissidents told us they thought he wanted to blunt that criticism by broadcasting the interview in Cuba. Of course, that was speculation.

The other intriguing development unfolding while we were in Cuba in 2002 was the work being done to launch an independent magazine, *De Cuba*. Although several religious magazines were permitted, it would be the first independent general-interest publication in Cuba since consolidation of the revolution. And, it would be written by journalists working outside the state-controlled media. These courageous journalists up to that point had been tolerated so long as they did not publish or broadcast their stories inside Cuba. Sometimes, of course, their stories played back to the island on Miami radio or in publications brought from abroad.

While listed in the first issue only as "advisor," Raúl Rivero was the magazine's intellectual father. Long a reporter for Cuba's official media, Raúl also is Cuba's best known poet. He was once a dedicated revolutionary whose poetry sang praise for the accomplishments of socialist Cuba, and he was trusted enough to serve as Moscow correspondent for the official Prensa Latina news agency. In 1991 he broke with the regime by signing a "Letter of 10 Intellectuals" calling for the release of political prisoners. He was the only one of the 10 who hadn't taken asylum outside Cuba. In 1995 he founded the independent news agency Cuba Press. For his courage he had received numerous international awards including a Reporters Without Borders award in 1997, a special Maria Moors Cabot citation in 1999 (which I pushed as a Cabot board member) and the position of vice president for Cuba of the Inter American Press Association, although he was unable to travel to our meetings. After he landed in prison he received the UNESCO's prestigious Guillermo Cano World Press Freedom Prize. European cities declared him to be under their protection and offered him political asylum.

Raúl told me at a breakfast, where I gave him several hundred dollars as a gesture of support as I had four years earlier, that the improvements then for independent journalists were "just show." He then laid out the plans for the magazine. "We are going to provoke them," he told me matter-of-factly. He detailed the stories planned for the first issue, which was scheduled for publication the next month, and said they would be straight, unbiased news coverage of events and topics that had not appeared in the state media. Included, he said, would be articles on a recent brutal murder of a five-member Havana family, the role of fear in Cuba, transvestites, and prostitution rehabilitation. Some cartoons also were planned. The project was being underwritten by a Spanish foundation. They planned 26 pages and a distribution of 2,000 copies throughout Cuba at 40 cents a copy. There was just one problem. Private mass media are prohibited by the Cuban constitution.

Raúl, of course, knew this. He told me there would be consequences after the first issue including confiscation of their equipment and a few nights in jail, but he thought Castro's charm offensive insulated them from show trials and lengthy prison terms. He was 180 degrees wrong. His own punishment was a 20 year sentence. He spent the first 11 months in solitary confinement and was finally released on a medical parole November 20, 2004, along with a few of the others after 20 months. The parole can be revoked at any time. The "isolation cell" was six-feet by five-feet with a bed, a toilet, a light and a boarded-up window. Prisoners are normally confined there as punishment for a maximum of 21 days. He lost 65 pounds while confined.

"Wherever I went, I was handcuffed," he told an interviewer the day of his release. "Like any other Cuban prisoner, I was entitled to visit with family eight hours a year. Eventually I was given phone privileges of 25 minutes every Thursday. The food was never good but I was allowed to supplement the prison diet with food from home. In the summer it was unbearably hot; in the winter cold and damp." He passed his time, he said, writing poetry, mostly about love, and reading. "I was only allowed to give my wife love poems that I had to give to a prison official to review first," he explained.

He said he became obsessed with not dying under any circumstances, which he also wrote about. He wrote about his relationships with others in prison. "You're locked up 24 hours a day and you can only read for so long. So you spend time telling each other the stories of your life. You learn everything about each other. You become close friends but you never get to see the other man's face. A prisoner can spend a year in jail alongside a man and never see his face."

President Castro, of course, had not lasted 43 years in power by losing battles like Varela and the new independent magazine, although Oswaldo Payá was not jailed along with the 75 dissidents. This was probably because he had recently been awarded the prestigious 50,000-euro Sakharov Human Rights Prize given by the European Union. His Varela movement continues, but extremely cautiously.

Shortly after our visit to Cuba, President Castro accused Washington of trying to "invent an opposition" on the island. "There is no (opposition) because they are like fish in an aquarium without water," he told the first session of the National Assembly after the Varela petition became public. "There is no oxygen for a counter-revolution, and each time there will be less."

Just weeks before Raúl's release, Castro suffered a serious injury to his left kneecap and right arm in a fall which sidelined him for months. Was the decision to release Raúl and a half dozen other dissidents on medical paroles somehow related? We probably will never know, but the *comandante*'s injury did bring to mind a humorous remark he made after another injury to his left leg two years earlier. He was sidelined then for three or four days and unable to attend a session of Cuba's parliament—the first he had missed in 25 years. "I must take care of my left leg," he said in an open letter to National Assembly President Ricardo Alarcón, "because with it I have made the best steps of my life."

What triggered the move against the independent journalists and other dissidents? Believing that international publicity offered protection to them, I spoke publicly at an IAPA general assembly in Lima just three weeks after leaving Havana about the plan for *De Cuba*, including Raúl's belief that punishment would be minimal. I also repeated this in a cover story for *The American Editor*, which came out in December. Long experience had taught me that publicity can be a protection. A year before Raúl's release, for example, Bernardo Arévalo Padrón, a dissident released after six years in Cuban prison, called the IAPA office immediately after his release to tell us our protests had resulted in better treatment. "They held off more and stopped beating me," he said. "The IAPA campaign saved my life."

It is doubtful the regime learned anything it didn't know from my revelations, but I may have focused their attention by giving the project international exposure—especially of the fact that the dissidents were telling foreign journalists they expected to get little or not punishment. I'll never know for sure. What I do know is that the 75 dissidents were arrested the next March 18, just two days after the Associated Press moved its first article about the magazine. Was that the trigger?

Undoubtedly there was more to the crackdown. From late 2002 an election process had begun that could likely set the stage for the selection of Cuba's next president if Castro is not available. The new National Assembly in March, just before the crackdown, elected the Council of State, which serves for five years. The two bodies will formally choose the next president. Also early in March 2003 six prominent activists announced a hunger strike and opposition leaders urged that Cuba's application for preferential trade treatment and assistance be rejected by the European Union. The crackdown followed.

The 2003 Iraq war undoubtedly also figured at least into the timing of the decision. With world attention on the race to Baghdad that began the day after the first arrests, Castro and his advisors could reasonably think their crackdown would be virtually lost in the headlines. In that, they were wrong. European Union financial aid was halted and relations between Cuba and the EU remain severely strained. The release of Raúl Rivero and a few others 20 months later came at the urging of Spain's new Socialist Prime Minister José Luis Zapatero, reportedly in exchange for Spain's commitment to work for improved Cuba-EU relations.

By the time AP moved that first story, *De Cuba* had published its second issue. The first came out in December, a month later than planned. The 250 copies were distributed through the 100 independent libraries that had been permitted as part of the Cuba Spring. The 50 photocopied pages included an examination of racism, a piece on differing views of political reform, a piece on Cuban Rastafarians and a cryptic essay by Raúl Rivero about making a statement. The second issue came out in late February, less than three weeks before the arrests.

Within weeks all 75 dissidents, including the 29 independent journalists, had been convicted in summary trials closed to the media. The key testimony was given by spies. Two reporters, Manuel David Orrio and Nestor Baguer, who had spent years working alongside Raúl in the independent journalist movement, testified against him, saying he and the others were paid by the U.S. Interests Section. The 80-year-old Baguer later told reporters he began working for the security police in 1960. He said he had not been allowed to tell even his family about his true work in the 43 years he had done it. He said he had known Raúl from childhood and had been a close friend of Raúl's mother. "I consider him a friend and I am very sad, but he deserved it because he chose the road of treason," Baguer said.

U.S. officials said their aid to the independent journalists took the form of Internet access, radios and newspapers as part of their democracy outreach, although the record shows that the U.S. Agency for International Development since 1996 had provided more than $20 million to U.S. groups working with the opposition.

There were a dozen government spies at the trials, among them some of the most prominent dissidents. The longtime assistant to one of the dissidents we'd met at Ambassador Cason's residence, the well-known economist Marta Beatriz Roque, testified against her.

Upon his release from prison, Raúl said he did not wish to emigrate. At 58, he said he hoped to be able to write in Cuba. "I have never wanted to leave here," he told reporters. "I am thinking about looking for a place to go work, teach, do something so that I can write the books I have to write." Among them, he said, would be a book about his prison experience.

Although he said he'd like to return to journalism, he admitted he didn't want "to work with the sword of Damocles over my shoulders, threatening me with prison again, because this has been an immense family tragedy." He saw little hope for the dissident journalists' movement. "Objectively, I can't now recreate what is destroyed," he said. Those aspirations "are waters that have run, as (the poet) Juan Clemente Zemea might have said. There is no one to renew this dream of an independent press. Many are in prison and the free ones want to emigrate."

Castro had won. The Cuba Spring was past. It would be known henceforth as the Black Spring. In truth, winter had returned.

19. Dominican Republic
Courtier to a Dictator

My best memory of the DR, as it should be, was the honor of being made a *Comendador* (Commander or Knight) by the nation and decorated by the country's president, the prolific writer and poet Joaquín Balaguer. I became a Knight of the Order of Christopher Columbus (*Orden Heráldica de Cristóbal Colón*). In a context so near the 500th anniversary of Columbus' 1492 discovery of America and arrival on the island, it was a remarkable experience for me. My status was bestowed for "eminent service to Humanity" and "meritorious service toward the unity and Development of the Peoples of America." The award is signed by President Balaguer and his Secretary of State.

Joaquín Balaguer by then had served three non-consecutive terms as president totaling 16 years and eventually was the author of 59 books. As President he was not without controversy, especially in the early years. He was lauded by President Ronald Reagan as "the father of Dominican democracy" and by President Jimmy Carter as setting "an example for all leaders . . . in changing his own country and his own people away from a former totalitarian government to one of increasingly pro democracy." His early political career was as a courtier of Dictator Rafael Trujillo, to borrow Balaguer's term from the title of his 1998 book, *Memorias de un cortesano de la 'Era de Trujillo.'* He served the notoriously brutal and corrupt Trujillo in numerous capacities, including as the figurehead President from 1960 to 1962.

Trujillo, who ruled for 31 years, was assassinated in May 1961. After mediation by the U.S. consul, a seven-member Council of State was formed, which Balaguer headed. Opposition to him led to chaos, and he went into exile in New York and Puerto Rico. An election was held, but then a military coup resulted in civil war. The United States intervened with 42,000 troops. Another election was held in 1966, which Balaguer won with U.S. support. He served via re-election until 1978.

The IAPA celebrated its 1977 annual General Assembly in Santo Domingo, the capital, which was organized by our second vice president, Germán Ornes, a lawyer and Dominican publisher. Balaguer's presidency was milder than the Trujillo era, but had a distinct authoritarian cast. Opponents were jailed and sometimes killed and opposition newspapers were occasionally seized.

Ornes—a friend of mine from numerous IAPA missions and other important IAPA projects—then was a champion of press freedom. He played a leading role in taking the case of obligatory licensing of journalists to the Inter American Court of Human Rights. He and others contended such statutes violated the freedom of the press provisions in the American Covention on Human Rights. The court agreed. But in his earlier incarnation, Ornes worked for the infamous dictator. In 1948 Trujillo founded the newspaper *El Caribe*, and Germán Ornes became its managing editor. He was named the publisher in 1954 and bought the paper that year. In 1955 he broke with Trujillo and went into exile. The paper was seized by the government. After Trujillo's assassination, Ornes regained control of the newspaper, but his reputation always suffered among some Dominicans due to his controversial history. Ornes, like Balaguer, was a bright, young and ambitious man in an authoritarian world where the best opportunity was playing the strong man's game. The account in Nobel laureate Mario Vargas LLosa's legendary account of the Trujillo dictatorship, *Feast of the Goat*, characterizes it. When we asked our friends Rafael and Francia Molina if the book was accurate, their quick reply: "It was far worse."

At IAPA's 1977 assembly, guided by Ornes, we encouraged Balaguer to respect civil liberties and continue building democracy. A year later he sought another term but was defeated by wealthy rancher Antonio Guzmán. The transition was the first in Dominican history of an incumbent peacefully surrendering the presidency to the opposition.

Balaguer was again elected in 1986. He had suffered from glaucoma for years and now, at age 80, was nearly blind. This third presidency was considerably more tolerant of opposition parties and human rights. Two years later IAPA had a second meeting, a Mid-year in Santo Domingo. IAPA held three more mid-year meetings in the Dominican Republic—in 1992, 2002 and 2016—the last two in La Romana and Punta Cana rather than Santo Domingo. The 1992 meeting again was organized by Germán Ornes and welcomed President Balaguer as the principal speaker.

Germán died from a heart attack in 1998 at age 78. The last two meetings were organized by my good friend Rafael Molina, who edited other publications and in the late 1970s and early 1980s was a diplomat. He served as the Dominican ambassador to the United Nations and later to the United States.

At the 2002 mid-year in La Romana, former U.S. President Bill Clinton spoke. Later that evening a memorable moment for me was being on the dance floor with Clinton as he held a Dominican female closely, apparently a friend.

20. Jamaica
Saving a Newspaper

One of my heroes rescued the oldest and most prestigious independent newspaper in Jamaica, *The Gleaner*, by forestalling bankruptcy in 1978. Oliver Clarke, a trained accountant, had joined the newspaper as managing director in 1976. We met and became good friends when he sought IAPA's help at our 1977 mid-year meeting in Cartagena, Colombia. He would later serve as IAPA president.

In the late 1970s Jamaica experienced unprecedented violence during the tenure of leftist Prime Minister Michael Manley. He had a close relationship with the dictator of nearby Cuba, Fidel Castro. More than 800 Jamaicans were killed in the 1980 election.

At one point Manley adjourned a cabinet meeting and was joined by his ministers and others in leading a mob attack on *The Gleaner's* building. They objected to coverage by the paper. "Next Time. Next Time!" they chanted, meaning if they revisited the newspaper there might be more than shouted words. Manley referred to *The Gleaner* as the "Call Girl on North Street" and described the editor, writers and Oliver as "pimps of imperialism."

The government withdrew advertising and diverted business to a supportive competitor. The ministers and departments were instructed not to buy *Gleaner* publications. Reporters became *personas non grata* and suffered beatings. At the time Karen and I visited, the newspaper facilities, which were new just a few years earlier in 1969, appeared empty and run down. The beautiful wood paneling of the offices now seemed decadent.

By July 1978, Oliver was desperate and had to seek financial support from Manley's opponents. He offered to the public $4 million in debentures to meet obligations and succeeded. Fortunately, Manley lost the 1980 election to opposition leader Edward Seaga and things changed.

Oliver would serve as host for IAPA's mid-year in 1984, where Prime Minister Seaga spoke, and again in 1999. At the latter, one of Michael Manley's ministers who had been in the mob on the Gleaner, P. J. Patterson, was now prime minister. At Oliver's invitation, he spoke at our meeting. Manley was now dead. Patterson had changed, too.

21. Haiti
Earthquake

On January 12, 2010, a catastrophic 7.0 magnitude earthquake wreaked havoc in Port-au-Prince, Haiti's capital. Although I had visited the country a time or two as a tourist, I do not speak French and had not been involved in IAPA's activities there. But the crippling blows to Haiti's major newspapers, *Le Nouvelliste* and *Le Matin*, drew my attention. I helped bring IAPA as well as ASNE into a consortium called the Haiti News Project to commission damage assessments and then raise funds, training and equipment for the country's independent media. The early belief was recovery seemed improbable.

The newspapers' buildings were damaged and *Le Nouvelliste's* presses were no longer usable. Both papers lost staff through deaths and attrition. Seventy-five percent of their advertising revenue was gone. Many businesses that were destroyed or severely damaged no longer wanted or needed to advertise. The consortium sent press technicians and identified banks that might make low-interest loans. *Le Nouvellliste's* publisher, Max Chauvet, had periodically attended IAPA meetings in the past and joined our group in Miami to provide first-hand information. The group coordinator, Joe Oglesby, made several trips to Haiti as well as attending an IAPA meeting.

I helped secure two fellows funded by the Knight Foundation to conduct on-site training on reporting and investigative journalism for the staffs. Nineteen media groups ultimately participated in the project. In addition to cash, donors contributed 37 computers, 52 laptop bags, four cameras and two printers.

After one year, our project and others and especially the efforts of Haitians themselves found the situation substantially improved. All the country's newspapers, albeit with smaller staffs, were again publishing and radio and television stations were back on the air. The slow return of newspaper advertising remained a challenge, as did political instability, disease and an extremely slow and painstaking recovery for the country.

22. Puerto Rico
Governor Intimidates

In late 1997 the owners of *El Nuevo Día*, Puerto Rico's largest and most influential daily newspaper, filed a lawsuit against the commonwealth's governor accusing him and his aides of violating their right of free speech. I played a small role by drafting a protest by the American Society of Newspaper Editors (ASNE) supporting them. I also provided information about a related judgement by the U.S. Supreme Court.

I knew the daily's editor, Luis Alberto Ferré, who participated in both ASNE and IAPA. His newspaper was scheduled to host the mid-year meeting of IAPA in San Juan the following spring.

The lawsuit challenged the use of government advertising and set an important precedent strengthening First Amendment freedoms on the island and possibly on the U.S. mainland. Gov. Pedro Rosselló had cancelled millions of dollars of advertising after investigative stories were published alleging government corruption.

I supplied information about a 1996 case my brother Dick Seaton had won in the U.S. Supreme Court. It established free speech rights for government contractors.

El Nuevo Día won in the lower courts and the case was settled by the government before appealing to the U.S. Supreme Court. The U.S. Court of Appeals in Boston ruled that using government funds to punish political speech runs afoul of the First Amendment. The ruling is binding in the states in the Boston circuit, which includes Puerto Rico. It may have influence elsewhere.

The case was ultimately settled out of court in 1999 when the government agreed to resume advertising but accepted no blame. It agreed to adopt a fair advertising policy affirming press freedom.

Interestingly, Gov. Rosselló spoke lauding the First Amendment at IAPA's 1998 meeting.

23. SIP = CIA????
Problematic

The resurgence of Latin American governments opposed to United States policy has brought with it renewed attacks on IAPA—including allegations of CIA funding of the society. Claims of CIA involvement are becoming as common as they were in the 1970s and 1980s. At the recent General Assembly in Buenos Aires a group of Peronist Party protestors distributed leaflets outside the meeting hotel: "SIP=CIA / FUERA YANKES." In Venezuela the allegations are routine at any IAPA session that includes Chavez government supporters.

My extensive investigation of this matter in publicly available documents and reports—including much declassified material—found no documented evidence of CIA funds flowing in any manner to IAPA. I ran across only one case of U.S. government funds coming indirectly. Nathaniel Davis, who served as U.S. ambassador to Chile from 1971–1973, writes in his 1985 book on those years that the U.S. information service (USIA) director Charles Z. Wick "acknowledged in 1983 that his agency had contributed, through third parties, 'to various organizations, such as the Inter-American Press Association, which under its charter does not take government money but got $50,000 from the federals through an intermediate group.'" The USIA is not affiliated with the CIA.

My study, however, did reveal numerous examples of IAPA member publications and/or their staffs receiving—knowingly or unknowingly—CIA funding.

The allegation of CIA funding to IAPA itself appears to have been driven primarily by two authors, Carl Bernstein of Watergate fame and Dr. Fred Landis, a Chilean-born North American psychologist who received his Ph.D. from the University of Illinois based on his thesis, "Psychological Warfare and Media Operations in Chile, 1970–1973." A 1982 article by Landis is often the source referred to today, but Carl Bernstein's 1977 essay in *Rolling Stone* came first and apparently influenced some prominent U.S. journalists including several of his colleagues at the *Washington Post*.

At one point in his piece, "How America's Most Powerful News Media Worked Hand in Glove with the Central Intelligence Agency and Why the Church Committee Covered It Up," Bernstein states without direct attribution: "James Copley was also the guiding hand behind the Inter-American Press Association, a CIA-funded organization with heavy membership among right-wing Latin American newspaper editors." The sentence is at the end of a section about the Copley News Service quoting from a *Penthouse* magazine article by Joe Trento and Dave Roman that had appeared two months earlier.

The *Penthouse* exposé states at one point: "Through his leadership in the Inter American Press, which had been described as 'pure CIA,' Copley cultivated the leaders of the right-wing Latin American press." While the *Penthouse* authors attribute many of their assertions to CIA sources, this one is not attributed. Nonetheless, given the similarity of the phrasing, Bernstein almost certainly appropriated it, taking "described (by no one in particular) as 'pure CIA,'" to another level: "a CIA funded organization."

While neither the *Penthouse* article nor Bernstein provides documentation or attributions for their assertions, they apparently did influence the *Post*'s Executive Editor Ben Bradlee and columnist Mary McGrory. In one of her columns, McGrory made the claim of CIA funding to IAPA, and when IAPA leaders asked Bradlee for a correction on the record, as I recall *Miami Herald* Executive Editor George Beebe telling me, he turned them down and said he was inclined to believe the assertion.

Also, in a 1997 report, gadfly Daniel Brandt published on his website, Namebase.org, a short history of journalism and the CIA in which he repeats the *Penthouse* allegation and attributes it to Trento and Roman.

In the early 1980s Fred Landis toured American campuses referring to IAPA as a "CIA puppet" that worked with leading newspapers to undermine leftist governments in Chile, Jamaica and Nicaragua. He spelled out this theory in the January/February 1982 issue of *Science for the People*, the magazine of a left-wing organization of the same name that emerged from the antiwar culture of the United States in the 1970s. In it he was somewhat more careful, referring to "the CIA-influenced Inter American Press Association." He quotes a December 26, 1977, *New York Times* article quoting a high CIA official referring to IAPA as "a covert action resource" of the Agency.

A month later he published the same article in the *Covert Action Information Bulletin*, Number 16, March 1982. As a result of these publications, his allegations have continued to receive wide currency in leftist circles. For example, on the website Spin Profile.org there is a page on IAPA which, along with a list of officers and directors, reports that "in all likelihood, IAPA was set up by the CIA and its affiliate organs." The substantiation is a lengthy quote from Fred Landis's 1982 article.

Landis's only documented source is the 1977 *New York Times* article. Interestingly, a careful reading of the article from the paper's on-line archive or on microfilm will not produce the reference. The four pertinent paragraphs, according to a 1986 editorial in the *Minneapolis Tribune*, apparently did in fact appear, but only in the *Times'* home edition. In it the *Times* quoted a Senate committee conclusion that the CIA orchestrated a 1970 protest against threats to press freedom in Chile, and the story says the IAPA joined in that protest.

This, of course, establishes only that IAPA did no more than play its normal role of speaking out to defend press freedom. Considering that the *New York Times* article, part of a three-part series, was published little more than a month after Carl Bernstein's *Rolling Stone* article and three months after the *Penthouse* piece, the fact that it does not assert CIA funding of IAPA suggests the authors, John M. Crewdson and Joseph B. Treaster, could not prove it had occurred.

In my own nearly four decades of active participation in IAPA—almost all of them as an insider—I have seen no evidence of any government funding beyond the occasional cocktail event sponsored at one of our meetings or a couple of grants from one of the independent, but government funded, German foundations. I have seen nothing that could conceivably be CIA funding. On the contrary, on occasion after occasion I have heard our members express in the strongest terms the imperative of avoiding government funding—especially from a covert source like the CIA.

I have no personal knowledge of the years between the founding of the modern IAPA in 1950 and my participation, which began in 1972. However, a book published in 2008 by Harvard University Press recounts the history of the CIA's clandestine PR campaign aimed at countering Soviet propaganda and influence. The book, *The Mighty Wurlitzer: How the CIA Played America* by Hugh Wilford, an associate professor of history at California State University, Long Beach, reviews in detail CIA front organizations in the 1950s and 1960s. His record of this anti-Communist period is rich with examples of cooperation by individuals and groups who continued a pattern with roots in World War II.

Wilford's examination reveals that the American Newspaper Guild accepted CIA money for its international activities, including in Latin America for its front organization, the Inter-American Federation of Working Newspapermen's Organizations (IAFWNO). In Europe it worked through the International Federation of Journalists.

His study also confirms that the publisher of *The New York Times*, Arthur Hays Sulzberger, agreed to permit the CIA to place agents in its foreign bureaus as correspondents or clerical staff as well as to have its legitimate staff pass along information on potential foreign agents. Henry Luce's *Time* magazine had similar arrangements.

At no point in the book does Wilford mention IAPA. To confirm that he found no information about any connection between the CIA and IAPA, I corresponded with him by e-mail. His response offers fairly compelling evidence that IAPA itself did not have any such relationship, although as we know, some IAPA members, including *The Times* and *Time* magazine, did have relationships and in several cases accepted CIA funding. "I've checked my notes," he wrote me, "and I don't have any data on the IAPA and CIA . . . I don't know of any links between the IAPA and CIA in the period with which I was concerned, that is the late 1940s to 1967."

It is possible that between 1967 and my entry into IAPA in 1972 there was some connection, but I doubt it. After exposure of several of the CIA front organizations in 1966 by *Ramparts* magazine, followed by many more by *The New York Times* and *Washington Post*, the agency's "Mighty Wurlitzer" went silent.

An exposé published in 1975 by former CIA agent Philip Agee, *CIA Diary: Inside the Company*, reveals names of agents and front organizations used during Agee's CIA tenure between 1956 and 1968 with assignments in Ecuador, Uruguay and Mexico. Agee also reports that the CIA "promoted the founding" of the International Federation of Journalists (IFJ) as an alternative society of journalists to the Prague-based International Organization of Journalists (IOJ). And he tells of the founding in 1960 in Lima of the Inter-American Federation of Working Newspapermen (IFWN) as a cover for the American Newspaper Guild. His only mention in the book of IAPA is to note that IFWN "is more like a trade union, as opposed to the Inter-American Press Association which is mostly composed of publishers." IAPA is not included in his Appendix listing of "organizations which, at the date of their mention in the main text, were either financed, influenced or controlled by the CIA."

The only entity with a direct relationship to IAPA listed by Agee is Editors Press Service, owned by Joshua Powers, then an IAPA director and member of the advisory council. This Appendix reference is as follows: "EDITORS PRESS SERVICE. CIA-controlled propaganda outlet based in New York. Material placed through CIA propaganda agents in Latin America." Agee mentions the CIA paying for coverage in Ecuadorean newspapers, but is not explicit about the manner or specific newspapers.

Quoting former CIA officials, *The New York Times* three-part series in 1977 mentions a number of IAPA member publications and their staffs with CIA relationships. These include Joshua Powers and his Editors Press Service, which, "as an established news and feature service with clients throughout Latin America . . . became a channel of dissemination for agency inspired propaganda." One former CIA man said Editors Press Service "was an outlet for what he called 'cliché stories, news stories prepared by the agency or for the agency.'"

Powers was interviewed for the series and acknowledges friendships and cooperation within the agency, but said he could recall only a single connection between Editors Press Service and CIA. In the mid-60s, he said, he used CIA funds to finance the travels in Latin America of one of his writers. That exile Cuban writer, Guillermo Martinez Márquez, had served as the 1956–57 president of IAPA. Martinez Márquez also was interviewed by the *New York Times* writers and said he "had never known that the money he received from Mr. Powers had come from the CIA."

Citing CIA sources, *The New York Times* series also reported that a dozen publications in Miami, primarily whose editors had fled Cuba after the Castro government came to power in 1959, were subsidized by the CIA through a front organization in New York called Foreign Publications, Inc. The subsidies—in some cases amounting to several million dollars—"reportedly included *Avance, El Mundo, El Prensa Libre, Bohemia* and *El Diario de las Américas.*" Most were at the time members of IAPA. The owners of *Diario Las Americas,* which was founded in Miami and still publishes, told me inclusion of their newspaper in the story was in error, a confusion with *El Diario de la Marina,* which had been published in Cuba. They wrote a letter to *The Times* refuting it, they said, but it was not published.

The CIA initially intended to distribute copies of the subsidized publications clandestinely into Cuba, according to the series, but its plans went awry, although the subsidies continued. The weekly *Bohemia* received more than $3 million.

The most widely known case of an IAPA member publication receiving CIA funding was Chile's *El Mercurio* in the early 1970s during the Allende government. The newspaper at the time was the victim of severe economic pressures, multiple law suits and tax claims filed by the government and of a six-day closure for running an ad that called the Allende administration "illegitimate." It said in 1971 it had lost 50 percent of its advertising revenue.

Details of the subsidy, which kept the newspaper afloat as an Allende critic, were revealed in the shocking 1975 Church Committee hearings and amplified in the 2003 National Security Archive book, *The Pinochet File: A Declassified Dossier on Atrocity and Accountability*. Between 1971 and 1974 the paper received millions of dollars. In a single year it was given at least $1.95 million. The newspaper is owned by Augustín E. Edwards, who served as IAPA president 1968–69.

Two cases often cited by IAPA critics are those of Nicaragua's *La Prensa* during the 1980s Contra War against the Sandinistas and Jamaica's *Gleaner* during Michael Manley's socialist government in the 1970s. In neither case are there documents confirming CIA subsidies.

Oliver Clarke, who at the time guided *The Gleaner* from virtual bankruptcy—stemming primarily from government policy—states categorically the newspaper did not receive CIA funding. It did obtain a guarantee for its private loans through the U.S. government's Overseas Private Investment Corporation (OPIC), he said, and he speculates the CIA might have made that possible without his knowledge.

Jaime Chamorro told an IAPA delegation in which I participated at the height of the Contra war that since the troubles began with the Sandinistas, *La Prensa* had received more than $250,000 from the National Endowment for Democracy—a quasi-private U.S. group that receives funds overtly from the U.S. Congress to support democracy abroad—money from a foundation supported by the German government, and $400,000 from a Venezuelan business man whose name he said he didn't remember. The latter was in the form of a "loan" but did not have to be repaid. He said that Interior Minister Tomás Borge, who had once worked as a distribution agent for the paper, had privately given his permission for the receipt of aid from all three sources. An additional $100,000 had come from Venezuelan President Luis Herrera

Campins, but it had not been "registered" with the government, although the Nicaraguan ambassador went with Jaime to receive it.

Jaime characterized the $400,000 "loan" as "presumably from the CIA," although he had no way of knowing for sure. He said a U.S. Embassy official told him about the money.

Although receiving less attention, another IAPA member newspaper, Emilio Filippi's *La Epoca* of Chile, took subsidies from the National Endowment for Democracy. His start-up daily received hard-won permission for the Pinochet government to publish after a favorable court ruling. It attempted to walk a line between government support and opposition adhering to a pro-democracy line, but it faced enormous financial challenges competing with the established pro-government media.

As mentioned earlier, another newspaper organization often linked to the CIA is the Copley Group, which was headed for many years by James Copley, IAPA president 1969–70. The *Penthouse* article by Trenton and Roman accuses Copley of collaborating with the agency during the Eisenhower administration by using the Copley News Service and its reporters as fronts. However, Copley's long-time weekly hometown competitor *San Diego Reader* reported in 2008: "Though their story has become gospel from many CIA critics, the Copley Newspapers have consistently denied its truth, and records that might back up the accusations remain classified, locked away or perhaps destroyed, by the CIA. But as the correspondence in the Nixon archives make clear, there was little doubt that Copley was willing to do almost anything the vice president asked of him."

Finally, allegations of CIA links to Jules DuBois, the long-time chairman of IAPA's freedom of press committee for whom IAPA's Miami headquarters building was named, are often leveled by IAPA critics. The 1977 *New York Times* series reported DuBois was "said to have been an 'asset'" for the CIA and was "described by one former official as 'well and favorably known' to the agency though never on its payroll."

A few paragraphs later in this discussion, which includes the names of several other journalists, the authors report that a former agency official "said a number of people were listed as assets 'who didn't even know they'd been recruited.'"

DuBois was the Latin American correspondent for the *Chicago Tribune*. Jack Fuller, who was the president of Tribune Publishing at the time the IAPA building was named for DuBois, said he asked the Tribune's Washington bureau—as a precaution before naming the building—to investigate DuBois' relationship with the CIA. The investigation found nothing.

Insofar as promoting press freedom is concerned, the IAPA and the CIA are often walking the same path, but that does not mean the IAPA is "CIA funded," a "CIA puppet," "CIA influenced" or an "asset of CIA" any more than President Obama's takeover of some banks makes him an "asset" of, say, Hugo Chavez.

That certain active members of the society have accepted CIA funds is problematic but not compelling. The IAPA Charter in its eighth and final provision states that "It is contrary to the existence of a free and independent press and to the principles of IAPA for newspapers to accept subsidies or any other form of economic help from governments." Meanwhile, the IAPA by-laws prohibit membership for media organizations or individuals that "adhere to totalitarian ideologies or advocate suppression of free expression." They also give the board of directors power, if five members petition for it, "to expel or to suspend" a member who appears to have violated the Charter or bylaws.

While these members may have violated the final provision of the Charter regarding government subsidies, other IAPA members have not seen fit to question their eligibility. They are not ineligible under the bylaw proscribing anti-free expression advocates. In fact, in most cases they have been strong advocates of freedom who are under siege from governments suppressing free expression. Under these circumstances, their violation of one provision of the Charter was not viewed as sufficient for them to be expelled or suspended. Had they been advocates of suppression, undoubtedly their fates would have been different.

24. Declaration of Chapúltepec
A First Amendment

The success of IAPA's aspiration to generate a Latin American version of the First Amendment vastly exceeded the expectations of all of us involved. It changed the landscape of press freedom issues in the region. Ten years after the Declaration of Chapúltepec was drafted, legislative and judicial reforms based on its 10 principles are the norm in most countries. The principles became embodied in international law when the Organization of American States adopted a version of the declaration known as the Inter-American Declaration of Principles on Freedom of Expression.

As a result of Chapúltepec, reported *Editor & Publisher* magazine on the declaration's 10th anniversary, "Latin American leaders who once slammed their doors in the face of IAPA fact-finders are now willing to travel to another country just to speak to them."

The declaration enshrines freedom of expression as an inalienable buttress of Latin American democracy. It was drafted in 1994 at the historic Hemisphere Conference on Free Expression in the monumental Chapúltepec Castle high above Mexico City. The conference brought together respected political leaders, writers, academics, constitutional lawyers and well-known editors and publishers. It was the result of more than a year of hard work examining challenges and pressures on free expression and freedom of the press in the democracies of the hemisphere.

As the 1990s opened and representative government began again to flourish in Latin America, we could see that many of the future challenges to the press would not be abusive dictators as had been the case for decades—although attacks on the press did not end—but rather restrictive laws and onerous court judgments emerging within the new democratic systems. Press freedom battles were going to shift from the confrontations we had long experienced with authoritarian regimes to courts and congress halls. The issues would be freedom of information and access, insult laws, criminal defamation and impunity rather than arbitrary detentions and closings. With these changes in mind, we convened the Mexico City conference.

The original idea was refined on a porch at James McClatchy's fabulous summer compound on Lake Tahoe. Jim was then chairman of McClatchy Newspapers and IAPA president. He and I envisioned a hemisphere conference on the role of the press in democracy. The concept evolved under our leadership into the historic gathering that, after three days of deliberations, hammered out the free press manifesto.

We set out to write a Magna Carta for press freedom in the Americas—and we did so. As Jim was fond of saying, it is a document not for the benefit of the media, but for all citizens, for the public at large. When Eduardo Ulibarri, editor of Costa Rica's *La Nacion*, and I crafted the original draft, we had a declaration of 20 principles. Eventually, we reduced these to nine, and the conference modified the nine and added one to make the total of 10. It adopted them by consensus, but probably could not have done so without the skillful leadership of the conference chairman, Javier Pérez de Cuellar, the distinguished former United Nations Secretary General. Because of its impact, the history of the declaration's origin is worth recording.

I had been appointed by Julio F. de Mesquita, my successor to the IAPA presidency, to head a new committee for raising funds. He named it the Foundations Committee. After several minor successes, I finally managed to secure a grant from the Knight Foundation for a total of $120,000, spread over three years, for a full-time professional to work with IAPA's Freedom of Press Committee. It was by far the largest grant received by IAPA in decades, and we had the good fortune to hire Ricardo Trotti, a bright young Argentine editor who had already published a book on press freedom in Latin America. Over the next dozen years Ricardo profoundly improved our freedom of press work. He also was the intellectual father and implementer of IAPA's important Impunity Project, later also funded by Knight.

I had worked on the Knight Foundation for funding for several years. When I was IAPA president, I once kibitzed in a conversation between Lee Hills and Augustine "Dooney" Edwards, both former IAPA presidents. Lee, who was then president of the Knight Foundation, bragged to Dooney about how large Knight's endowment had become and what the foundation could accomplish. "How about sending some money IAPA's direction?" I interrupted. Lee, somewhat startled by my impertinence, responded that because of IAPA's history with foundation money and his personal involvement, I'd have to get money elsewhere before he thought he could help us. Years before,

IAPA had gone through a $400,000 Ford Foundation grant without accomplishing much other than publishing a couple of books.

The next two years I managed to obtain small grants from the Tinker Foundation, the Reuter Foundation, the Hewlett Foundation, the Ramos Foundation and a couple of others. None was of the size I think Lee hoped for, but in the spring of 1992 Knight approved that first large grant. Then, in early July that year, Lee sent me a note suggesting I try to re-ignite interest at Chicago's Robert R. McCormick Tribune Foundation. Colonel McCormick had been an early supporter of IAPA and his successor, Don Maxwell, also had been active. His Latin American correspondent, Jules Dubois, headed IAPA's Freedom of Press Committee for the first 15 years of its existence, from 1950 to 1965. The *Chicago Tribune* served as host in 1952 for the second IAPA General Assembly held in the United States. "The foundation seems to be doing more and more things outside its immediate bailiwick," Lee wrote.

Serendipitously, I had recently had a conversation with an old friend, Neal Creighton, whom I'd met when he was commanding general of Fort Riley, the military post near my Kansas home. Maj. Gen. Creighton was now president of the McCormick Tribune Foundation. The foundation had not previously ventured into funding international activities, but Neal had invited me to Chicago to discuss a possible relationship. We had a common interest in Latin American, where he had held U.S. Army posts in both the Dominican Republic and Panama. In the 1980s I had included him in a fact-finding trip to Central America with my congressman, Rep. Jim Slattery. As things evolved, my relationship with Neal was to have an enormous impact on IAPA and its accomplishments.

We agreed I would visit Chicago in early September. I asked IAPA president Jim McClatchy to join me. He went far beyond joining. He invited Karen and me to visit his Lake Tahoe compound for his annual Labor Day picnic and arranged for his jet to pick us up in Kansas. He said we would have time to brainstorm various possibilities we might present to the foundation.

In the same weeks Lee Hills wrote me about reigniting interest with the Tribune crowd and Neal Creighton invited me to Chicago, Jim McClatchy was having an exchange of letters with H. Brant Ayers, the colorful editor and owner of *The Anniston Star* in Alabama. Despite his non-metropolitan setting, Brandy has the same passion for the international world that I do, and unhesitatingly tries to infect others with it. I first met Brandy on ASNE's 1986 trip to the Soviet Union, and we have been friends since. At my encouragement he became active in IAPA and has served several terms as a director.

Brandy had sent Jim a book about emerging issues in Latin America, and in his thank-you letter, Jim lamented the fact that the authors did not display much concern for the role of a free press in efforts to establish economic stability. In response, Brandy suggested the Twentieth Century Fund, where he was a trustee, might take an interest in a book about "the role of the Latin American press as a catalyst for political change and as a nurturing agent of fragile democracies."

Jim picked up on Brandy's suggestion and asked whether the Fund would be interested in, rather than a book, co-sponsoring a conference on the subject of the press as a catalyst for political change. He suggested the fund could bring important scholars or corporate executives or political leaders to join press leaders at such a conference. Brandy responded that he would forward the idea to the Fund's staff and that he thought, because the Fund's focus is on U.S. public policy, there would more likely be interest if such a conference focused on how U.S. public policy should be constructed to effect a positive "role of the press in creating a new economic climate."

Jim sent me copies of this correspondence in mid July and asked for comments. I responded that a Hemisphere Conference was a "brilliant" idea, but that tailoring it to developing U.S. policy would be inconsistent with the mission of IAPA. Nor was I comfortable with a focus on the role of the press as a catalyst for political change. Such an approach, I wrote him, "smacks of an agenda that we might be uncomfortable with later. It brings to mind the 'social responsibility' theories currently in vogue in some Latin American countries."

But at its core Jim's vision led to the Declaration of Chapúltepec. "Important for IAPA would be an effort to build a South American general endorsement of free speech coming from a conference important enough to attract a lot of leaders, a truly international event," he had written. That is exactly what took place. Jim and I talked by telephone refining this idea over the next month and by the time we met at Lake Tahoe, we had set a goal for the conference to produce a document which could serve as a continental "Magna Carta" for free speech.

We believed the recently unleashed press in Latin America was now probing in places it could not before, and the public was learning about corruption of which it had been unaware. It was starting to think democracy brings corruption. In some cases leaders were beginning to look for ways to curb the press. A broad understanding of the role of free speech and press, we believed, was crucial to the survival of the fragile new democracies.

In Chicago, Jim and I joined board members and staff of the McCormick Tribune Foundation for dinner at a downtown club Tuesday, Sept. 8, 1992. Among them were Charles Brumback, president and CEO of the Tribune Company, and Jack Fuller, editor of the Chicago Tribune. We told them about eight possible projects.

Looking to what we believed to be the most important needs of IAPA, we did not present the hemisphere conference as our top priority. It was not even second. We told our dinner companions supplementing the Knight Foundation's grant was at the top of our list because it would be declining each year. Second was a project we hoped would get U.S. editors more involved in IAPA. The conference was our third priority. Our dinner hosts were very encouraging about an enhanced relationship with IAPA and the evening was extremely pleasant, but there were no commitments. We were driven back by Neal Creighton and his assistant, Dick Behrenhausen, to Cantigny, the late benefactor's former estate, where we were staying.

The overnight there was of special meaning to me because my great-uncle, Edward S. Beck, had been McCormick's managing editor for more than 30 years. I could envision Uncle Ned meeting with the Colonel there in his impressive library or talking with him by phone on deadline. Not bashful about such things, I mentioned the connection on several occasions, as I had earlier in conversation with Jack Fuller. Whether my connection to E. S. Beck helped me get foundation support for IAPA and other causes, I may never know for sure, but I've always thought so.

Incidentally, on the drive back to Cantigny, Dick Behrenhausen, another old Fort Riley connection of mine who would later succeed Neal Creighton as head of the foundation, asked if I'd be interested in bringing *The Manhattan Mercury* into the foundation's Communities Program. The program matched local fundraising dollar for dollar. I said I would consider the possibility but expressed fear such a campaign in a small city like Manhattan might undermine the local United Way. I did not follow up with Dick until the following summer when parts of Manhattan were devastated by the Flood of 1993. We launched a Neighbors in Need campaign that raised nearly $400,000 including the match, which was about as much as the United Way campaign totaled that year. Manhattan's relationship with the foundation continued for years and with the match—later trimmed to $1 for every $2 raised locally—provided over the next decade more than $4 million for local youth programs and the poor.

Within two weeks of returning home from Chicago, I received a letter from Neal: "I personally was quite interested in the idea that you mentioned of having a conference which would come out with a statement of principles for freedom of the press in Latin America," he wrote. "If such a conference could be held at Cantigny, I think our Board would enthusiastically provide the necessary monetary support. Let me know if you think that this might be a viable project to pursue."

Pursue it with enthusiasm we did. Yet without Neal's vision and initial push, I doubt there would be a Declaration of Chapúltepec. McCormick's journalism program director, Vivian Vahlberg, soon visited our IAPA office in Miami; but even several months after our Chicago visit, letters were exchanged about other possible projects. Neal and Vivian came to Miami in January for a meeting with IAPA's key leaders, this time to discuss the hemisphere conference. They still wanted the conference at Cantigny, but we were firm in our desire to hold it in Latin America, possibly in Santiago, Chile, to offset a threatening anti-free press UNESCO conference planned there, or San José, Costa Rica, due to its long identification with democracy in the hemisphere.

On February 8, 1993, Vivian called with the uplifting news that our grant request had been approved. She mentioned the desirability of obtaining follow-up funding from other sources—preferably in Latin America. She also said the foundation board wanted to limit its focus outside the country to Latin America and would like to visit there to become familiar with the challenges facing the press. I would help arrange that trip, which was taken in conjunction with the conference at Chapúltepec.

As things eventually turned out, the foundation not only provided full funding for the conference, the staff told us if we needed extra funds to "do it right," the money would be available. I had prepared a budget for $110,000 and asked initially for $100,000. The foundation supplemented that with another $30,000. As a result of our remarkable success, the McCormick Tribune Foundation for many years was the sole funder of the Chapúltepec project.

A great deal of work went into pulling off the conference, which took place in March, 1994. Along with Bill Williamson, IAPA's executive director, Jim and I oversaw the work of David Hume, a former Reuters correspondent who was hired to coordinate the preparations. Bill managed the finances and contact with IAPA members. In addition to producing the original draft of the principles with Eduardo Ulibarri, I solicited background papers from key IAPA members on various key issues confronting the press in the region. I wrote one myself on the history of press freedom in Latin America, which is the basis for parts of the Introduction to this memoir.

We came up with the idea of getting Javier Pérez de Cuellar to chair the conference. To establish contact, Jim McClatchy attended a speech the former secretary general gave in California and made a point of seeing him afterward. Our Peruvian colleagues in IAPA also were important in securing his participation. We were also fortunate to recruit through other IAPA colleagues a number of other celebrities. Among them were Mexican author Octavio Paz, the Nobel Prize winner, prominent Mexican writer Enrique Krause, and former Ecuadorian President Rodrigo Borja.

The site of the conference was the idea of Alejandro Junco de la Vega, who was IAPA president in 1993 when we received the grant. He suggested the Chapúltepec Castle as an alternative to San José or Santiago, both of which were seriously considered, and the thought of a "Declaration of Chapúltepec" seemed to ring right with everyone. It said "Latin America," perhaps even "indigenous Latin America."

As the conference in the majestic castle unfolded, it became clear not everyone would endorse the principles. The former Ecuadorian president, for example, was not prepared to take the political risk of offending his country's College of Journalists, a mandatory guild, by signing on to the ninth principle, which insists membership in such groups be voluntary. For a while we wondered whether we would be able to succeed in producing the declaration. That's when the skillful Pérez de Cuellar suggested we approve the principles not by voting but rather by consensus. That move led to the Declaration, although Rodrigo Borja and perhaps one or two others did not sign the final document.

We also struggled mightily to keep drafts in both Spanish and English up-to-date as changes were suggested. Ultimately, subtleties could not be matched in both languages.

We had to resort midway through the conference to making the Spanish version official and promising we would later do our best to produce an accurate English translation. My wife Karen, a former university Spanish language instructor, and I produced the English translation as soon as we returned home.

The language problem was one of many issues that had to be resolved on the fly—a situation not made easier by the fact that David Hume, the conference coordinator, became ill and was unable to provide much help as the conference progressed. It was with a considerable sense of relief—but also victory—that the declaration was adopted on the morning of March 11, 1994.

Our next step initially was both to promote the principles of the declaration at the local level in individual countries and to internationalize Chapúltepec. We weren't quite sure how to go about it, but the day after the conference some of us had a breakfast meeting with Mexican President Carlos Salinas at Los Pinos, the presidential residence. He asked what we'd been doing in Mexico City, and we told him. Then, in another totally unplanned and serendipitous development, someone asked if the president would be willing to sign the declaration. "Let me read it," he said. At first it seemed no one had a copy, but then—in another example of sheer serendipity—one of our younger members found a copy in his pocket. President Salinas read it and signed that copy.

His decision to sign Chapúltepec gave us the idea of seeking other presidential signings. It was apparent that a president who endorsed Chapúltepec by signing would more likely support the principles and cooperate with proposed legal reforms aimed at making a country's laws consistent with them. It also gave us hope that we might somehow advance the principles into the legal framework of the Americas. So we were on two tracks: national and international.

At the international level, we set out to have the principles adopted by the OAS system. We began working with the Inter American Human Rights Commission and eventually the OAS General Assembly. They were receptive partners, especially the Commission. The result was, first, the ground-breaking creation by the Commission of the Office of Relator for Freedom of Expression, and subsequently the adoption of the Inter American Declaration of Principles on Freedom of Expression, which is a Chapúltepec clone with a few modifications.

As we gathered presidential signatures in conjunction with additional hemispheric conferences and nation-by-nation conferences, we were advancing on our local track. These national forums examined the laws of each country against the Chapúltepec principles and in many cases have led to advances in the cause of freedom of expression in the countries where they have been held. We published in book form a compendium of these comparisons. Heads of state of at least 29 of the hemisphere's 35 nations have signed and embraced the declaration. Of major countries, only Canada, Venezuela and Cuba are without signatures—the latter because we have not sought endorsement.

Working with Jack Fuller of the *Chicago Tribune*, I managed after several false starts to arrange for U.S. President Bill Clinton to sign the Declaration. He signed in conjunction with his appearance at the 1995 annual convention in Dallas of the American Society of Newspaper Editors. Jack had been a class-mate of Bill and Hillary Clinton at Yale Law School and could get messages directly to the president. We originally ran into resistance from the U.S. De-partment of Justice, which was opposed to Clinton's signing out of concern that his doing so might be used against the government in U.S. courts. But Jack persuaded Clinton personally that his signature, as was the case of the other head-of-state signatures, would not carry the force of law. He was the 12th head of state to sign.

That Dallas ASNE meeting was a high point for me not just because Clin-ton signed the Declaration. It also was the meeting where I was put on the ladder by its board to become ASNE president. I had been a board member since 1991, but the key to my selection probably was that I had managed to bring to Dallas both the president of Mexico, Ernesto Zedillo, and the prime minister of Canada, Jean Chrétien. Their appearances along with President Clinton meant we had all three heads of state of the new North American Free Trade Agreement (NAFTA) countries. It was the first time three heads of state had appeared at an ASNE convention. I was successful only because of my IAPA friends. Alejandro Junco de la Vega, who had arranged for use of the Chapúltepec Castle, helped me with Zedillo; and Bill Thorsell, editor-in-chief of the Toronto *Globe and Mail*, who at the time was active in IAPA, put me in touch with the right individuals in Chrétien's government.

As the success of Chapúltepec gained momentum, I wrote two additional grant requests to the McCormick Tribune Foundation which were approved. The second of those was for nearly $500,000 and, because of its size, resulted in a very fractious debate within the IAPA leadership. The chairman of the so-ciety's Freedom of Press Committee, Danilo Arbilla of Uruguay, tried to stop the project. He feared the Chapúltepec campaign was growing so big it would supersede his committee. He, along with several others, also believed our goal of having the principles adopted as "customary law" by the Inter American Human Rights Court was unrealistic. As a result of a lot of sensitive diplomacy by then IAPA president Dave Lawrence, publisher of *The Miami Herald*, Danilo ultimately became a strong advocate of Chapúltepec and, much to his credit, led the successful campaign to have the principles adopted by the Inter American Human Rights Commission—his alternative to the "customary law" strategy.

After the country-by-country forums where we compared each nation's laws to the principles, we narrowed the focus to, first, the judiciary and then the congresses. In each case we held hemisphere conferences and then forums in each country. The grant proposal for the later judiciary and legislative phases of Chapúltepec were written by the IAPA staff under the direction of Alejandro Miró Quesada C., who succeeded Jim McClatchy as chairman of the Chapúltepec Committee.

In subsequent years the project received nearly $500,000 annually from the McCormick Tribune Foundation, which was justifiably proud of the results. In the decade after the foundation turned its attention toward helping the press in Latin America, it invested more than $17 million there with IAPA and other organizations. Included was $2.3 million toward a six-story IAPA headquarters in Miami. This strong support came not only under the guidance of Neal Creighton, but also that of Dick Behrenhausen when he succeeded Neal.

The impact of the Declaration of Chapúltepec has strengthened a doctrine of press freedom that is now permeating legislation, judicial decisions, international tribunal rulings and, of course, public thinking throughout the Americas. Each individual country grapples with the nuances of its own individual law and history, but most are moving press freedom forward. While there have been setbacks, here are some positive examples: National courts have implemented the Inter American Court's decision against the licensing of journalists in several countries. The Human Rights Commission has ruled in numerous cases in support of press freedom. In Panama, the gag law was repealed and a freedom of information act passed. In Costa Rica, the Insult (*Desacato*) Law was repealed, professional secrecy established by the courts and penalties eliminated for republication of stories distributed by other media. In Guatemala, the monopoly on television licenses was broken. In Mexico, freedom-of-information laws have been passed at both the national and state levels. Jamaica has adopted a freedom of information statute. In Colombia, a special prosecutor's office has been set up to pursue crimes against journalists. In Chile, access has been established by the courts and the seven insult laws have been eliminated or reformed. The Honduran Supreme Court eliminated that country's insult laws from its Criminal Code. In the Dominican Republic, action began to overturn its restrictive laws. Peru's and Ecuador's congresses adopted access laws, and a presidential decree established an access law in Bolivia. Governments and congresses in Argentina, Nicaragua, Uruguay and Guatemala considered access laws. In Brazil, major reform of laws affecting the press tool place. Freedom of information laws—including access to legal proceedings—were studied in other countries. Several courts adopted the standard of actual malice.

The hemisphere judicial summit in Washington in 2002 fostered a dialogue with Supreme Court justices from throughout the hemisphere on the issues of press freedom. U.S. Chief Justice William H. Rehnquist received the participants at a reception, and Associate Justice Stephen Breyer delivered an eloquent address on the importance of press freedom. Subsequently, nation-by-nation judicial conferences were held throughout the hemisphere. I helped set the stage at the Mexican conference that led to the new access law there. My address outlined the history of freedom of information in the United States. I also participated in judicial conferences in Colombia and Ecuador, where IAPA President Jack Fuller and I met with President Lucio Gutierrez and received from him a promise to issue regulations implementing the recently passed access law, which he later did.

The next phase of the Chapúltepec campaign bringing together congressional leaders and the press also produced remarkable results. The hemisphere conference in the summer of 2004 in Washington brought together the presidents of virtually every congress in the hemisphere with the exception of Cuba. Alaska Sen. Ted Stevens, president pro-tem of the U.S. Senate, represented the United States. He arranged for the Latin American leaders to visit the floor of the U.S. Senate and, because early in his career the senator had worked for my uncle, Fred Seaton, at the Department of Interior, he included me.

The conference started on Mother's Day. We had difficulty finding a senator available to welcome the delegates. At my request a friend, Sen. Pat Roberts of Kansas, who once worked as a student reporter for *The Manhattan Mercury* and more importantly was chairman of the Senate Select Committee on Intelligence, bailed us out.

I gave the wrap-up speeches at both the judicial and congressional hemisphere summits, basically reviewing our accomplishments.

The next phase of Chapúltpec was to develop an ethics statement for the press. This delicate project was led by Jack Fuller, the former president of Tribune Publishing and a leading authority on journalism values in the U.S. Jack's seminal book, *News Values: Ideas for an Information Age*, has been translated into Spanish and distributed throughout the region. As one of the five directors of the McCormick Tribune Foundation, Jack's support was crucial to Chapúltepec's success.

The Declaration of Chapúltepec is important. It has nourished and interacted with an increasing body of freedom of expression doctrine in the Americas. It inspired the office of OAS Relator on Freedom of Expression as part of the Inter American Commission on Human Rights as well as adoption of the OAS Declaration of Principles on Freedom of Expression. Before Chapúltepec, there had been a couple of important decisions on press issues by the Inter-American Court on Human Rights. There have been several since. Now there is a growing body of doctrine judges and legislators can refer to when interpreting and writing the law.

The Declaration of Chapúltepec is a dream come true. It is now the gold standard. It is routinely cited as such by journalists and politicians throughout Latin America. But it must be nurtured continuously, as has been done for 25 years. It has to be rekindled relentlessly to keep it growing—to keep this bastion of freedom of the press alive.[1]

-----

1. My participation as a leader in producing the Declaration and nurturing its later development is without question the most important accomplishment of my five decades toiling within Latin American journalism.

I still treasure the letter I received a week after the 1994 conference from the McCormick Tribune Foundation's journalism director, Vivian Vahlberg, who wrote:

"Kudos to you on a tremendously successful conference, which was due in no small part to the diplomatic skills, credibility and extensive knowledge you brought to the undertaking. You made an enormous difference."

Conclusion

The histories in this book of my courageous colleagues and friends—champions of press freedom all—reveal remarkable individuals facing prodigious challenges.

I think first of Raúl Kraiselburd and Bob Cox in Argentina's "Dirty War." Raúl lost both his father and son as a result of his fight for his newspaper. Bob faced nearly overwhelming odds to report on the "disappeared" and ultimately had to leave the country when credible threats targeted his children.

Alejandro Junco changed the face of Mexico by pushing journalism to new and higher standards. He could easily have lost everything in doing so.

Roberto Eisenmann took similar risks and helped bring down a dictator.

Pedro Chamorro did the same at the cost of his own life.

Aldo Zucolillo fought a battle with Alfredo Stroessner and won.

Christian Edwards survived a horrendous kidnapping because he was in the media.

José Rubén Zamora risked his life time after time to bring truth to light.

Juan Manuel Santos became president of Colombia and won the Nobel Peace Prize.

Yet with many of them and others there have been inconsistences on the principles I advocate. Such is typical of the chaotic relationship Latin America has had with human and civil rights and especially freedom of the press.

The challenges to consistency come from diverse sources—ideology, money, affiliations, even sex. Compromise has not been uncommon. But in my view those featured in this book are champions of the cause. As in any field, history can be messy.

A couple of my heroes have switched sides on the principles, initially working against them and those who advocated them. Others saw their economic wellbeing as more important. I have tried to tell how these compromises occurred. Others were taken in by concepts of equality and fairness that superseded press freedom and democracy.

Journalists and their supporters are fundamental to democracy. They do the watchdog work of exposing abuses of power in both the public and private sectors. They put searchlights on corruption and inequitable practices. Without that work, democracy withers.

The Inter American Press Association in Latin America, as well as the American Society of Newspaper Editors in the United States, have played central roles in fostering a free press that supports this critical role. I have had the privilege to be a participant in these efforts.

Journalism independent of government normally requires a hybrid of capitalism and democracy. Without the former, journalists directly or indirectly work for the state. Yet sole worship of economic interests can also undermine the journalism and free expression so fundamental to democracy. In some instances the press has been taken over in the name of private interests to design an illusion that hides and censors the real reality.

This, too, has led to compromise on my principles. But, as former U.S. Secretary of State Henry Kissinger has said, "Policy to promote democracy needs to be adapted to local and regional realities, or it will fail. In the pursuit of democracy, policy—as in other realms—is the art of the possible."

That is what has happened in Latin America. Violence often is the reality democracies must face, and a debate takes place on how much a government should restrain the press. Such situations tend to result in principles compromised. Government abuse, history and ideology also play roles. I have described how this occurs, yet how these courageous editors and reporters have had important roles in building their emerging democracies. Nearly all the countries my colleagues helped are today functional democracies with credible elections, respecting generally the rule of law, individual liberties and minority rights. The future will require similar commitments to freedom of the press. Heroic leaders will have to step forward. The challenges, while different, will be many and perhaps more difficult to overcome.

A battle exists today of whether citizens want liberal democracy in its classic form, with the guarantee of individual rights including an unencumbered independent press, or the offerings of populists who attack the press without hesitation or accuracy and subvert the courts and even the electoral process.

This alone is daunting. But the disruption of traditional media by contemporary challenges from the Internet—especially the undermining of the economic models of the printed press and television—make the future of press freedom more uncertain.

Twitter, Facebook, Google and other social media pose a new world. With politicians and anyone else having what amounts to a personal megaphone to push their own take on reality—without the vetting of professional reporters and editors—democracy as we know it is unlikely to remain the same.

New heroes for freedom are essential.

Appendix
More Historical Roots

To understand fully the modern struggles for liberal institutions like press freedom in Latin America, I believe one must examine not only the 19th century independence movement in its context but also look back to the 16th century origins of the struggles in Spain and Portugal. The political ideas underlying the indigenous societies encountered by the conquerors also undoubtedly are relevant, especially where Native Americans still predominate today, such as in Mexico, Guatemala, Bolivia, Ecuador, Colombia and Peru.

In the United States and the continent's other English-speaking countries, while differences exist, the role of the press in democracy is generally accepted to be free and unfettered—a watchdog of society. In this form it can provide the unvarnished information and ideas necessary for self-government. Few limitations are placed on the press in these countries. No special obligations are given to the press. The philosophical underpinnings to this approach assume that, given the chance, good ideas will drive out bad ones. This assumes that the press must be given the right to be both wrong and irresponsible. The first and strongest defense against abuses by the press is more press—meaning competition and free debate.

The American Revolutionary concept of unqualified press freedom was in stark contrast to the Old World legal tradition, existing at the time in England, Spain and elsewhere, of lèse majesté, the assumption that the ruler and his or her officials can do no wrong. Criticism of political officials was considered "seditious libel," a criminal offense. If a writer said that a royal person or crown servant was corrupt, he was not allowed to defend himself by producing evidence of corruption. Truth was no defense because the criminal harm lay in lowering esteem. The greater the truth, the greater the libel, as the saying went.

While press laws in the English speaking countries vary in length and substance, most are of few words and fewer caveats. England today has no press law whatsoever and depends on unwritten common law as interpreted by the courts. The United States law is limited to the blanket statement in its constitution, "Congress shall make no law . . . abridging the freedom of speech, or of the press." There are in the United States and elsewhere laws guaranteeing access to official records and public meetings. There are also judicial precedents that established rules, without inhibiting press freedom, of libel to protect individual reputations as well as control of pornography. There also is a narrowly defined ability for the state to protect itself and the public order where a clear and present danger exists. In a phrase, this concept is often characterized as "freedom from."

In contrast, Latin American countries historically took a "freedom to" approach. They have followed the European Continental tradition, inherited from Rome, France and Spain, of trying to regulate and codify everything—in some countries down to the smallest detail. A list at the time of the colonial wars of independence from Spain contained more than 5,000 books that were prohibited in the region. The impulse to codify finds its democratic justification in the founding document of European Continental democracy, the Declaration of the Rights of Man and of the Citizen of 1789. Article 11 reads: "Free communication of thoughts and opinions is among the most precious rights of Man. Thus, all men may speak freely, write and publish, *provided they be responsible for any abuse of this freedom in cases determined by law*" (emphasis added). This is still French constitutional law.

The rhetoric of democracy has lived in Latin America for longer than in any other part of the world except North America. Yet some words and phrases used in Latin America carry important distinctions compared to their use in other regions. Such key terms as popular sovereignty, representative government, the popular will, participation, individual rights, even democracy itself often mean something somewhat distinct in Latin America from the English language interpretation of the same terms.

The earliest medieval parliaments in continental Europe, for example, appeared in Spain. Citizens of cities developed rights of self-government and met in municipal assemblies to decide on public affairs.

At the time of the conquest of America, the rights granted citizens in their townships began to crumble as Charles V centralized Spain. In 1519 the townships rose in revolt, although unsuccessfully, to defend their rights and political assemblies. Their clearly stated aim was a constitutional, democratic monarchy based on popular representation. But the outcome was an authoritarian order imposing itself on progress toward a democratic order. As the founding fathers of the Spanish American republics achieved independence, monarchy was in disrepute and despotism unacceptable. The democratic concepts of their Iberian heritage were in vogue in the form of the European Enlightenment and the American and French revolutions. They looked to the Spanish Constitution of 1812, the first ever written, known popularly as "La Pepa." It called for a constitutional monarchy including freedom of the press.

Established in the midst of the Peninsular War with France by the Cádiz Cortes, Spain's first sovereign assembly, the Cortes Generales, "La Pepa" lasted only two years. It was revived from 1820 to 1823 and again in 1836–37. While never fully implemented, it served as a model for several Latin American and Caribbean nations. Prominent figures from Mexico, Chile, Peru and Ecuador participated in its drafting. Original monuments to it were torn down in 1814 with the exception of an obelisk in St. Augustine, Florida, which still stands.

In most cases the liberators also used constitutions patterned, at least in part, after the U.S. model. The constitution writers often used the structure, organization and sometimes even the language of the U.S. Constitution, but they tacked on the French Declaration of the Rights of Man and the Citizen and normally turned to the legal and constitutional codifications of Napoleon and the Spanish Constitution of 1820.

That the Old World concept of a strong central authority in defense of an undisturbed status quo evolved alongside a nascent liberal model of individual liberties is not surprising in the context of the social and racial makeup of the times. The founders feared the consequences of unfettered liberalism. American and French Revolutionary themes of liberty and equality could only be seen by most of the founders as threatening in societies where whites were a minority and the vast nonwhite majority, mostly illiterate, was not prepared for republican and democratic government. Democratic Caesarism, which also could trace roots to the French Revolution (Bonapartist era), allowed the elites to talk about equal rights and yet maintain hierarchical political and social structures that reflected the Old World roots. Only the next generation of liberal political leaders would begin to focus on transforming the vast majority of their countrymen through education into an informed, democratically oriented and engaged citizenry.

At least in their origins, many constitutions in Latin America did not serve primarily as social compacts or a set of ground rules for the conduct of public life. They tended to be lengthy codifications; and like the old Spanish and Portuguese laws, they mixed general precepts with regulative specifics and were viewed as documents to be put into effect in the future. Few citizens were concerned that many provisions were held in abeyance for years. In this context, many Latin American revolutions were regarded more as something to be permanently institutionalized, not as a point of departure for an open-ended process. The result was a perpetual struggle in many countries between idealistic theories of government and the reality of immediate practical needs. Soon constitutions and laws in these countries, including safeguards for free expression, were set aside. Despotism, interrupted by revolution and assassination, became the prevailing form of government in many of the new nations.

There were exceptions, such as Chile and Costa Rica. After its initial period of independence, Chile began a gradual emergence of parliamentary stability interrupted only in recent decades. When the Spanish rule collapsed in 1821 in Costa Rica, a sort of town-meeting democracy replaced it. Brazil evolved on a somewhat distinct track as well because it had 69 years of constitutional monarchy after independence, but the roots and ultimate unfolding of its constitutional history are similar to its neighbors of Spanish heritage.

Today, each Latin American country has evolved in its unique way, but most now live under political institutions that are truly democratic, even if often fragile. The earlier threads of colonial and continental heritage remain in their political cultures. Constitutions still tend to emphasize logic from the code law tradition, to be anticipatory and to remain idealistic. As a result they are less rooted in experience, and the public and political leaders in these countries sometimes demonstrate an inclination in times of crisis for limiting freedom of the press.

Following these traditions, most press laws and many constitutional press provisions first proclaim press freedom and then provide for its restriction, sometimes in great detail. They reflect what Tina Rosenberg has called "magical liberalism." This phenomenon reached a certain pinnacle in the early 1990s when the Legislative Assembly of El Salvador passed a law obligating publication and broadcast of all public statements, political ads and other messages of political parties. The law also prohibited the media from damaging the "private image" of leaders, dead or alive. In the words of Octovio Paz: yesterday's attitudes with today's ideas.

In 2013 the Ecuadorian Congress set the bar even higher (or perhaps lower) when it passed a communications law creating a state watchdog to regulate media content. The law, with loosely defined regulations, requires "accurate and balanced" coverage and prohibits "discrediting another person . . . (or) reducing his or her creditability." In the law's first two years the government's watchdog (Supercom) brought 506 cases resulting in 313 punishments including fines as high as $350,000. It created the novel notion of "media lynching," defined as affecting someone's reputation without sufficient evidence.

The influences of the indigenous cultures pre-dating the Spanish and Portuguese on this evolution are problematic to document. Over five centuries Native Americans have lived under their Inca, Maya and Aztec masters, their Spanish conquerors, Catholic dominators and, since national independence, governments that exploited them. In many cases that has meant a perpetual state of servitude and bondage. It undoubtedly also has meant at the local and especially family levels—those closest to the native populations themselves—that influential factors from long ago continue to carry weight.

Little detail about earlier native political structures and ideas is known earlier than a generation or two prior to arrival of the Europeans. Their values undoubtedly reinforced the authoritarian inclinations of the conquistadors and their successors, but with subtle differences that have undoubtedly influenced the liberal concepts now grafted onto them.

After the conquest, native peoples have been portrayed as quiescent and exploited at the bottom of a caste system, which was often the case. However, they also have participated in the various political settings since the conquest, particularly through armed rebellions and other acts of resistance. Their pre-Conquest relationships also were more complex than is widely thought.

In the Inca world, for example, the pre-conquest political system was not as absolutist as often imagined or, for that matter, as brutal as in the preconquest Mexican culture. The Inca Empire, established less than a century before it was conquered by the Spanish, was achieved in part without warfare. The Inca technique was to send in spies, then through the help of bribery with concubines and textiles, win over the old chiefs and assure them they could keep their positions if they joined the empire. Recalcitrant tribes often were not killed but resettled in a comparable environment to work on imperial projects at the opposite end of the empire. Explorer Hugh Thompson describes the empire as more of a huge trading association than a formal empire: "(the Incas were) like an aggressive modern corporation that offered overwhelmingly compelling reasons to each client tribe why it had to join—consumer benefits."

The Incas were an anonymous small tribe in the Cuzco valley until sometime around 1438 when the Inca Yupanqui took the throne after leading the tribe in a battle for survival. He adopted the name Pachacuti (Transformer of the Earth) and within a generation the Incas dominated the Andes. The leading indigenous political party today in Ecuador is the Pachacutic Party.

A powerful motive for the Incas aggressive territorial expansion was their unusual tradition of inheritance. On the death of the emperor his properties would be kept intact as a site in perpetuity for his mummified body. A group of relatives and retainers would look after it and his estate. His successor, usually a son, would have to acquire his own lands and build from scratch.

Of course, the Inca practices were not without brutality and exploitation. A factor in the success of the Spanish conquerors, whose tiny force might easily have been overwhelmed, is that, as was true with the Aztecs earlier in Mexico, half of the tribes in a position to stop them bore more hatred for the Incas than for the new invaders. Uprisings by holdouts even after the initial conquest failed similarly.

The more important explanation of the Spanish success rests with the animals they brought to America. European diseases, especially smallpox but also waves of diphtheria and measles, killed far more Indians than arms did. They also set the stage for the devastation the Spanish found upon arrival. Carried down the coast of South America from Panama, they almost certainly caused an epidemic, which killed the Inca Huayna Capac and half the population in around 1527. His death resulted in a succession war between his sons Huáscar and Atahaulpa that left the empire in virtual wreckage. The Spaniards simply exploited what was left. In doing so they undoubtedly grafted their own institutions onto those already present in the indigenous world.

The Mexican pre-Conquest world also was authoritarian with power exercised vertically by a single leader, but the brutality was far worse. The practice of human sacrifice was widespread and resulted in a hatred of the Aztecs by their client states similar to the Inca problem that contributed to the Spanish success. Large numbers of their sacrifice victims were extracted from the clients, who in some cases actually joined the Spanish against Moctezuma's armies.

This history of the indigenous populations undoubtedly played out in a willingness to take orders and accept authoritarian rule generally, but also probably underlies resistance that would come to the surface in the form of rebellion, which can be seen in many countries today that have significant native peoples. Mexico, of course, experienced a full-scale revolution in 1910 that brought Native Americans into leadership and transformed the country permanently.

Today, indigenous populations are growing in influence in civil society, especially in the Andean countries. They are encouraged and heavily influenced by nongovernmental organizations (NGOs), especially religious groups, often of foreign origin. These groups strongly advocate their rights as legitimate and powerful political actors. This relatively recent phenomenon extends even to Mexico, where outside groups took up the cause of the Zapatistas in Chiapas.

The roots of this change can be traced as far back as the 1960s Alliance for Progress, an initiative of the Eisenhower administration that was renamed and advanced by President Kennedy. It was intended to foster democratic stability in the Cold War context by advancing social and economic development through land reform and other measures. Instead, ironically, it promoted instability that led to the resurgence of military rule. It also resulted in an empowerment of native populations and stimulated interest among foreign nongovernmental organizations.

Among the many challenges to press freedom today in Latin America, especially as compared to the United States, are the customs and traditions of the indigence roots accepting authoritarianism and discouraging individualism. Not only do the Old World feudal restraints brought from Spain and Portugal make a difference, the long history of authoritarianism in pre-conquest America undoubtedly plays its role.

Gratitudes

I began this book after the late Stephanie Abramson, the extraordinary spouse of my best friend and college roommate, urged me to record my experiences. She said my work in Latin America had impact and encouraged me to write them for others who might take up the cause of press freedom.

My devoted wife and cherished companion Karen, a retired university Spanish teacher with a good memory who willingly joined me on most of my Latin American ventures, reviewed every word and offered numerous improvements. My son Ned, a journalist with extensive experience at all levels, copyedited the entire manuscript with important suggestions.

My good friend and tennis buddy Bill Richter, a former political science professor at Kansas State University where he also served as associate provost for international programs, was my final reader and offered excellent edits and revisions.

I am forever grateful to all of them for their patience, enthusiasm and encouragement as well as making the book more readable and understandable.

My many friends, colleagues, and mentors of the Inter American Press Association and the American Society of Newspaper Editors (now called News Leaders Association) aided me throughout my career and helped me in innumerable ways.

I also appreciate help I've had from employees of Seaton Publishing Company, especially with images and maps. As well, I am grateful to University Press of Kansas and especially its managing editor, Kelly Jacques, for design, production and printing.

I respectfully dedicate this result to all heroes of press freedom everywhere.